Mastering Change
Winning Strategies
For Effective
City Planning

Mastering Change

Winning Strategies
For Effective
City Planning

BRUCE W. McCLENDON
RAY QUAY
Foreword by
ANTHONY J. CATANESE

PLANNERS PRESS

AMERICAN PLANNING ASSOCIATION
Washington, D.C.
Chicago, Illinois

The cover illustration is reprinted from Kevin Lynch's
book, *What Time Is This Place?*—copyright 1972 by MIT
Press.

Copyright 1988 by the American Planning Association
1313 E. 60th St., Chicago, IL 60637
ISBN 0-918286-48-4
Library of Congress Catalog Number 87-70796

To
Lola Mae Thomas
Roy Quay
and
Nancy

Contents

Acknowledgments

The catalyst for this book was a simple request by David Sawicki, director of the City Planning Program at Georgia Institute of Technology, and Alida Silverman, of the League of Women Voters of Atlanta-Fulton County, Georgia, to develop a paper and present a lecture in Atlanta on the subject of citizen participation in effective city planning. The intriguing and challenging part of their request was their emphasis on and interest in getting a new perspective on how to make planning more effective in their community.

While there are numerous but almost random references to effectiveness in planning literature, we found that the best-selling book, *In Search of Excellence: Lessons from America's Best-Run Companies*, by Thomas Peters and Robert Waterman, Jr., provided the most suitable structure for framing and structuring our investigative research and analysis. We owe an immeasurable debt of gratitude to Peters and Waterman and acknowledge that in the absence of their work, there would not have been *Mastering Change*. Their findings gave us the basis for our hypothesis that successful planners and planning organizations shared common traits and encouraged us to investigate the applicability of transferring successful private sector management principles and practices to the public sector.

Anthony Catanese, dean of the College of Architecture at the University of Florida, has written extensively on the need for planners to become more effective, and he willingly reviewed our first and subsequent drafts. His enthusiastic interest, advice, support, and encouragement sustained us through the times when we wondered if the thousands of hours we were investing in our research would ever amount to anything. We will be forever indebted to Dr. Catanese.

C. France McCoy, of the Municipal Legal Studies Center of the Southwestern Legal Foundation, and Robert Freilich, Hulen Professor of Law in Urban Affairs, University of Missouri–Kansas City School of Law, who was the program chair for the 1985 Institute on Planning, Zoning and Eminent Doman, graciously provided us with a public forum to present and discuss some of our preliminary research and findings. Janice Moss expertly and with care edited the lengthy paper we presented at the Institute and laid a solid foundation for our subsequent manuscripts.

Chester Newland, editor-in-chief of *Public Administration Review*, published by the American Society for Public Administration, allowed us to use that publication's public management forum in the summer of 1986 to discuss some of our ideas for making planning more effective. John Clayton Thomas, of the L. P. Cookingham Institute of Public Affairs at the University of Missouri at Kansas City, accepted the chapter on innovation as a paper for discussion at the sixteenth annual meeting of the Urban Affairs Association.

Frank So with the American Planning Association was an early supporter of our work. He provided insightful advice and guidance and included a program on "Excellence in Planning" at the 1986 annual conference of the American Planning Association in Los Angeles.

Wolfgang G. Roeseler, director of the Center for Urban Affairs at Texas A&M University and author of *Successful American Urban Plans*, supported and encouraged our efforts and gave us valuable suggestions and guidance. Other reviewers who freely gave of their time and contributed to our findings were Ralph E. Thayer, James Duncan, Norman Standerfer, David Brower, Floyd Lapp, Paul Sedway, George Raymond, Leon Eplan, Roger Hedrick, Allan Hodges, and J. Lee Rodgers, Jr..

We are sincerely grateful to the many planners, city managers, and educators we interviewed during the course of our research. Their assistance and the examples they provided in support of our findings made our final manuscript richer and more rewarding. During the course of our research, we were impressed with the plain old-fashioned common sense displayed by many of the planners with whom we talked. It often seemed that they almost instinctively knew what would and wouldn't work in their communities. These planners were masters of their profession. They had developed, over a period of years, skills and practices that had been fundamental to their success and advancement. In a sense, they were the winners in the natural selection process that is characteristic of most careers in the planning profession. In so many ways, this book is their story and we are indebted to them for their accomplishments.

We also want to extend a special thank you to the extraordinary public officials that we met and often worked with over the years who provided us a unique perspective and insight into the public interest and the political decision-making process. This list includes: Bob Bolen, mayor of Fort Worth, Texas; Jan Cogeshell, mayor of Galveston, Texas; Henry Cisneros, mayor of San Antonio, Texas; Maury Meyers, Mayor of Beaumont, Texas; Jack Burke, chairman of the Butte-Silverbow City-County Planning Board, Butte, Montana; Charles Cartwright, chairman of the Corpus Christi Planning Commission; Richard Greene, mayor of Arlington, Texas; Kay Granger, chairman of the Fort Worth Zoning Commission; Tommy Warren, chairman of the Beaumont Planning Commission; and Carolyn Stiles, chairman of the Galveston Planning Commission.

Over the years we have had the benefit of working for some of the most respected managers in the city management profession. This list includes Ray Riley, Paul Rice, Tom Mullenbeck, William Kirchhoff, Karl Nollenberger, Buford Watson, and Douglas Harman. These individuals helped shape the work ethic and activist's values that made us more effective planners. Douglas Harman must also be thanked for providing the cartoons in this book and for reminding us not to take ourselves too seriously.

Finally, we are forever indebted to Mike Williams, who assisted in the preparation of the graphics, and to Christi King who typed, retyped, and reretyped what must have appeared to be a series of never-ending drafts of this book. Thank you, Christi.

Foreword

When I first told my parents, some years ago, that I wanted to be a city planner, I both broke their hearts and confused them. I broke their hearts because they saw no future for city planning and did not think that I could support myself at it. I confused them because they had no idea what a city planner was or did. My parents, I suspect, were quite typical in their feelings and understanding of planning and planners. Yet, recently my parents, who live in central Florida, told me: "We wish we understood the need for planning then as we do now. We would have encouraged you." I like to think that my parents are again typical in their feelings.

After a long and less than smashing run, planning has reached a new plateau in the United States. It is now seen as both a necessity and an opportunity. It is a necessity because leadership is needed that can transcend the short-term expediency. Planning is an opportunity because the country has witnessed a series of mistakes and losses in the built environment that cannot be repeated. Planning is widely regarded as a process that allows the opportunity to do things better.

In order for plannng to work better, there will have to be a number of major changes. These changes have to do with process, techniques, organization, and management. Perhaps most importantly, planning must be more concerned with effectiveness and implementation rather than principles and theory. A major problem has been that precious little can be found in the literature dealing with such changes. Most of the planning literature tends to be utopian, radical, theoretical, or dogmatic—all of which provide for good reading but little applicability. In the world of *realpolitik*, most planning books are met with mild disdain.

Something extraordinary has been done by Bruce McClendon and Ray Quay. They have been outrageous enough to suggest that not only can planning be more effective through changes in tactics and strategies, it can actually lead to *excellence*. They have gone beyond rhetoric and written a guide for planners to pursue excellence in city planning. This guide deals with astonishing common sense as well as phenomenal new thoughts. No ideologues, McClendon and Quay present their work in a straightforward, pragmatic, and highly readable way. This is all the more fascinating because McClendon and Quay are not academics, critics, or observers of planning; they are, by golly, practicing city planners. They have made the extraordinary commitment to take the time from their practice to write this incredible book.

The ideas in this book are a synthesis of the search for excellence that occurs in many places—business, government, and institutions. The authors have been able to integrate their ideas and then find real examples for planning practice that show the utility and applicability. That feat absolutely requires both insider knowledge and wide familiarity with current practice. Perhaps only Bruce McClendon with the help of Ray Quay could have produced such a work.

I hope this book becomes a standard for planning practice. I hope it spawns more works by practicing planners who are willing to make a commitment to excellence. This book signals a whole new direction for the literature of planning.

Anthony James Catanese
Dean, College of Architecture
University of Florida

Preface

Winning isn't everything; it's the only thing. VINCE LOMBARDI

Unlike Vince Lombarbi, we do not believe that winning is the only thing, but we do believe that planners should place a higher priority on winning and be less willing to accept ineffective roles. The planning profession is at a crossroads. Planners can continue to strive for relevancy, influence, and effectiveness and learn from the innovative and entrepreneurial achievements of successful planning agencies, or they can revere the tainted failures and ineffective practices of the past. We believe that many planners are seeking to become more effective and are trying to make a difference by improving the way they practice. Our simple objective in writing this book was to help planners learn from the successful experiences of others and to identify, develop, and promote strategies and tactics for achieving excellence that results in more effective planning.

This book may provoke academic debate because of the ease with which we use the term "effective planning." In *The Effective Local Government Manager*, it was noted that "effective is often equated with success."[1] We agree wholeheartedly with this definition. Peter Gent, a popular author and former football player for the Dallas Cowboys, said that "winning is matter of opinion but losing is a cold reality." Winning means success and success for planners, according to Alan Altshuler, means "direct influence on policy decisions and the prestige that follows from recognition by others of that influence."[2] Wolfgang G. Roeseler, author of *Successful American Urban Plans*, found that there was a simple test for determining success in local government. He concluded that "just as in your own life you consider yourself successful if you achieve what you set out to do, so does the body politic."[3]

xvii

Webster's New Collegiate Dictionary defines "effective" as "producing a decided, decisive, or desired effect."[4] The companion definition for "effect" is "to cause to come into being" or "to bring about often by surmounting obstacles."[5] Combining the two definitions and applying their meaning to planning results in the creation of the following composite definition for effective city planning: *It is planning that produces a decided, decisive, or desired outcome that is often achieved by surmounting obstacles.* The League of Women Voters of Atlanta-Fulton County, Georgia, developed the following, more complete definition of effective city planning:

> It is planning based on a long-range view of the city as a whole with all of its (sometimes competing) interests and on goals for the city in light of that long-range view and the realities of the city. It is planning based on good, complete data about the city. It is planning that results in implementation because the goals are clear and good and generally agreed upon so that planning can influence the political decision making.[6]

Robert Einsweiler, of the Humphrey Institute at the University of Minnesota, conducted a series of interviews in 1980 with the leading planners in six major cities across the country. He found that they shared the following vision of the role of planners in the future of city planning:

> They outline a "new process" of planning, whose characteristic is that it operates "inside the system." They want a "seat of influence," and seek it through a "direct relationship to . . . key decision makers." They require of a planner that he or she be "more of a pragmatist than an idealist," that he or she be "as interested in strategies . . . as . . . in goals." The product of planning becomes "shorter range and more pragmatic."[7]

Peter Marcuse of Columbia University is critical of this emerging view of the role of planners. He argues that the profession is in retreat in the United States today and he contends that ". . . a technocratic approach to planning that considers effectiveness per se the object of planning, without asking what is being effected, for whom, at whose cost, and why, is an approach to planning that betrays the best ideals of the profession."[8]

Leonard Reissman, in an essay entitled "The Visionary: Planner for Urban Utopia," argued that "an urban problem for the visionary includes anything that violates his high standards of morality and aesthetics" and that "his solution is usually nothing short of a massive reconstruction of metropolitan society."[9] You would have to be greener than Kermit the Frog not to know that this unrealistic philosophy is based on a fundamental misunderstanding of both the role of the planner in the decision-making process and the incremental way in which public policy is really made. As noted by Charles Lindbloom in "The Science of Muddling Through," "policy does not move in leaps and bounds . . . it proceeds through a succession of incremental changes."[10]

Effective planning doesn't mean abandoning the traditional values of the profession. Planning must continue to be a champion of civil rights, health, conservation of resources, efficiency, equity, and justice. But to be an effective champion of these ideals, we must win. Planners must effectively represent these values and make them become part of the political process. To believe that planners must sacrifice idealism for pragmatism, or that being effective is a betrayal of the profession, is to accept defeat. We believe that to achieve excellence in planning, planners must be effective in helping people realize their goals and ideals.

Our bottom line is that excellence in planning will result in more effective planning and vice versa. "Cutback planning" will be the order of the day for those planners and agencies that fail to make the transition and learn from the winning, successful, effective agencies that have prospered by providing excellence in planning.

This is how our search—a personal search of how we could maintain our ideals, our own utopian desire for excellence, and still be effective—began. In our search, we found that more often than not, those who had achieved excellence, whether in the public or private sector, also shared this commitment. But rather than just talk or write or think about it, or even understand it, they did it. They made their ideals a reality. In our mission, we have attempted to document these accomplishments and relate them to specific strategies and tactics that can be understood and used by other planners.

We want to emphasize that we made no attempt to survey the profession comprehensively or to analyze statistically all of the management principles and practices that are referenced in this book. Our approach was simply to review the appropriate literature and to use our extensive network within the profession aggressively to search for excellence and to try to determine the who, what, where, when, how, and why it seemed to occur.

Many of our observations and conclusions are based on our personal experiences or what we observed in the many places we worked and lived. Our combined experience in the public and private sectors was in the following cities: Butte, Montana; Lawrence and Merriam, Kansas; Chicago, Illinois; Lake Charles and Alexandria-Pineville, Louisiana; Kansas City and St. Joseph, Missouri; and Mesquite, Beaumont, Corpus Christi, Houston, Austin, Arlington, Galveston, Waco, and Fort Worth, Texas.

In our research for this book, we interviewed many planners who willingly and with candor shared their successes, frustrations, and failures. One of our early reviewers suggested that we should concentrate exclusively on success stories. While this was, in fact, our original objective and we desperately wanted to be positive in our approach, we soon discovered that it was just as essential to look at some failures or what we often referred to as almost successes. However, we did not go out of our way to look for failures. Almost all of the planners we interviewed or sought information about were highly respected and emulated professionals. These planners were eager and willing to tell us about their important victories, and in most cases they were just as interested in telling us about some of the not-so-successful experiences in their careers—with one frequent exception. Most planners did not want to talk about unsuccessful situations in the communities where they were presently employed. Several planners indicated they were experiencing problems, but in their minds these were only temporary setbacks that had to be overcome. They may have lost a recent battle, but they were confident that the war would be won. Successful planners are not quitters and more often than not, they don't lose; they just run out of time. As most successful planners, opera devotees, and sports fans know, "It's not over till the fat lady sings."

One of the important lessons we learned from our interviews was that failure didn't deter these successful and respected planners. In fact, it became increasingly clear to us that failure made them better and more effective planners. We are also candid enough to admit that many of the failures we mention in this book are our own or just as easily could have been ours. Thomas Peters and Robert Waterman, Jr. report in *In Search of Excellence* that managers often "fail their way to success."[11] We too found that an aggressive willingness to take risks, to experiment, and to learn and benefit from failure and mistakes were common characteristics of most successful planners. It has certainly been characteristic of our careers.

A brief word of explanation about our writing style is in order. We have used an anecdotal case study approach and, where possible, have tried to use humor to make this book enjoyable for practitioners. When we believed that particular information was relevant or useful to the reader, we provided names, places, and dates. On some occasions, anonymity was necessary in order to avoid needlessly embarrassing individuals or adversely affecting someone's job.

This book is based on the premise that the past experiences of planners can provide an important tool for formulating strategies and tactics for more effective planning. Further, these stategies and tactics have potential application in most planning programs throughout the country. Our findings offer planners an opportunity to become aggressive participants and accountable managers of more effective plannng programs.

However, too many in the planning profession have failed to understand the magnitude of the changes that have taken place in the economic, social, and political environments and the magnitude of the response that is required. Our argument is that these changes have rendered our past responses even less effective than before and that planners must eagerly and aggressively seek innovative ways to improve their effectiveness. If we are to become more effective, we must embrace and learn to benefit from change.

Anthony Catanese suggested in *The Politics of Planning and Development* that planners should change the way they look at politicians and that equally valuable changes and revisions are needed in the basic practice of planning. Planners must begin to develop and take advantage of new and more effective technologies and adapt their old tools and techniques to become more responsive to changing social, economic, and political conditions. Catanese also calls for planners to "develop the more recently defined role of *manager of change* in contrast to the ancient role of *master planner*."[12] We would go one step further and propose that planners must become change masters. By this we mean that planners and planning agencies must become more adept at the art of anticipating the need for and of leading productive change in local government. In *The Change Masters*, Rosabeth Moss Kanter explains that change masters are:

> . . . the right people in the right place at the right time. The *right people* are the ones with the ideas that move beyond the organization's established practice, ideas they can form into visions. The *right places* are the integrative environments that support innovation, encourage the

building of coalitions and teams to support and implement visions. The *right times* are those moments in the flow of organizational history when it is possible to reconstruct reality on the basis of accumulated innovations to shape a more productive and successful future.[13]

Our work is not a step-by-step "how-to" book. Instead it is an outline of patterns and characteristics and guiding principles that can help planners understand change, the opportunities it presents, and what specific strategies and tactics might be most effective for their specific situations.

Reinvigorating the planning profession will be a challenging task for planners. Our presumptuous approach can be likened to the entrepreneurial style of Ross Perot, the maverick former board member and largest shareholder of the General Motors Corporation. He found that revitalizing General Motors was like teaching an elephant to tap dance: "You find the sensitive spots and start poking."[14] We believe we have found plenty of sensitive spots and that positive, lasting results will be produced from our systematic poking and prodding.

With the planning profession at a crossroads, it is our duty to roll up our sleeves and push a little harder. Push the profession, ourselves, and our organizations to get involved and make a difference. The city planning profession has built a firm foundation over the past ninety-four years and is blessed with that most important resource: its people. All of us who are a part of this special profession have the opportunity and responsibility to shape its destiny. This is our modest contribution.

1

Mastering
Change

We have entered an era where change is a permanent factor. Some cities will prosper and some will be victims, dependent on how they deal with change. Success in the future will depend on a sense of planning using a different set of road maps (than) we've used in the past. HENRY CISNEROS

The principal theme of our work is that doing planning well and much more effectively will be increasingly critical to planners and the planning profession. Political and socioeconomic conditions have been changing; the federal government no longer provides much of the financial assistance for planning and planning mandates that historically have supported the growth and prosperity of the profession. When such support diminishes, many unprepared planning agencies and programs languish and a few even vanish. Some of the planners who have advocated "smaller is better" have been given the chance to be better. The respect for planning in some communities has sunk so low that if the planning director walked on water, the newspaper headline would declare, "Planner Can't Swim"! One planner noted that the only difference between the Titanic and the agency he used to work for was that the Titanic had a band.

Planning agencies which operate in environments where cutback planning has been the order of the day are like a pig with an artificial hip. When the farmer was asked why his pig had an artificial hip, he explained that it was a special pig. The farmer's tractor had once turned over and pinned him to the ground and the pig, seeing that the farmer couldn't move and would bleed to death from a lacerated leg, rushed back to the farmhouse. The pig oinked and ran around in circles until he attracted everyone's attention and then led them back to the accident in time to save the farmer's life. After hearing this and several other equally remarkable stories of the heroics of this extraordinary pig, the farmer was asked what this had to do with explaining the pig's artificial hip. His answer was simply that "a pig this good, you don't eat all at once."

Unfortunately, too many planning agencies are like the pig in this allegory. Their traditional products and services have protected the public's health and safety, optimized the use of tax dollars, supplemented or leveraged local funds with various grants, and improved the general quality of life of many communities. Yet their reward has been a partial disemboweling of the agency—cuts in staff and operating funds. Many of the agencies that are waiting for the final ax to fall are tired bureaucracies more concerned with survival than the search for excellence.

George Steiner, author and expert in the field of management, concluded in *Strategic Planning* that "years ago the managerial emphasis in the typical organization was on operations," but that today, "because of a turbulent and rapidly changing environment, the ability of an organization to adapt properly to environment, internal and external, is becoming critical in survival."[1]

In high school biology classes, many of us heard that if a frog is placed in a beaker of very hot water, the frog will immediately leap out of the container. However, if a frog is placed in an unheated beaker of water and a bunsen burner is used to slowly raise the temperature, the frog will not jump out and will be boiled alive. In many organizations, the staff's threshold of awareness is set so high that changes in the outside environment are not detected in time to avoid disastrous consequences.

Many planners are learning that the old ways of doing things no longer work—if, in fact, they ever did. Robert Walker was critical of the general ineffectiveness of city planning in his landmark book, *The Planning Function in Urban Government*, which was published in 1941.[2] Anthony Tomazini, professor of city and regional planning, University of Pennsylvania, concluded in a paper presented at the 1985 annual meeting of the Association of Collegiate Schools of Planning (ASCP) that city and regional planning has lost "its flexibility to change dramatically the subject matter of the concern, the process of its explorations, and the tools of its inquiries."[3]

Planners have two choices. They can react to change as a threat and fear it, hoping to ride it out. Or they can make fundamental, structural adjustments and welcome change as an opportunity and control that change to their advantage.

Some planners, like the old gunfighter or the last of the buffalo hunters, seem not to realize that a change has come over the land. They now stand on the edge, railing against what is, longing for what was, and not knowing the difference. General George Patton always advised his troops to keep moving. He contended that the SOB who ordered "hit the deck" killed more men that way because they became like ducks in a shooting gallery. His theory was that if you move you at least have a chance.

Our research has revealed that successful planning agencies have, in fact, kept on moving and have been able to earn respect and influence by developing new entrepreneurial skills and practices in response to the needs of their clients. Conventional conservative wisdom holds that it is safer to stay with the tried and true, but these agencies have prospered by reviewing their basic premises, jettisoning outmoded programs, products, and services, and developing innovative, flexible, dynamic, and experimental risk-taking approaches to city planning. Functioning in an increasingly unstable, accelerative, and even revolutionary local government environment, these successful planning agencies are more than mere survivors; they are overachievers who have taken control of their destinies. Their successes have been founded on the development of aggressive management strategies and tactics and a commitment to excellence. They are truly masters of change.

The 1986 National League of Cities' City Innovative Conference focused on the creative approaches that cities of all sizes are taking to increase and improve services, trim costs, and respond to new challenges in their communities. Bill Evans, vice-president and director of public sector services from Creasap, McCormick, and Pagent told the participants that "they must be willing to challenge long-held assumptions—figure out what is no longer true or useful, and make changes in procedures and services accordingly."[4]

Bruce McDowell, of the Advisory Commission on Intergovernmental Relations, noted that the federal government's divestiture of regional planning councils and the loss of federal aid has resulted in an accelerating search by regional planners for adaptive strategies to ensure their survival and success. He warned that regional planning councils must adapt their programs to reflect changing conditions and recommended eliminating services, increasing productivity, "getting back to basic politically acceptable regional activities supported by state–local partnerships, and focusing upon innovative areas of activity that are attracting public attention and public acceptance."[5]

In support of McDowell's prescription for success, an ACIR survey and study on the roles of metropolitan planning organizations found a dramatic recent "shift from the planning-oriented 'national emphasis' of regional planning councils to the local 'service provider' and 'local entrepreneur' styles" of operation.[6] The study concluded that the adaptive regional council will be the one that survives.[7]

Competition is the American way, and the planning profession has suffered because the competitive spirit hasn't been instilled in enough public sector planners and managers. Competition heightens awareness and sensitivity to changes in the environment; that is one of the reasons why the private sector is quicker and more aggressive than the public sector in changing its mix of products and services.

For example, Zebco, which stands for Zero Hour Bomb Company, began its corporate existence in the 1930s as a manufacturer of time bombs for oil field drilling. Today Zebco is synonymous with fishing; it manufactures the world's most popular brand of fishing reel. Over the years, Zebco employees have responded to changing markets and foreign competition by cutting waste, improving quality, and increasing productivity. Juanita Parker, who has worked for twelve years on the Zebco assembly line in Tulsa, says that she can't go to Japan for a job so she is committed to doing a better job here and putting out reels fast enough so that the company makes a profit. Another employee noted that everyone is conscious of his or her job and the fact that the company has to stay competitive or risk being forced out of the fishing reel industry.

Competition can be found in almost every aspect of our day-to-day lives. For instance, an environmental planner and an economic development planner were hiking in a wilderness area in Montana when they noticed an obviously hungry grizzly bear approaching from the timberline. The economic development planner dropped to his knees, took off his hiking boots, and put on a pair of running shoes he had retrieved from his backpack. With an air of superiority, the environmental expert chastised his colleague for failing to know that he couldn't outrun a grizzly bear. The planner finished tying his shoe laces and said, "I don't have to outrun the grizzly; I just have to outrun you!"

The essence of competition is a contest between rivals. The challenge for the manager of a planning agency is to create a competitive work environment that builds and promotes friendly, positive competition. We believe that the creation of a team-based competitive work environment involving performance pay incentives and an expectation of excellence is an important strategy for more effective planning.

Successful managers know that expectations can influence behavior. This phenomenon is known as the Pygmalion effect. In Greek mythology, Pygmalion was a sculptor who fell in love with a statue that he had created to fulfill his own expectations. The statue was brought to life by his prayers to the gods. Individuals create images of what can be and, if they believe those images, they can become self-fulfilling prophecies.

Donald Schon concluded in his book, *The Reflective Practitioner: How Professionals Think in Action,* that there is a crisis of confidence in professions like city planning.[8] What is needed is increased recognition and awareness of the exciting potential of the planning profession—a potential that is within the reach of almost any planner. One of the purposes of this book is to raise the expectations of planners, managers, and decision makers and to challenge them to make planning more effective.

COPPING OUT

Man must cease attributing his problems to his environment and learn again to exercise his will, his personal responsibility. ALBERT SCHWEITZER

A critical first step on the long road to becoming a more effective planner is the willingness to accept responsibility for the way you are. In the comic strip "Peanuts," Lucy blames her missed fly balls on the sun, the moon, the wind, the stars, and even on toxic substances in her baseball glove. She always has some excuse for her shortcomings as an outfielder. Excuse making is how we deal with the human dilemma of fallibility. Many unsuccessful and even some successful planners believe that their professional careers and the effectiveness of their planning programs are predominantly determined by nonrational external factors that they cannot control or influence.

One planner we interviewed said he had been forced to resign his position as the director of an agency because the commission and council were badly divided and he had too many bosses to be effective. However, the subsequent planning director was able to develop an effective program because he recognized that when you have too many bosses, you also have none. During the course of our research, several planning directors shared the view that there is inadequate local support for planning and that they simply are waiting for a shift in public opinion or a change in the composition of the planning commission or legislative body so they can develop more effective planning programs. This passive attitude conflicts with the experiences of many successful planners and it conflicts with our evidence which indicates that in most communities there are controllable internal management factors that have a dominant role in determining the effectiveness of local planning programs. Almost without exception, we found that successful, winning planning agencies had well thought out internal management strategies and aggressive work programs; the losers had excuses.

Our findings and investigative analysis seriously conflict with the findings and opinions of several respected scholars. Alan Altshuler's main thesis in his chapter on political restraints and strategies in *The City Planning Process* was that the city planner "controls so little of his environment that unquestioning acceptance of its main features is a condition of his own success."[9] We have concluded, however, that acceptance of political constraints does not mean passivity and defeat. Effective planners recognize and tolerate constraints, but they also show great energy, creativity, imagination, and skill in adapting to constraints and using strategies and tactics to successfully overcome obstacles and restrictions.

Francine Rabinovitz concluded in 1969 that the degree to which planning influences decisions is said to depend on three factors: organizational, technical, and political conditions."[10] More recently Caner Oner took this concept one step further by conducting a survey on planning effectiveness by asking ninety planning officials and a like number of graduate planning school faculty members to evaluate and rank a list of factors that were assumed to influence the effectiveness of planning. Only one of the top seven factors was an internal factor that could be influenced by the manager of the planning agency or department. Robert Einsweiler conducted interviews with a dozen planning directors in central cities in 1980 and found by using the nominal group technique that the highest priority rankings of factors that influence planning effectiveness were "legal powers, expectations of the chief administrator, and the local economy."[11]

In both the Einsweiler and Oner surveys, only one of the many factors assumed to influence the effectiveness of local planning was an internal management factor that the planning manager could, to some degree, control. In essence, the limiting of the survey selection to factors that were predominately external predetermined that circumstances local planners could not control would be responsible for the successes and failures of planning programs. Thus positioned, these surveys naturally support the view that planners should not be held responsible or accountable for the effectiveness of their local planning programs. Yet our research indicates that nothing could be further from the truth.

Stephen King's book, *It*, is a story of adolescent search for love, identity, and belonging. Seven outcasts fight against a shape-shifting monster that lives in the local sewer system and feeds on the town's children. In a sense, their encounter with It is a metaphorical encounter with growing up. It is as much a symbolic monster as it is a real one. It assumes the shape of its victim's worst fear and appears as a mummy, werewolf, giant spider, crawling eye, and giant bird. It is almost as vulnerable to lack of fear as it is to physical weapons. The challenge of the young adversaries fighting It is overcoming their fears of believing in themselves.

In many ways, planners are like the adolescents in King's story. The doubts and fears of too many planners are symbolized in the form of unethical public officials, an unsupportive manager, budget constraints, inadequate state legislation, or an uncaring public. Battling these monsters proves to be a formidable and often impossible task for some planners. Lacking the faith and sense of self-respect that has historically sustained the profession, they lose their fight and willingly accept ineffectiveness.

What we are really proposing is a catalyst for a transformation in the way that public planners approach the practice of their profession. We are convinced that the vast majority of planners can control the degree of their effectiveness to a much greater extent than traditionally has been thought. Success depends on the ability of planners to develop management strategies that fit both the internal and external environment in which they operate.

CREDO OF EXCELLENCE

A review of some of the programs instituted in local governments around the country confirms that management practices based on the Excellence philosophy have been successful . . . . INTERNATIONAL CITY MANAGEMENT ASSOCIATION

The format and methodology for this study is based on the landmark book, *In Search of Excellence*, by Thomas Peters and Robert Waterman, Jr.[12] Their book identified what makes corporate organizations more effective and offered what the subtitle calls "Lessons from America's Best-Run Companies." Our research used as its starting point the eight attributes that Peters and Waterman found to be characteristic of successful companies with particular emphasis on a bias for action, closeness to the customer, and autonomy and entrepreneurship.[13]

Many of the specific examples that will be presented to support the management strategies and tactics suggested for achieving planning excellence and effectiveness will come from the private sector because this has been the focus of the search of excellence movement. There is an obvious trend toward adapting transferable corporate management techniques to local government management. Daniel Nissenbaum noted in his article, "Tracking the Pursuit of Excellence," that:

> Peters and Waterman's book . . . has had an effect on local government management that is rivaled by few other public sector oriented books. . . . The values that the book espouses, of "closeness to the customer" risk-taking and entrepreneurialism, and "sticking to the knitting," hold true for local government management as well as Fortune 500 companies.[14]

Nissenbaum, assistant to the director of the International City Management Association (ICMA) said that many managers have adapted the credo of excellence and have made numerous changes in their management practices.[15] ICMA has developed a training program that is designed to help local government managers translate the thinking described in *In Search of Excellence* into criteria and strategies for more effective management. Under this program, local government employees are introduced to the basic practices that are characteristic of successful companies and they explore ways these practices could be applied to the management and operation of their agencies and departments.

At the 1986 ICMA annual conference, participants from the 1985 conference's workshop on excellence provided convincing evidence of the dramatic influences that the movement has had on local government managers. Nissenbaum reported that participants from such diverse cities as Fort Worth, Texas; Randolph, New Jersey; Lancaster, South Carolina; Westminister, Colorado; Woodridge, Illinois; and Lewiston, Idaho, experienced "a marked increase in employee morale, a goal or performance orientation toward programs and services, improved internal communication, and a basic regeneration of spirit and enthusiasm."[16]

PROPOSED EXCELLENCE IDENTIFICATION SYSTEM

The establishment of performance benchmarks is an important link to excellence and increased effectiveness in almost any area of performance. Since 1984, ICMA has given an annual award for excellence to an individual who best exemplifies that the role of the professional in city government is to enhance the *effectiveness* of elected councils. Unfortunately, the interest and excitement on the part of public managers about promoting and recognizing excellence is not shared by many planners.

In fact, there is so little interest in promoting any form of excellence in planning that in 1983 the American Planning Association (APA) downgraded its annual awards program to a biennial awards program—though that decision was reversed a year later. The three practicing planners on the twenty-one member board in 1983 led the support for an awards program. Opposition to developing a new awards program was based on budget concerns and a belief that planners did not want their dues being used for such purposes. The opinion of a majority of the board was buttressed by the results of a market survey of both members and nonmember planners that revealed that an annual awards program was the least valued service provided by APA.[17] Yet the same survey showed that determining and maintaining the standards of the profession was ranked third in importance to planners.

The conclusion that we draw from this is that while planners want planning to be recognized and protected as a profession, a large number of planners who are just muddling through know there is nothing special or unique about the way they perform their jobs; they have no appreciation for or commitment to the concept of excellence. Under the circumstances, an awards program recognizing excellence in performance would be both wasteful and potentially detrimental to any planner who lacks self-respect and a sense of pride in the quality, relevance, and effectiveness of his or her performance—planners receiving awards for excellence would have a competitive advantage over less effective planners. We believe in the value of recognizing excellence and we are going to do our best to raise professional standards and public expectations of planning.

While we enthusiastically support the excellence movement, we are not suggesting that all private sector management practices and techniques are universally transferable to the public sector. The public sector operates under political limitations that preclude the wholesale transfer of private sector management principles and practices. But despite these constraints and the obvious differences between the public and private sectors, our research and findings prove that the efficiency and effectiveness of planners and planning agencies can and has been improved by using basic private sector management principles and practices.

Brian Rapp and Frank Patitucci conclude in their book, *Managing Local Government for Improved Performance: A Practical Approach,* that "strategies and means of improving performance in private business can and should be applied to local government."[18] Similarly, Joseph Vitt, Jr., former director of the City Development Department in Kansas City, Missouri, says that he "became convinced that planning agencies and planners could become more effective if the best concepts of the management profession—that is, things that industrial managers and business managers were telling us and were using in their own professions—and the basic concepts of the planning profession could be combined and integrated within an organization."[19] Additionally, Allan Hodges, a professional associate and planning department manager of the consulting firm of Parsons Brinckerhoff Quade and Douglas, Boston, and a former vice-chairman of the AICP Commission, contends that "the skills required in private business are often the same as required by aggressive public planning agencies."[20] In summary, our professional experiences, the experiences of our colleagues, and review of planning literature have shown clearly that successful planning agencies share many of the most common traits and characteristics of successful businesses.

2

A Bias
For Action

Unless and until planning goes to work today, plans for tomorrow aren't likely to do much good. FRED BAIR

The first common characteristic shared by most successful corporations is a bias for action. "Do it, fix it, try it" was the favorite axiom of Thomas Peters and Robert Waterman, Jr., who contended that "the most important and visible outcropping of the action bias in excellent companies is their willingness to try things out, to experiment."[1]

In west Texas, the first one to see a rattlesnake kills it. No study or plan is needed to decide what to do, how to do it, and who is responsible for doing it. Initiative is prized and, in fact, is essential to one's health, safety, and welfare.

In one city, a group of residents asked their city concil to block a building permit for a pawn shop that was to be located next to their neighborhood. A thirty-day moratorium was imposed by the council and a public hearing was scheduled so that the zoning ordinance could be amended to exclude pawn shops from the neighborhood commercial zoning district. The planning staff analyzed what appeared to be a simple issue and in less than a week prepared a staff report that recommended deleting pawn shops from the district in question. At the public hearing, legal representatives from the pawn shop industry asked for an immediate end to the moratorium and for a continuance of the hearing so that the matter could be given further study. Several members of the zoning commission supported postponing any action and suggested that the scope of the study be expanded to include, first, the compatibility of all the uses that were permitted in the neighborhood commercial district and, second, an evaluation of the appropriateness of the overall pattern of commercial and industrial zoning near residential areas. Instead of addressing the issue before them, they compounded it.

The commission continued the hearing but at the very next council meeting, pawn shop owners from across the state and their legal representatives packed the council chamber and demanded an end to the moratorium. The outnumbered residents, including the president of the neighborhood association who had been personally sued for libel by the state pawn shop association, begged the council to protect their neighborhood. The council was frustrated and upset about being placed in a no-win situation, and one councilman angrily lashed out at the zoning commission for failing to take action and for making the problem more difficult to resolve.

This example is characteristic of the decision-making process in too many communities. Instead of killing the snake, they organize a large committee, hire a consultant who knows a lot about snakes, and then talk about it at length while the snake gets larger and more difficult to handle.

Unfortunately, many unsuccessful planners working in local government planning agencies appear to have a bias for inaction because they believe that most of the critical problems they deal with are of such scale and complexity that vague, impractical, or esoteric solutions are often the only solution. Ernest Bonner, the former planning director of Portland, Oregon, contends "there is nothing that is so complex that it cannot be stated very simply."[2] Yet even for simple problems, many planners are tempted to formulate complicated solutions because much of their education, technical expertise, and experience has been with complicated problems that required complicated solutions.

Some large, unsuccessful corporations also have a bias for inaction. Their problem, as identified by Peters and Waterman, is "the all-too-reasonable and rational response to complexity in big companies: coordinate things, study them, form committees, ask for more data (or new information systems)."[3]

Cities are complex, too, and there is often a perceived need for complex planning and coordination mechanisms as a way to bring about order and understanding. But in many planning departments, as well as large corporations, the process is greatly overdone; inevitably, such complexity leads to lethargy and inertia. As

noted by Norman Williams, Jr., in *American Land Planning Law:*

> (i)t is a reasonably safe bet that many (and perhaps most) large American planning agencies have file cabinet after file cabinet full of reports and statistics which they have never found any way to use, because no one thought out ahead of time precisely what it was necessary to know, before making decisions on specific planning problems . . . : some planners have developed an almost conscious technique of using research to avoid decision making—always wanting more information before they can make up their minds about anything, and thereby condemning themselves to wallow forever in a sea of statistics.[4]

An obsession with data collection can adversely affect a planning department's ability to produce timely, useful recommendations and advice. Alan Altshuler concluded in his classic book, *The*

City Planning Process, that planning studies must consist of more than factual analysis; they must include at least a few conclusions.[5] However, he noted that the conclusions could be of the following several kinds:

> Planners may content themselves with stating that problems exist. They may state piously that the facts demonstrate the need for more planning. Or they may go on to propose specific courses of action.[6]

Incredible as it may seem, the primary conclusion of some planning studies is that additional planning studies are needed. In his critique of planning in the Minneapolis-St. Paul region, Altshuler found that much of the St. Paul land use plan exemplified the strategy of recommending more planning. He concluded that "the plan as a whole was so abstract ... that it attracted no comment whatsoever."[7]

The alternative to this relatively ineffective strategy is to concentrate on being more responsive to the current problems of local decision makers. It means tackling the difficult, pressing problems that everyone agrees need to be resolved. One of the essential techniques for this approach to planning is the application of the "chunking" principle.

CHUNKING
Command large fields, but cultivate small ones. VIRGIL

Peters and Waterman observed that "chunking" was an underlying principle associated with a bias for action. Chunking "simply means breaking things up to facilitate organizational fluidity and to encourage action."[8] Whether they were called teams, task forces, project centers, or quality circles, these small groups, formed to achieve specific tasks, had the same objective—identifying, attacking, and managing problems on a priority basis. In essence, the right people are brought together on a problem and are expected to solve it in a relatively short period of time.

We interviewed several planners who had worked their ways up from small cities with small staffs to bigger cities with larger staffs, and they reported that it was far easier to be effective and to do more meaningful work in smaller communities. They concluded that the smaller the community, the more "plannable" it was. But what our research revealed was that planners in small communities were more focused. They spent more of their time working on critical, short-term problems and projects that required immediate action. They were more effective not necessarily because of their small city environment but because they had a bias for action and were more responsive to the needs of the people in the environment they were serving.

The same fundamental strategies that produce results in small cities can be applied to larger cities. Regardless of the size of the organization, Peters and Waterman noted that small groups "are quite simply, the basic organizational building blocks of excellent companies."[9]

Many planning agencies have already successfully applied the chunking principle. Baltimore, Maryland; Beaumont, Arlington, and Fort Worth, Texas; Windsor, Connecticut; and San Jose, California, have project review committees or development teams that expedite the consideration of new development concepts and ordinances in addition to the review and evaluation of specific problems or projects. Baltimore, Plano, and Austin, Texas, use a permit expediter who troubleshoots for projects and has the authority to intervene in the permitting process. In Austin, a process manager with extensive experience in both the public and private sectors has the responsibility of coming to the aid of applicants whose projects have become stalled. The mission of the process manager is to determine who, what, or where the problem is and to get the project moving again. The city of Los Angeles uses a housing expediter to encourage development of housing for low- and moderate-income persons or families.

Phoenix is experimenting with quality circles and has about fifteen employee groups which meet regularly to look at ways to improve their jobs and reduce costs. In the spring of 1985, the Dallas planning department created a hot spot planning program. These hot spot plans are short term (two- to three-month) studies of specific developing areas where there are conflicts between commercial and residential uses. Hot spot plans are assigned to planners based on their availability, expertise, and familiarity with the area. A small ad hoc work group is established for the plan composed of business, property owner, and citizen representatives. Specific recommendations are developed on a case-by-case basis for resolving individual adjacency problems. The common traits shared by all these cities is that the time associated with each problem project is kept relatively short and it is given priority attention by an appropriate individual or small group of individuals until resolved.

TEAM BUILDING

Being part of a team is not a natural human function; it is learned. PHILIP B. CROSBY

In *Managing for Excellence*, David Bradford and Allan Cohen concluded that "achieving excellence demands the development of a high performance team" and that such a team "produces high-quality solutions, provides coordination among members, and is the vehicle for shared responsibility in managing the department."[10] A sharing attitude based on mutual trust and respect is an essential prerequisite for effective team building. When trust is missing and there are interpersonal fears, suspicions, and doubts, an organization is in serious trouble and team building does not work. Read the words of one planner we know (who shall remain anonymous) and hope they are never said about your agency:

> We have to watch each other all of the time, fighting for power, struggling for existence. That is not fun! To add to our woes, we have planners in our agency trying to abolish our organization (they have been here a while, are frustrated, and are job hunting). I was suspicious of "funny" things going on, talked to my boss and other top management. We were right, and these people admitted to doing the bad things that we thought they were doing. One of our planners was writing legislation to submit to the state legislature to abolish our agency. Our main enemies are not the developers, but are other planners.

In our experience, planning is most effective when operating in an environment that encourages and rewards flexibility, responsiveness, and spontaneous teamwork. Group or team solutions are superior to individual responses and multidisciplinary teams produce superior results. Effectiveness depends on leadership being shared, with different planners taking on leadership roles as new situations arise. Communication must be up, down, and lateral—and lateral communication is the most critical.

Robert Herchert, former Fort Worth city manager, believes that "teamwork is the most direct route to positive change in managerial and organization effectiveness."[11] Larry Black, city manager of Rockville, Maryland, believes that the team approach is the surest way to achieve excellence. In his experience, the group product, whether it is achieved by using task forces or top management, is "usually superior to what any one of the group participants could have produced individually."[12]

Illustrative Planning Department
Professional Position Hierarchy

SOURCE: Lauber, Job Descriptions for Planning Agencies;
(Planning Advisory Service Report No.302,
American Society of Planning Officials, May 1974)

Figure 2–1

This figure illustrates the relative levels in the
planning department's professional planning hierarchy;
it does not necessarily indicate who reports to whom.
It is not uncommon, particularly in smaller planning
departments, for a single individual to supervise several
planners at different job levels: e.g., a senior planner
might directly supervise both associate and assistant
planners, as illustrated in two different ways on the
right side of the figure.

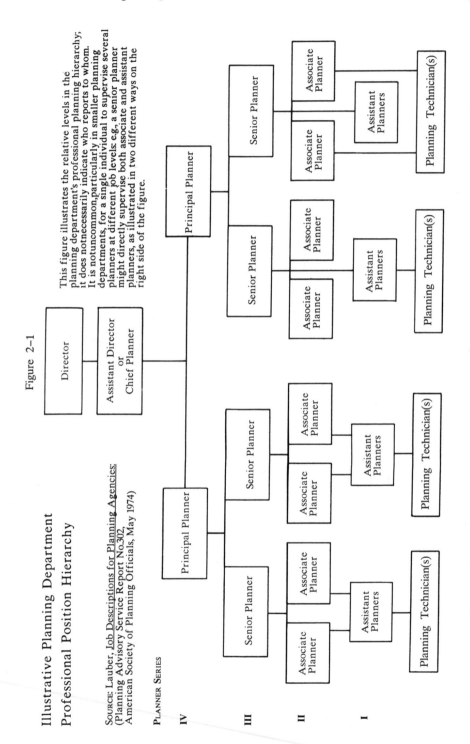

Peters and Waterman noted that the true power of the small group lies in its flexibility and size. They support the research evidence that optimal group size is about seven and added that "teams that consist of volunteers, are of limited duration, and set their own goals are usually found to be much more productive than those with the obverse traits."[13]

In *Corporate Revolution*, Roger Hayes and Reginald Watts concluded that traditional, large corporate hierarchies are no longer effective. They found that in successful firms the emerging form of the organization is more slender, with flexible management modules that can easily and more rapidly respond to changing market demands.[14] Big business is looking hard at what makes small businesses more effective and is reorganizing itself along the lines of smaller companies. In contrast, there appears to be a trend toward proliferation of titles and expansion of the vertical positions in the hierarchy of many planning agencies. Donald Spaid, former planning coordinator for St. Paul, noted that in government, the communication has to be horizontal, not just vertical, and yet "our structures are designed for vertical communication, almost at the penalty of insuring that we do not get any horizontal communication."[15]

Figure 2-1 illustrates the typical hierarchical arrangement of planning positions in larger agencies. However, some planning agencies are streamlining their vertical organizational structure to promote more flexibility, responsiveness, teamwork, and entrepreneurial behavior. In recent years, the hierarchical structure of the Fort Worth planning department was slimmed down and compressed so as to decrease supervisory responsibilities and increase opportunities for more individual autonomy, responsibility, and authority for lower level planners. (See Figure 2-2.) The number of core divisions or management modules was increased from two to four, and a strategy of interdivisional team building for aggressively attacking emerging problems was established. The assistant director was assigned the primary responsibility for tackling critical short-term problems and opportunities. He has the authority to form short-term strategic planning teams using any of the staff from any of the four divisions in the department. He also is responsible for preparing requests for plannng programs, projects, and services, and for soliciting proposals from any planner interested in taking a leadership and management role for a short-term interdisciplinary strategic management team.

Figure 2–2

Fort Worth Planning Department

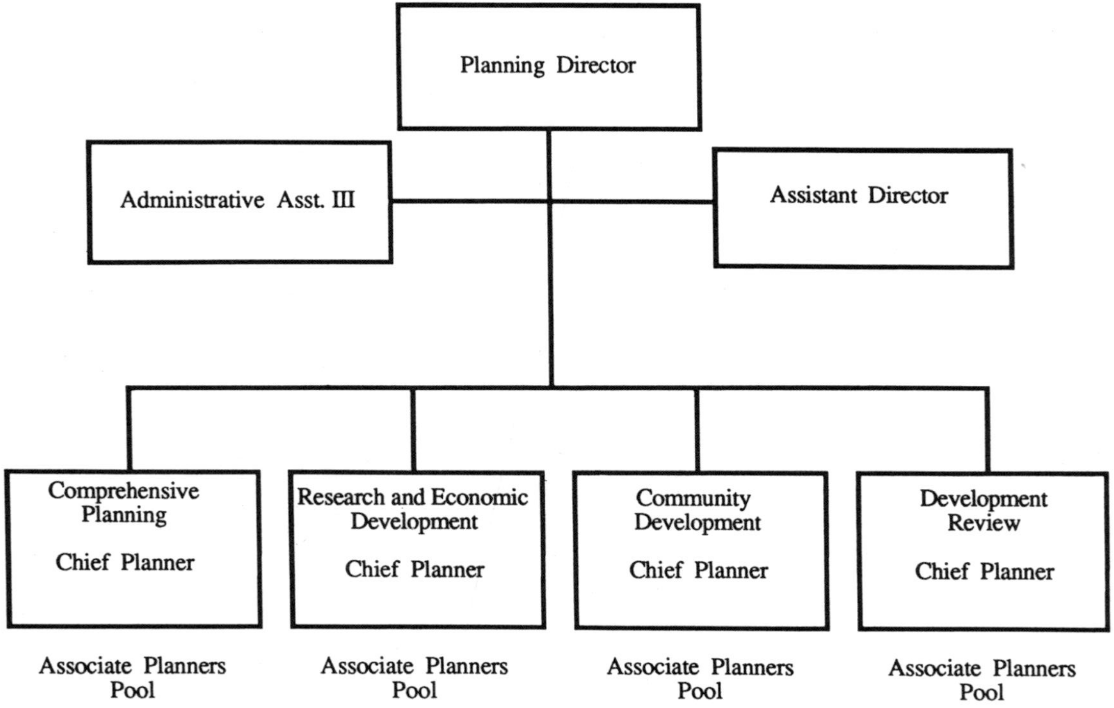

The Fort Worth planners are expected to take turns serving on strategic management teams in addition to fulfilling their customary responsibilities for the divisions to which they are assigned. They are challenged to increase productivity in their regular division duties so that more time is available to volunteer for short-term team projects. This means that the emphasis on rapidly resolving highly visible, current problems is not achieved at the expense of the objectives of the annual work program.

In *Re-Inventing the Corporation,* John Naisbitt and Patricia Abrudene found that using flexible and fast small teams is a popular and effective approach and that the teams "can accomplish even more when people with different talents and perspectives come together to work on a problem."[16] Similar findings were reported by many planners and local government managers across the country.

An extraordinary example of the successful use of small, cross-disciplinary teams in the public sector is provided by Phoenix, Arizona. There, a value management resource group works from the city manager's office as a team of internal consultants which combines interdisciplinary industrial engineering and behavioral science skills to help departments solve various operational and management problems.[17]

While we were able to find several examples of successful team building, we also came to the conclusion that these situations were a relatively rare phenomenon. We further concluded that what team builders really need is a good theoretical description of the characteristics of an ideal team that can be used as a model for team

Bureaucratic Lament

The image of the classic government department is one of hierarchical, pyramidal organizations with permanent functions and lines of career progression. Everybody is graded and has in-step rating. Everybody's salary is fixed and everything is set up like an old-fashioned machine. That organizational form worked in a traditional industrial, Second Wave environment. But tomorrow's tasks can no longer be carried out efficiently by such factory-style organizations.

Toffler, "Toffler Laments," Management 54 (U.S. Government Printing Office, Vol. 4, No. 2, 1983).

development in any organization. Fortunately, we were able to find a truly outstanding model in *Managing for Excellence.* The following is a summary from that book of the ideal characteristics of an effective team:

> Everyone knows his/her own and others' tasks well enough so that nothing falls through the cracks; everyone knows who is, and who should be, doing what.

> Trust is so high that the group does not need to meet on every issue. Because all members know, and are committed to, the same overarching goal and know each other's attitudes and positions on issues, any member can act in the department's name when necessary, without seeking everybody's approval. Each member is confident that no one, including the boss, would act without consultation unless there was a good reason—such as prior general agreement, special expertise, legitimate time pressures, or unavailability of affected parties. And the person who does act would know that others would back any action.

> Such a group would not be very "group-y" or clinging and would not waste time meeting on trivial issues or limiting those who had taken individual initiative. A lot of individual work would be assigned to be done outside meetings, with reports and recommendations brought back to the team.

> Members who were clearly more expert than the others in certain areas would be given great latitude to make the decisions on those matters.

> Nevertheless, if issues cross several areas or affect the department as a whole, members would seriously address the issues together, fight hard and openly for their beliefs, insist that their concerns be addressed, yet also pay attention to the needs of the department as a whole. Everyone would be comfortable wearing at least two hats, one for their area and one for the department.

> Although skilled at persuasion and willing to fight hard over important differences, members would feel no obligation to oppose automatically initiatives from other members or the manager. There would be no competition for competition's sake. Members would enthusiastically support the positions or ideas of others when they happened to agree. Furthermore, when they were in opposition to one another, the battles would center on issues, not personalities. Differences would be considered legitimate expressions of a person's experience and job perspective, not indicative of incompetence, stupidity, or political maneuvering.

> Despite members' willingness to fight when necessary, the climate is pervasively supportive, encouraging members to ask one another for

help, acknowledge their mistakes, share resources (people, information, or equipment), and generally further everybody's performance and learning.

The group pays attention to successful task achievement and to individual members' learning; members are not restricted to areas where they have total competence and hence can't acquire new expertise, nor are they so overloaded with learning experiences that group performance seriously suffers. Cautious members are pushed to venture into less secure areas, while overreaching members are reminded that new opportunities can't supplant ongoing responsibilities.

Perhaps most important, the group has self-correcting mechanisms; when things aren't going well, all members are ready to examine the group's processes, discuss what is wrong, and take corrective action. Whatever the problems—overly lengthy meetings, inappropriate agenda items, unclear responsibilities, lack of team effort, overly parochial participation, or even poor leadership practices—the group takes time out to assess its way of operating and to make mid-course corrections. Individual members as well as the manager feel free to raise questions of team performance. Nevertheless, the group is not so overly self-analyzing that it neglects its main tasks. High task performance remains a central concern.[18]

Obviously this ideal profile of an effective team would be difficult to develop in reality, but it does provide a goal toward which team members and team builders can aspire and a benchmark for evaluating performance. Most important, it provides a pattern of correct behavior that should help in overcoming the significant obstacles to the development of truly effective teams. The bottom line is simply that effective teams are crucial to achieving excellence and, therefore, it is absolutely essential that we pay the price and make the extraordinary commitment necessary to build effective teams.

But despite the bright promise of team building and the successes reported in both the public and private sectors for the multidisciplinary small team approach to problem solving, there are still some planners who continue to be advocates of the status quo. Not understanding that status quo is Latin for "we're in deep trouble," they eagerly advise their colleagues to hang on to outdated, ineffective practices and processes. Typical is the advice given in an article in *Planning* magazine on how to choose the right job. The author recommended that job seekers should be cautious if they discover that they will be responsible to several people or will have to "coordinate" with others. He stated that, "Management textbooks call this a matrix arrangement. I call it chaos."[19]

This particular planner is quick to see the potential for conflict and confusion that is possible in matrix management but, unfortunately, he fails to realize or appreciate the phenomenal benefits that it also produces. Our advice to young planners is just the opposite of his. Seek out employment in organizations offering integrative, participative management experiences with multidimensional responsibilities. With matrix management, there is a sharing of authority and responsibility, increased potential for achieving recognition and status, and more opportunity for self-development and self-fulfillment.

Avoid organizations that have traditional hierarchical structures with clearly defined and segmented compartments walled off and protected from one another—section from section, division from division, department from department. Such a structure inhibits any organization's ability to successfully adapt to change. In *The Change Masters*, Rosabeth Moss Kanter called "segmentalism" antichange and anti-innovation because it compartmentalizes actions, events, and problems, and keeps each piece untouched and isolated from the others. She argues that "segmentalism" and the classic unitary chain-of-command authority are designed to protect against change, to prevent deviations, and to ensure that individuals have sufficient awe and respect for this course to maintain their role in it without question. In contrast, Kanter, a professor at Yale University's School of Management, found that in matrix organizations with fluid nonhierarchical structures—including project teams and other professional or quasi-professional self-managed work teams—traditional authority virtually disappears with valuable results. For instance, she notes that with the resulting integrative, participative approach to problem solving, individuals are willing to reach beyond the boundaries of their jobs, to work collaboratively with others in search of a higher level of performance, to combine ideas from unconnected sources, and to embrace change as an opportunity to test limits.[20] We have more to say about organizational structure and self-development in Chapter 5.

We are strong advocates of organizations using an integrative team approach to problem solving, but an important cautionary note is in order for the effective planner. As suggested by John Darrington, city manager of Rawlins, Wyoming, always bear in mind that "management teams, task forces, or committees should not be used to put off or prolong a decision or recommendation, but rather to focus time, attention, and talent on specific objectives in a predetemined time frame."[21] This idea is summed up well by a Chinese proverb: "To talk much and arrive nowhere is the same as climbing a tree to fish."

EFFECTIVE PLANNING COMMISSIONS

Commissions are composed of laymen who make recommendations or decisions involving millions of dollars in real estate and the environments in which we live, and deal with technically complex issues touching upon profound and fundamental concerns of society. WARREN J. JONES

The propensity for voluntary citizen participation in governmental affairs in the United States is a founding principle that has been a hallmark of twentieth century local government. In most cities across the country, planning and zoning commissions are easily the most visible, influential, and controversial of all local citizen advisory groups.

In one particular community, the planning commission was at the center of influence and power, deeply involved in several controversial issues. The members were so busy and important that the following joke made the rounds at city hall: A man is told by his doctor that he only has six months to live. The man pleads with his doctor to do something, anything, to prolong his life. His doctor can suggest only one thing: for him to be appointed to the planning commission. The doctor explains, "I can promise you, it will be the longest six months of your life."

Since the appointment of the first planning commission in 1907 in Hartford, Connecticut, there has been debate about the proper role and responsibilities of commissions and commissioners. From their inception, almost exclusive emphasis has been placed on semiautonomous citizen planning commissions. These independent commissions were intended to insulate city planning from political and administrative influences. Knowledgeable citizens were to be drawn into public service by appointment to the planning commission. They were to formulate long-range comprehensive plans for guiding the growth and development of their communities. It was believed that such an approach to city planning was needed because the local municipal legislative authorities were too political and too involved in the pressure of day-to-day problems to be able to carry out long-range planning responsibilities.

A scathing indictment of independent, autonomous planning commissions was rendered in 1941 by Robert Walker in *The Planning Function in Urban Government.* He argued that planning commissions were politically ineffective, an obstacle to professional planners, and called for major reforms in this area of planning.[22] More recently, Anthony Catanese commented that:

> The first two decades of organized planning and zoning commissions were virtually ineffective, because they were composed of well-meaning amateurs and patricians with a sense of noblesse oblique who were more intent upon embarrassing politicians than playing politics.[23]

There have been substantial changes regarding this aspect of planning. The most popular current concept of this city planning function involves having the planning commission advise the council, with the professional planners serving in a staff role to the chief executive (either the manager or mayor) and in an advisory role to the planning commission.

The influence and effectiveness of planning commissions varies from community to community. Planning commissions can be the epitome of effective chunking or an impediment to innovation and action. As reported in *The Language of Zoning,* planning commissions in some places:

> Have considerable power by playing an important role, not only in shaping public policies, but also in administering land-use controls; in other areas, planning commissions have been abolished or relegated to a minimal advisory role.[24]

Some commissioners believe they are to serve at the beck and call of the elected officials and should not initiate problem-solving efforts unless so instructed. Some commissions are satisfied with the status quo or fear rocking the boat and they can be a serious impediment to any action. William Lucy, an associate professor in the School of Architecture at the University of Virginia, has found that in policy making and planning "the most thorough way for opponents to block an idea is for them to be well-placed and to refuse to play the game." This partly explains why opponents to planning frequently seek membership on planning commissions. A particular commission in a medium-sized city in the Southwest exhibited what can only be described as an Alamo complex. They defiantly notified the new, aggressive planning director that nothing was broken, so there was nothing that he should try to fix. They made it clear that there would be no negotiations and no compromise. A line was drawn in the dirt; they dared the planning director to step over it.

In the above situation, the planning commission's attitude reflected that of a majority of the city council. The council was exceedingly pleased with the status quo and was satisfied with a "do-nothing" commission. The planning director, whose philosophy was, "If it hasn't been fixed, it's probably broken," struggled with the unyielding and stifling commission for two years and finally resigned to take a better position in another city. A year later the following feature editorial appeared in the local newspaper:

> [The city] at this point in history lacks energy, it lacks creativity, and bottom line, it lacks the guts to make radical changes in the way it views itself and the world around it. . . . We have a sorry bunch of public officials. I call them "sorry" in that they don't seem to be able to take the long-range view. . . . A recognition by elected officials that long-range planning is important, that goal setting is important, and that courage to stand up to special interests is important would signal a critical change in attitude.

Planning commissions can be an obstacle or impediment to an effective planning program, but they can also be an asset. In the right organizational context, commissioners who show ready acceptance of fluidity can become part of a truly remarkable problem-solving entity and have a profound impact on achieving excellence in planning.

In November 1986, Becky Black, chairperson of the seven-member Bannock County Planning Commission in Pacatello, Washington, was recognized as the planner of the month by the *Western Planner* for her leadership role on the commission and her influence on the planning profession.[25] She earned this award the hard way, as you can tell from the following short story that appeared in *The Western Planner*:

> The first planning and zoning commission meeting Becky attended was rather long and arduous. In the first decisions of the evening she found herself voting contrary to the majority of the commission. During a short break at mid-meeting, one of the older members of the commission (no longer on the commission) took her aside and told her in a fatherly manner that that was not the way things were done. He offered the friendly tip that usually everyone "kind of went along together" in order to get out earlier. Retrieving her jaw from the floor, Becky replied politely that she didn't wish to cause trouble but may not be able to be part of the tradition.[26]

Black indicated that her greatest challenge on the commission was "to find and keep the balance between the rights of private property owners and the general public."[27] David Allor, writing in *The Planning Commissioners Guide,* suggests that being an effective commissioner requires "balance in the interpretation of the opinions of others, compassion in the giving of advice and the making of recommendations, neutrality in negotiation of disagreements, and fairness in the granting of permissions and the imposition of restrictions."[28] While these obviously are desirable traits for individual commissioners, the effectiveness of the commission is greatly influenced, if not dominated, by its organization structure, operational characteristics, and political circumstances. The following is a brief list of the most important characteristics of successful commissions:

- The selection of commission members provides broad-based representation (a cross section of community, background, talent, and abilities).

- The commissioner selection process places emphasis on community spirited membership that is representative, caring, and responsive to community needs.

- There are policies, rules, and procedures for terminating inactive members.

- Orientation is provided for new members by the staff and commission. Day-long retreats are particularly effective.

- The commission is well-organized, with clearly defined goals and objectives and established priorities. This is essential if the commission is to function as more than a mere "zoning commission."

- There is good communication characterized by openness at meetings and positive relationships between commission members, staff, and the general public.

- There is effective realization and utilization of outside resources.

- There is receptiveness as evidenced by open-mindedness, flexibility, and willingness to change or to compromise.

- There is an understanding and acceptance of responsibilities as evidenced by a willingness to work to face difficult issues, to stay informed, to listen and learn, and to give the time necessary for the job.

- There is a commitment to striving for a group consensus on issues through cooperation, teamwork, and the development of commission policies. This is particularly valued by elected officials.

- There is able leadership characterized by well-run meetings, good preparation, effective agendas, active committees, good attendance, promptness, respectful membership, and a pleasant atmosphere at meetings.

- Meeting times, dates, and places are selected for maximum convenience to the general public.

- Regular evaluations of the effectiveness of the commission and staff are provided.

- Members have a personal commitment based on concern, dedication, a feeling of usefulness, and an acceptance of self and others.

- Productive membership is achieved through perseverance and a willingness to accept risk, vision, and enthusiasm.

- There is an educated and knowledgeable commission that receives continuing education through workshops, conference trips, and published materials.

The chair has a major responsibility for shaping the operational characteristics and level of performance of the planning commission and should be committed to an objective recruitment process, an informed commission, interesting meetings, and a cohesive working atmosphere. It is important that the chair be sensitive to the need for a balanced, representative board and actively and objectively recruit appropriate individuals with interest, knowledge, and talent. The members should understand the purpose and goals of the commission and be provided with a mixture of training programs, workshops, seminars, outside speakers, and trips. The meetings should be informative and stimulating. The chair should delegate and assign individuals with talents and abilities to specific tasks or subcommittees and encourage open discussion and debate. Lastly, a cohesive atmosphere must be created conducive to the establishment of effective working relationships—one that is based on trust and respect and willingness to take risks and accept changes.

Any type of citizen advisory group in local government can be improved by emulating the organizational and operational characteristics of successful commissions. However, the critical role and responsibility of planning and zoning commissions demands an extraordinary commitment to excellence and a willingness to maximize effectiveness. Planning commissions can be stodgy, paperbound, and bureaucratic, or they can function as an action-inducing chunk. It is doubtful if an elected city council could function in such a capacity.

PRODUCTION OF PRODUCTS AND SERVICES

Performance can make an administration. Planning can wreck it. ROBERT MOSES

A bias for action also requires a commitment on the part of city planners to the production or delivery of products and services. Richard Milbrodt, city manager, South Lake Tahoe, California, has found that "citizens and council members need to see, feel, and touch results."[29] For years planners wasted time arguing whether planning was a process or a product. As Anthony Catanese warned in *Planners and Local Politics:*

> (t)he basic problems with the planning process are that it promises to do too much, takes too long, covers too many problems, is too complicated, and produces results that are largely vague and esoteric.[30]

In addition, the planning profession's traditional emphasis on and excessive concern with the process has often created a general mind set for many planners that minimized the role, value, and importance of the product that they subsequently produced. The

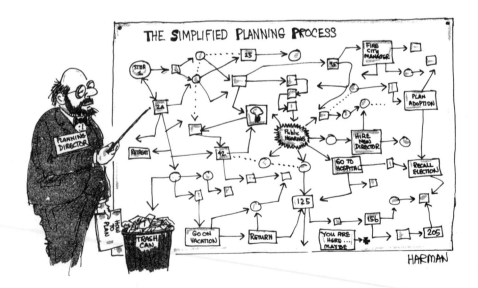

typical planning process is almost always diagrammed as a circular, never-ending, repetitive process (see Figure 2-3), in contrast to the strategic planning process (see Figure 2-4). It's easy to believe that the product or solution that results from the lengthy application of the traditional planning process is incomplete because updating and recycling is constantly needed. You don't have to worry about getting it right because you are still working on it. In this situation it is difficult to develop much enthusiasm for implementing the tentative solution. It is placed on the shelf, and the planning staff sits back and waits to see if anything happens to it.

In *The City Planning Process*, Alan Altshuler suggested that "the job of the city planner is to propose courses of action, *not* to execute them"[31] (emphasis added). Uninformed planners could easily interpret this to mean they should not get their hands dirty. After all, if planners are only responsible for planning and not doing, then they are certainly not responsible for what others might or might not do with their plans. "A more fruitful way of looking at planning," according to John Friedmann in *Retracking America*, "is to see it as a way of linking scientific and technical knowledge to *actions* in the public domain"[32] (emphasis added).

In contrast to Altshuler's views on the role of the planner, Margarita McCoy, professor of planning at the California State Polytechnic University in Pomona, advocates and teaches that planners are responsible for harvesting the fruits of their labor. In an article about her winning the 1986 Distinguished Service Award from the American Planning Association, McCoy was quoted as saying:

> Planners have to move beyond the "Johnny Appleseed" approach (of) writing plans and then leaving it to someone else to carry them out. . . . Instead, they must stay and work the land, as farmers do, to carry the plans out.[33]

Making a difference is a recurring theme for successful planners. According to Harold Koontz and Cyril O'Donnell in *Principles of Management: An Analysis of Managerial Functions:*

> Planning is deciding in advance what to do, how to do it, when to do it, and who is to do it. Planning bridges the gap from where we are to where we want to go. It makes it possible for things to occur which would not otherwise happen.[34]

In the private sector, it is recognized that planning should be a process that makes things happen—that produces desired outcomes. Russell Ackoff concluded in *A Concept of Corporate Planning*

Figure 2–3

Policymaker and Citizen Inputs into the Classical Planning Process

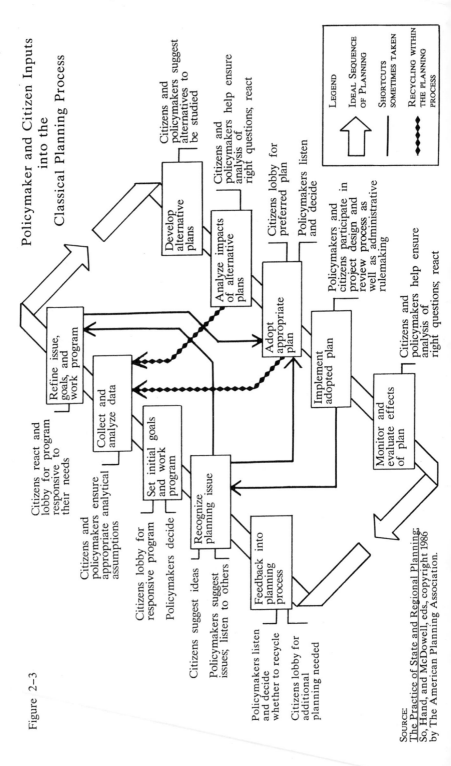

Citizens react and lobby for program responsive to their needs

Citizens and policymakers ensure appropriate analytical assumptions

Citizens lobby for responsive program

Policymakers decide

Refine issue, goals, and work program

Collect and analyze data

Set initial goals and work program

Recognize planning issue

Develop alternative plans

Citizens and policymakers suggest alternatives to be studied

Analyze impacts of alternative plans

Citizens and policymakers help ensure analysis of right questions; react

Adopt appropriate plan

Citizens lobby for preferred plan

Policymakers listen and decide

Implement adopted plan

Policymakers and citizens participate in project design and review process as well as administrative rulemaking

Monitor and evaluate effects of plan

Citizens and policymakers help ensure analysis of right questions; react

Citizens suggest ideas

Policymakers suggest issues; listen to others

Feedback into planning process

Policymakers listen and decide whether to recycle

Citizens lobby for additional planning needed

Legend

IDEAL SEQUENCE OF PLANNING

SHORTCUTS SOMETIMES TAKEN

RECYCLING WITHIN THE PLANNING PROCESS

SOURCE:
The Practice of State and Regional Planning; So, Hand, and McDowell, eds, copyright 1986 by The American Planning Association.

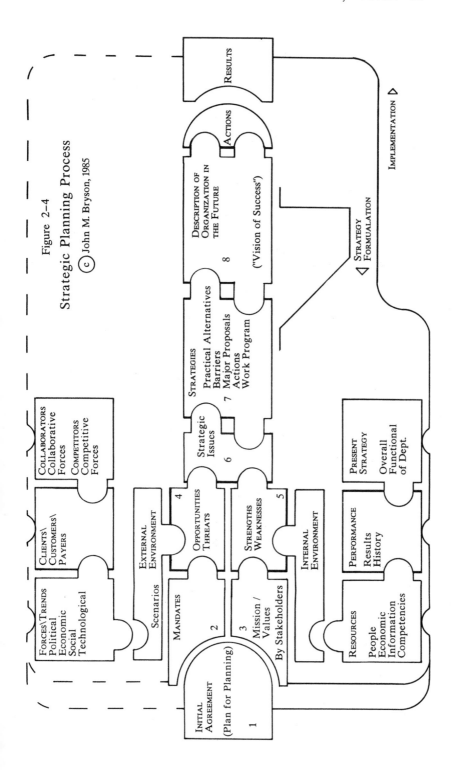

Figure 2–4

Strategic Planning Process

ⓒ John M. Bryson, 1985

that "planning is the design of a future and of effective ways of bringing it about."[35] Carol Barrett, former planning director for Annapolis, Maryland, and currently director of community development for the Greater Washington Board of Trade, observed that "(u)nlike planners, business people don't believe the process is the product; they're always saying the equivalent of 'where's the beef?' "[36] Thomas Dark, assistant city administrative officer for Shreveport, Louisiana, demonstrated that many others in the public sector also recognize the importance of performance when he wrote that "it's more important to fix the streets than to have a procedure telling us how we fix streets."[37]

In *Elements of Physics*, Alpheus Smith and John Cooper pointed out that "during the eighteenth century, supporters of Huygens argued that light was a wave motion, while followers of Newton held that light was a stream of particles."[38] This wave-particle duality was a source of great confusion until the development of modern quantum mechanics, which "now considers that light possesses a sort of dual personality, part wavelike and part particlelike."[39]

While the debate in planning over whether planning is a process or a product has not raged quite as long as the conflict over the properties of light, it is still an important issue to the planning profession. In our experience, planning, too, shares dual properties, and effective planning requires a commitment to both a process and a product. In an ineffective planning agency, the process is often a surrogate for substance. The biggest challenge is to make sure that the planning process doesn't overpower everything else, that an obsession with planning doesn't start to interfere with doing business. Always remember that "doing is to planning as catching is to fishing." To paraphrase Roscoe Pound, "city planning, like law, is judged by result, not by its logical processes."

Based on his experiences as the commissioner of budget and planning for Atlanta, Georgia, Leon Eplan found that "planners are taught how to produce plans, but little emphasis is placed on how to get those plans implemented."[40] He believes that planners have the responsibility of preparing plans and then figuring out how they are going to carry them out. For planners to meet their responsibilities, Eplan contends, "they have to write ordinances; they have to lobby; they have to be willing to change; and they have to refine, interpret, and cost-out."[41]

A good example of one planning department's efforts to explain the local planning process and to focus attention on the critically important link between plan preparation and plan implementation is demonstrated in the following excerpt from a recent planning document from the city of Fort Worth:

> An "issue/action oriented" planning process was used to develop the Mid-South Revitalization and Redevelopment Plan. The first step in the process involved working with owners and residents to identify the significant problems and issues in the area. This phase was followed by surveys of existing land use, population, and socioeconomic characteristics, structural conditions, and ownership patterns of housing, streets, utilities and community facilities in order to provide a data base for the Plan. Next, goals and objectives were developed to provide guidance and direction to the staff and to facilitate the monitoring and evaluation of the success of implementation proposals and actions. The culmination of this process was the development of specific policies and proposals for resolving the critical issues in this area and for achieving the goals and objectives that had been agreed upon.
>
> Implementation, monitoring, and maintenance will be essential to the success of this Plan. Upon the adoption of the Plan by City Council, it will be necessary to prepare an "action plan" that will include a step-by-step program for implementation. Annual measurable objectives will be established on a priority basis, and implementation responsibilities will be assigned.
>
> The goals, objectives, policies, and proposals in the Plan are not static or end-state. As conditions in the area change and new problems emerge, the Council may need to reconsider and alter the Plan. Some proposals may even turn out to be unrealistic or unworkable.
>
> An effective Plan will depend on a commitment to reviewing and updating it on an annual basis. Properly done, the annual review refreshes memories and provides for an accounting of our successes and failures during the year. It also encourages all parties to set their sights on the major steps to be taken during the next year to carry out the goals, objectives, policies, and proposals in the Plan. The Plan is not the final product. It is only a resource that can be used to aid in solving problems and improving the quality of life in this area. The Plan will be judged by its results, not by its processes.[42]

Peter Drucker noted that "the test of a good plan is whether management actually commits resources to action which will bring results in the future."[43] Clients of the plan should be asking the decision makers and the managers of the organization, "Have you put your best people to work on implementation, and who are they?" Very little is ever accomplished unless scarce resources, both personnel and financial, are concentrated on a small number of clearly defined priorities. Next it is essential that responsibility be recognized, accountability assigned, a deadline imposed, and the resulting performance evaluated. Drucker correctly points out that the result of the decision-making process "is not knowledge but strategy" and "*its aim is action now.*"[44]

Los Angeles is one of the more well-known cities where there has been growing dissatisfaction with the lack of results from planning. *Planning* magazine, reporting on the resignation of Calvin Hamilton, the long-time planning director of Los Angeles, reported that "homeowners blamed him for not implementing the master plan," and prominent local politicians said that he was "highly regarded as a thinker" but was "out of date in an era when implementation was so important."[45] *Los Angeles Times* reporter and columnist Sam Hall Kaplan summed up their complaints by noting that:

(a)s development has nibbled away at their quality of life, casting shadows and spilling traffic into neighborhoods, residents have been growing more and more frustrated with the city's planning process, or what they prefer to call a lack of process. . . .[46]

Recently, in a city in Montana, a developer seeking to speed up the review process submitted to the planning commission three minor plats in lieu of a single major plat. Plat approval was necessary so that he could proceed with the construction of a K Mart store that would bring 200 new jobs to the area and inject $3 million into the local depressed economy. The planning director opposed the procedural short-cut, which was permitted by the ordinance, primarily because "approving the plat would set a precedent that other, less cooperative developers might take advantage of."[47] As common sense might suggest, the plat was approved and the local paper triumphantly reported that 200 jobs would be coming to town because council members were more concerned about getting things done than about procedure.[48] Expecting elected officials to choose process or procedure over jobs is an invitation to ineffectiveness. The local planners could have suported this project and proposed strengthening the ordinance to avoid possible abuse by less scrupulous developers. Instead, they promoted the impression that as planners they were more concerned about procedure than results.

In contrast to the preceding example, a planner on the East Coast told us the following story. A state governor was trying to demonstrate his "can-do" ability and wanted to be able to announce before election day that a long-sought and much needed bridge was going to be built. The secretary of transportation employed a planning consultant firm to review the state's environmental laws, and the consultants found a technical loophole that would permit the draft environmental impact report for the project to be accepted as the final report. In addition, a way was found to speed up the publication and public review timetable since all unresolved issues could be mitigated. Although the state environmental secretary didn't like being pressured, he and his staff were impressed with the project and the inventiveness of the consultants, and they decided to go along with the findings. The project was approved in record time, no regulations were violated, and the public interest was protected and served. Unfortunately, this example of results-oriented planning tends to be the exception rather than the rule.

The general public often has a negative perception of planning and planners. In recent years, one critic of planning in Fort Worth, Texas, wrote a series of letters to the mayor and council. He pleaded with them to "please restrict the planning department from wasting time and tax money on land use plans and studies" and suggested that "planners were detrimental to community development because they were only interested in satisfying personal egos or idealistic training." He noted that what was needed was to "actually see real results of such activity [planning]." He observed that:

> . . . younger planners wish to appear necessary, useful, meaningful, important, and very vital to society. Perhaps this usefulness is to continue one's job and to create an apparent necessity or to make work in order to continue one's present occupation. The big question is in this area: is the public being served by great shuffling of colored papers and verbalization? What is the immediate and especially the long-lasting effect toward all of those who are actually producing something?

Obviously, a bias for action is not the same as a bias for busywork. However, rather than being faulted for laziness, many planners readily accept being labeled idealistic and ineffective. Bureaucratic empire-building and make-work programs intended to demonstrate a planning presence and involvement in community problems are no substitute for concrete products and useful services. Sam Hall Kaplan contends that many planners he has known are intelligent, well-meaning, and sensitive to community concerns but, in a scathing indictment of the profession, he adds that:

> Like public planners elsewhere, when it comes to taking an initiative and implementing an idea, or simply supporting one, they seem to disappear behind a pile of printouts and projections. . . .[49]

Many successful planning departments feature at least one high-visibility planning project with short-term value in addition to their conventional projects and services. Promotion of a steady stream of useful products builds support for planning and minimizes the number of people who ask, "What have you done for me lately?" Alan Altshuler found that one reason the St. Paul planning department under the direction of David Loeks was very successful was because Loeks emphasized the production of a series of attractive pamphlets and reports. Altshuler noted that:

> (T)he St. Paul planning staff . . . did almost no original research, and never had more than two trained planners free from zoning and administrative chores; but in the final two and one-half years of Loeks's tenure it published seven handsome reports. Two were presentations of census data (one on population, one on housing); two explained and "sold" programs of other agencies (urban renewal and freeways); and three proposed procedural, as opposed to substantive, policies.[50]

Unfortunately, many planning agencies concentrate too heavily on complex projects with long lead times and limited short-term application, or even worse, they become enmeshed in potentially unsolvable problems. As Fred Bair, a noted planning and zoning authority, pointedly observed:

> I have seen any number of cases where planners could have taken hold of a problem right under their nose and done something intelligent to solve it, but chose instead to engage in lengthy research as to the shape of things to come while the problem grew beyond manageable proportions. That kind of approach doesn't make much sense.[51]

FOCUS AND SIMPLIFY

The question is not whether decisions must be made on the basis of simplified assumptions about the real world; it is rather which complicating factors shall be deemphasized, how significance shall be judged, and what the substance of the assumptions shall be. ALAN ALTSHULER

To build respect, support, and effectiveness, planners must concentrate on a limited and manageable number of definable, concrete, and solvable issues. Focus first on the one or two issues that seem to

You Need Simplicity

Only an obvious idea will work today. The overwhelming volume of communication prevents anything else from succeeding.

But the obvious isn't always so obvious. "Boss" Kettering had a sign which he placed on the wall of the General Motors Research Building in Dayton: "This problem when solved will be simple."

"Raisins from California. Nature's candy."

"Moist and meaty Gainesburgers. The canned dog food without the can."

"Bubble Yum. Number yum in bubble gum."

These are the kinds of simple ideas that work today. Simple concepts expressed with simple words used in a straightforward way.

Often the solution to a problem is so simple that thousands of people have looked at it without seeing it. When an idea is clever or complicated, however, we should be suspicious. It probably won't work because it's not simple enough.

The history of science is a history of the Ketterings of this world who found simple solutions to complex problems.

Reprinted with permission from Ries and Trout, <u>Positioning: The Battle for Your Mind.</u> Copyright 1981 by the McGraw-Hill Book Company.

---

be most critical. Then proceed by breaking down complicated issues and problems into a series of simple, resolvable matters. Many decision makers in local government are not unlike the successful corporate president who disliked long memos and told his staff to "boil it down to something I can grasp." Even the most complicated problem can be understood and resolved if presented as a series of simple problems. An appropriate Chinese proverb is, "Settle one difficulty and you keep hundreds away." Planners need to learn to place an emphasis on solving one difficulty at a time to increase their perceived value and effectiveness.

Planners and decision makers have no realistic alternative to the strategy of focusing and simplifying. Charles Lindbloom provided the following definitive explanation of why this approach is essential to public administrators and policy analysts: "Limits on human intellectual capacities and on available information set definite limits to man's capacity to be comprehensive. In actual fact, therefore, no one can practice the rational comprehensive method for really complex problems, and every administrator faced with a sufficiently complex problem must find ways drastically to simplify."[52]

POLITICAL CONSIDERATIONS

The question is no longer whether planning is part of a political process, rather how planning can be made part of good politics. Good planning and good politics are an unbeatable combination for a working democracy.
ANTHONY CATANESE

Planning and politics are closely related. In *Thinking Strategically: A Primer for Public Leaders*, Susan Walter and Patrick Choate concluded that "politics, although often used as an excuse for poor government management, no more makes government unmanageable than competition and rapid change makes business unmanageable."[53] Planners need to stop using politics as an excuse for ineffectiveness and come to realize and accept that it is an essential, integral part of an effective planning process.

Leon Eplan contends that "planning is a political process" and that "the person who does not realize that every planning decision is a political decision is not going to get very far."[54] Melvin Webber went so far as to suggest that "there are no scientifically or technically correct answers, only politically appropriate ones."[55] Donald Spaid, former planning coordinator for St. Paul, argued that "if we are going to have a city that is developed in accordance with the plan, the planner and politician are going to have to get in bed together."[56] He points out that he "never met a planner who actually built something; *it is the political process that causes things to be built.*"[57] Even the more moderate view expressed by Lisa Peattie holds that:

> planning without a political force behind it becomes a paper exercise and politics without planning becomes a politics of symbols or personalities: we say that this candidate or that movement lacks a program.[58]

Anthony Catanese and Paul Farmer edited a series of essays and interviews with seven successful nationally recognized planners in *Personality, Politics and Planning*. They found that each of these planners made it known that they were working for political leaders and within a political arena.[59] It is clear that effective planners must be sensitive and responsive to political considerations. Linda Dalton, former chair of the Seattle Planning Commission, described in the *Journal of the American Planning Association* how in less than ten years, "... Seattle's executive planning agency changed from a promising new office to a defensive unit fighting for its survival."[60] Dalton concluded that some of the factors responsible for the decline of the planning agency were outside the influence of the agency's directors; however, there were significant areas where effective leadership could have had a positive influence. In particular, noting the implications for other planning agencies, she concluded that:

> Agency leadership must negotiate a modest scope or set of activities that ultimately serves the broader purposes of planning but also produces some periodic *output* and meets the ongoing needs of the executive and legislative branches and line departments.[61]

Public officials need to be perceived by their constituents as effective service providers. In *Urban Politics and Public Policy*, Robert Lineberry and Ira Sharkansky pointed out that local governments are seen as service institutions, not places for settling the great issues of the day; they "are supposed to 'get things done,' picking up the garbage, providing fire and police protection, fixing potholes in streets, telling neighbors to fix houses in disrepair, and generally making services available to citizens."[62]

Speaking on "What Elected Officials Want From Planners" at the October 1985 annual conference of the Texas Chapter of the American Planning Association, Dallas city councilman Craig Holcomb stated that he wants "fast, private answers to current problems and ideas for the future." At the same session, Austin city council member Sally Shipman, who was also a member of both the commission of the American Institute of Certified Planners and the board of directors of the American Planning Association, urged planners to generate and express ideas and to remember that councils understand and appreciate "straight talk" delivered in concise, simple reports.

Several years ago, while a member of the faculty of the Graduate School of Management at Vanderbilt University, Dennis Rondinelli pointed out that "with the increasing complexity of urban decision making, political leaders and urban administrators are demanding from planners pragmatic assistance with policy formulation and implementation."[63]

Incorporating Political Factors Into Planning Analysis

Political analysis has several meanings. In one sense political analysis refers to the acceptability of the alternatives to the political system. How will politicians, decision makers, and voters respond to our client's preferred alternative? This question cannot be answered in isolation, however, since our client (as well as ourselves) is part of the political process and can affect the outcome of policy decisions. Political analysis, therefore, has at least three meanings in policy analysis and planning. There is the analysis we do to help clients discover preferences. There is the analysis of how the political system will respond to the preferred alternative. Finally, there is the analysis of the actions we and our client might take to cause the preferred alternative to be politically acceptable to other participants in the decision and implementation process.

Patton and Sawicki, Basic Methods of Policy Analysis and Planning, p. 283. Copyright 1986, Prentice-Hall, Inc., Englewood Cliffs, N.J.

Pragmatic assistance requires adherence to some form of chunking. Grand visionary schemes and long-range comprehensive plans too often are irrelevant and easily ignored in the political decision making process. Rondinelli suggested that planners ". . . must isolate components of urban problems and reduce them to calculable proportions. Policy planners must indicate how resources can be mobilized and focused on remediable aspects of problems. . ."[64]

Many planners are appallingly ignorant of local political decision-making processes. It can be argued that the finger of blame for the deficiency can be pointed toward those educational institutions that fail to teach urban politics, but the ultimate responsibility must be shouldered by individual planners. It is like the story of the rube who had never seen a train and found himself walking down a smooth logged path between two metal rails that cut through a rugged forested area. Suddenly, from out of the woods, a train, belching smoke and making a ferocious noise, appeared. Running along the tracks until he was exhausted, the man was finally overtaken by the train and violently knocked into the bordering trees and rocks. A hunter who came to the man's assistance pointedly asked why he hadn't jumped off the tracks. The man replied "Wal, ah knew iffen ah couldn't outrun that rascal on smooth ground, ah didn't have no chance atall in the brush!"

How many times do technocratic planners have to be run over before they learn that political decision makers use a process that is different from the conventional planning process and that this fact has to be taken into account in order to be effective? Professor Howell Baum interviewed a number of planners for his book, *Planners and Public Expectations*, and found that "planners exercise limited power in decision-making because they misunderstand the ways in which decisions are made in bureaucratic organizations and in the political process."[65] Effective planning depends on an awareness of and sensitivity to the political and organizational interests of those involved in the decision-making process. Figure 2-5 from Dennis Rondinelli's classic article "Urban Planning as Policy Analysis: Management of Urban Change," provides a description of the categories of skills and knowledge of the various relationships which are needed by planners seeking to become effectively involved in the typical political policymaking process. The effectiveness of planners greatly depends on obtaining the necessary skills and knowledge and an understanding of the manipulating processes of political interaction. Intervention and participatory involvement in the political decision-making process is critical if planners are to be effective and actually influence public policies. After all, planning as described by John Friedmann "may be simply regarded as reason acting on a network of ongoing activities through the intervention of certain decision structures and processes."[66]

Figure 2-6 depicts the stages in the theoretical intervention process as developed by Jerome Kaufman, chairman of the planning department at the University of Wisconsin-Madison. Kaufman contends that "the choice of strategies and tactics should evolve from a careful analysis of a mix of behavioral, attitudinal and resource characteristics of the key individuals and groups."[67] Carl Patton and David Sawicki, in *Basic Methods of Policy Analysis and Planning*, offered to unskilled planners the following tips about political analysis:

1. Determine whether the obvious problem is only a symptom of a larger controversy.

2. Make sure you look for underlying issues and related problems.

3. Check your sources of information. Much political data is anecdotal, second-hand, and vague. Use several sources if possible, and question the validity of sensational data.

Figure 2-5

Skills and Knowledge Needed in Urban Policy Making

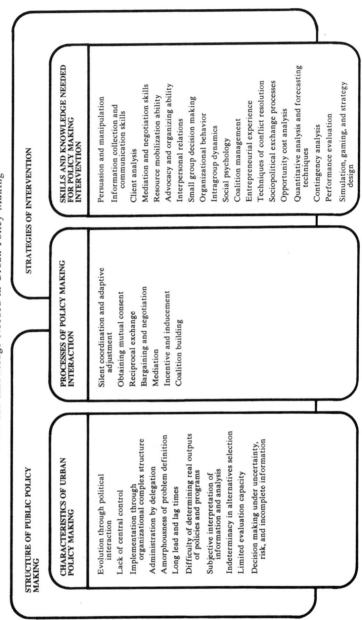

STRUCTURE OF PUBLIC POLICY MAKING

STRATEGIES OF INTERVENTION

CHARACTERISTICS OF URBAN POLICY MAKING

Evolution through political interaction

Lack of central control

Implementation through organizational complex structure

Administration by delegation

Amorphousness of problem definition

Long lead and lag times

Difficulty of determining real outputs of policies and programs

Subjective interpretation of information and analysis

Indeterminacy in alternatives selection

Limited evaluation capacity

Decision making under uncertainty, risk, and incomplete information

PROCESSES OF POLICY MAKING INTERACTION

Silent coordination and adaptive adjustment

Obtaining mutual consent

Reciprocal exchange

Bargaining and negotiation

Mediation

Incentive and inducement

Coalition building

SKILLS AND KNOWLEDGE NEEDED FOR POLICY MAKING INTERVENTION

Persuasion and manipulation

Information collection and communication skills

Client analysis

Mediation and negotiation skills

Resource mobilization ability

Advocacy and organizing ability

Interpersonal relations

Small group decision making

Organizational behavior

Intragroup dynamics

Social psychology

Coalition management

Entrepreneurial experience

Techniques of conflict resolution

Sociopolitical exchange processes

Opportunity cost analysis

Quantitative analysis and forecasting techniques

Contingency analysis

Performance evaluation

Simulation, gaming, and strategy design

Source: "Urban Planning as Policy Analysis," *Journal of the American Institute of Planners*, copyright 1973.

Figure 2–6

Steps in the Recommended Intervention Planning Process

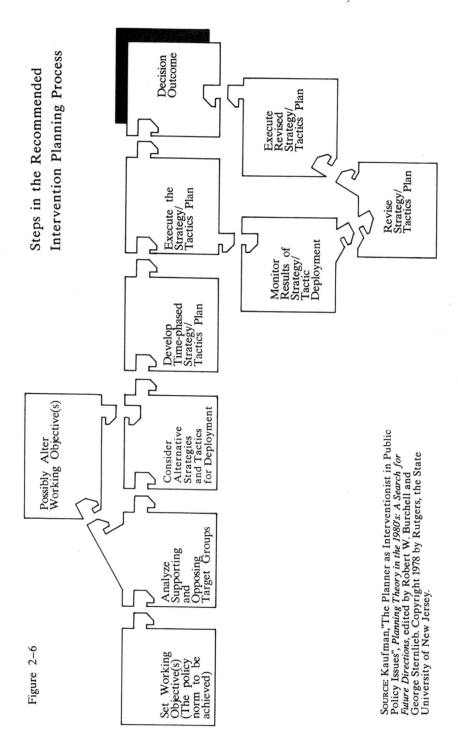

Set Working Objective(s) (The policy norm to be achieved)

Analyze Supporting and Opposing Target Groups

Possibly Alter Working Objective(s)

Consider Alternative Strategies and Tactics for Deployment

Develop Time-phased Strategy/Tactics Plan

Execute the Strategy/Tactics Plan

Decision Outcome

Execute Revised Strategy/Tactics Plan

Monitor Results of Strategy/Tactic Deployment

Revise Strategy/Tactics Plan

SOURCE: Kaufman,"The Planner as Interventionist in Public Policy Issues", *Planning Theory in the 1980's: A Search for Future Directions*, edited by Robert W. Burchell and George Sternlieb. Copyright 1978 by Rutgers, the State University of New Jersey.

4. Take advantage of internal review. Does your account of the political situation ring true to other analysts? Do they interpret past events in the same way?

5. Remember that political data are only part of the fact base. Do not let this aspect of analysis displace other important components.[68]

In *The Progressive City: Planning and Participation, 1969-1984,* Pierre Calvel, of Cornell University, describes the accomplishments of a number of cities and concludes that progressive ideas caught on because local planners and politicians learned to leave their traditional technical roles. In particular, Clavel observed that "(p)lanners in these cities learned to deal with conflict situations" and that "requires political commitment."[69]

Myles Rademan, former director of community development for Crested Butte, Colorado, and a 1985 Kellogg National Fellow, predicted that a fundamental shift in thinking is required in order to save planners from being "consigned to a purgatory of perpetual irrelevance."[70] His solution to the creeping malaise of ineffectiveness that characterizes the planning profession is: ". . . that planners align themselves locally with those factions and groups expressing action-oriented, positivistic community views. They might be developers, neighborhood associations, or private entrepreneurs. We must absolutely shake our image as faceless technicians, and be prepared to dirty our hands and souls in the hurly-burly political arena."[71]

The early experiences of the independent planning commission established in New York City in 1936 by municipal charter demonstrates that a bias for action must be balanced by an awareness of political considerations. Rexford Tugwell, the commission's first chairman, was a prominent figure in the history of planning. Tugwell wrote later in his career that if politics is the art of the possible, then it is "only when the planner . . . gets beyond the sphere of what the politicians consider possible that he is a planner at all."[72] His personal view of the New York city council can best be illustrated by the following comment from his diary, written after his resignation as chairman of the commission:

> (they) can be counted on to do their best to prove that Hitler is right; that legislators are corrupt, always anxious to be subservient to any special interest, always ready to act against the public interest.[73]

Tugwell lacked the political skills and tact necessary to direct a successful planning program and, as a result, he was able to accomplish the rare feat of alienating politicians, bureaucrats, business-men, civic groups, and the general public alike. Mark Gelfand, as-sociate professor of history at Boston College, observed that "Tugwell's excursions into public housing, zoning, and master planning would be marked by frustration and defeat."[74]

Jon Peterson, associate professor of American history at Queens College of City University of New York, reported that the political origins of the nation's first comprehensive city plan—the McMil-lan Plan for Washington, D.C.—"underscores the critical role of power and politics in the making of workable comprehensive plans, then and now."[75] He concluded that the history of planning gives clear evidence that ". . . successful planning must be regard-ed as much as a complex political art as a knowledge-based field of endeavor."[76]

In *The Planning Function in Urban Government*, Robert Walker con-tended that planning agencies would not be successful unless they could develop more harmonious personal relations with political decision makers and the personnel in the various operating agen-cies of local government. Walker believed that planning agencies would not survive if they remained intent on promoting their own autonomous policies. In the second edition of his book, he suggest-ed that the following three alternative roles were available for planners:

1. To flail away ineffectually in the public forum,
2. To deal with issues of slight importance (i.e., zoning to protect property values, or designing individual public works), or
3. To serve as the *confidential* advisor of incumbent officials.[77]

Walker noted that while most planning agencies had selected the second alternative, he believed that the third alternative was the only option that would produce meaningful involvement and effectiveness for planners. To increase their influence, a growing number of planners are now learning to respect and to take advan-tage of the political aspects of local decision making. Ann Leviton, former director of the Whitman County Regional Planning Coun-cil in Colfax, California, said that her hardest lesson was "that peo-ple don't always do the rational thing and that almost everything is political."[78] Susan Brody, planning director for Eugene, Oregon, re-cently noted that over the years she has learned the importance of having a sharp political sense.[79] In a similar vein, Michael Carroll, vice-president of community development for Lilly Endowment, offered the following political advice to planners when he was deputy mayor of Indianapolis:

> Deal with the decision-making process on its own ground. Do not attempt to implement a decision on the basis of the planning rationale behind the decision. Argue on the basis of the political sensibility of that decision. . . . Argue that you have attempted to define the public interest in such a way that you touched base with all of the groups that are likely to be affected by the decision, and argue that this is the best compromise you can arrive at with the least negative consequences. Those are very important parameters for the decision-making process.[80]

To identify areas of agreement and differences about how planners approached their jobs, Hamid Shirvani, currently dean of the College of Architecture and Planning at the University of Colorado at Denver, in 1985 interviewed eleven successful practicing planners in positions of authority around the country. Based on the interviews, Shirvani concluded that, "These new planners have become political animals; they know how to try to expand their roles, yet they recognize the built-in limitations they face. They have learned through experience how to be of influence."[81]

Action-oriented planning must be based on a commitment to meaningful effective intervention and involvement in the political decision-making process that results in an immediate solution to a current, pressing problem; it also must have an incremental impact on more complex, longer term issues. This approach, as espoused by Leon Martel in *Mastering Change*, "requires taking a long-term perspective and adopting long-term strategies, yet at the same time having the ability to be flexible, to adapt quickly, and to make appropriate short-term tactical responses."[82] In local government it is exemplified by the philosophy of Gale Wilson, the nationally recognized city manager of Fairfield, California, who says that "my vision for the future tells me how to act in the present."[83]

The political reality, according to Charles Lindbloom in his classic essay, "The Science of Muddling Through," is that "democracies change their policies almost entirely through *incremental* adjustments. Policy does not move in leaps and bounds."[84] The key challenge for planners is to relate these incremental advances to a broader vision of the future.

Joseph Vitt, Jr., former director of city development in Kansas City, Missouri, said that one of the major strategies of his administration was to look "for programs and projects that are action-oriented and that can be implemented, even partially, in the short run because of the incremental nature of the environment in which we operate."[85] He described this strategy as "purposeful incrementalism," meaning that decisions are going to be made on a day-to-day basis and that his agency was "interested in giving some purpose to those incremental decisions and in guarding them within some kind of general framework."[86]

The challenge for the planning director is "to walk the line between providing good information and good judgment and good recommendations on problems that are immediate and pressing," according to Paul Farmer, deputy planning director for Pittsburg, while "at the same time providing a long-range outlook and a reasonable kind of judgement on long-range policy directions."[87] It does not resurrect the old issue of incrementalism versus the ad hoc as long as we follow the advice given by Israel Stollman, executive director for the American Planning Association, who stated that "(t)he qualification of the comprehensive planner, if that planner is to be the best incrementalist, is to know what it is, in the long run, that must be accomplished bit by bit."[88]

Alan Altshuler noted that while it can be argued that planning in the service of discrete political clients is the only kind of planning that can be effective in our system of government and that "in effect, many city planners are acting in accord with this theory today," he found that "they have not permitted themselves to say so."[89] In his words, these successful planners "are unwilling to raise this dictate of expediency to the status of basic dogma" because it would be a repudiation of the profession's traditional idealism and "require a rethinking of their entire conception of the proper role of government in a free society."[90]

While agreeing that attention to the political needs of decision makers will make it possible for local government to pursue goals with greater efficiency than at present, Altshuler expressed concern that the use of this strategy will encourage planners "to eschew all but the most noncontroversial values and the most predictable effects of actions."[91] He was particularly concerned that "if the idea takes hold that a principal component of 'good' planning is political success, the temptation is great to choose 'easy' political paths."[92]

Our solution to the apparent dilemma of having to choose between being effective and upholding the profession's traditional righteous role is simply to recognize that the service philosophy that provides the foundation for success in the political arena can just as easily be provided to other potential customers and clients. It only requires an awareness of the need to expand the client base and to apply the "repositioning" and "focusing" strategies to serving their needs as explained in Chapter 3. Our view is simply that planners who are effective in their relationships with political decision makers are successful because of their ability to service the specialized needs of such clients. Effectiveness is not determined just by whom you are serving, but also by the strategies and tactics used to meet the needs of those clients. Once you understand that there is a whole universe of decision makers who are potential clients for your services and that you are able to transfer the strategies and tactics that produced effective results for public officials to your other clients, you will find that the theoretical underpinnings of the profession are strengthened and in no way diminished by this approach to planning. Effectiveness does not depend on abandoning a commitment to public service. In fact, it's just the opposite. True, meaningful, public service depends on developing an effective planning program—not on martyrdom.

STRATEGIC PLANNING

(There is) increasing interest in borrowing the business concept of strategic planning as an approach to planning cities. FRANK SO

Strategic planning is a tightly focused process that concentrates on selected issues, considers resource availability, assesses strengths and weaknesses as well as threats and opportunities within the community, and most important of all, is *action-oriented*. As explained by George Steiner in *Strategic Planning*, it provides a basis for "making better current decisions to exploit the opportunities and to avoid the threats."[93] Strategic planning does not attempt to make future decisions but rather to concentrate on present decisions while contemplating the future. The concept originated as a military undertaking and was later applied to private sector endeavors beginning in the late 1950s at companies such as General Electric.

In an article on strategic planning in *Planning* magazine, Frank So, deputy director of the American Planning Association, identified the following relevant characteristics of strategic planning:

> The strategic planner exploits existing data and past studies and never uses the lack of data as an excuse for inaction;
>
> Strategic planning relies on knowledge that is widely known and shared and stresses the use of intuitive solutions;

It challenges fundamental assumptions and is a way of promoting creative and innovative thinking;

It separates those things about which you can do something from those that you can't do much about;

It places a priority emphasis on the solving of issues of the most importance;

It provides an improved understanding of mission and purpose and in local government it can provide a vehicle for improving managerial effectiveness.[94]

Jerome Kaufman of the department of urban and regional planning at the University of Wisconsin-Madison, reported at the 1986 annual conference of the American Planning Association that proponents of the strategic planning approach believe it differs from conventional public planning in several ways. Those differences include the belief that strategic planning is more action-, results-, and implementation-oriented; promotes broader and more diverse participation in the planning process; places more emphasis on understanding the community in its external context, determining the opportunities and threats to a community via an environmental scan; embraces competitive behavior on the part of communities; and stresses assessing a community's strengths and weaknesses in the context of opportunities and threats.[95]

In cooperation with Arthur Anderson & Company and the International City Management Association, Public Technology, Inc. has been working in recent years with four communities to test possible applications to local governments of such corporate planning concepts as strategic planning. The four communities are Fort Worth, Texas; Kansas City, Missouri; Fort Collins, Colorado; and Prince George's County, Maryland.

Public Technology, Inc. began leading the Fort Worth chamber of commerce, the school district, and the city through a strategic planning exercise in 1984. The three entities considered and evaluated various issues within the community to determine the focus of the effort. After considerable debate, they selected two broad categories of issues: economic development and education. Two task forces were established to research, analyze, and present recommendations on economic development and education issues using the following steps in the strategic planning process:

• Scanning the environment to determine how external forces would influence events,

- Selecting key issues whose successful resolution would be critical,

- Setting broad goals to establish the direction of strategy development,

- Performing indepth external and internal analysis to look at forces affecting the achievement of goals,

- Developing goals, objectives, and strategies with respect to what could be achieved and how it could be accomplished,

- Developing an implementation plan to carry out strategic actions, and

- Monitoring, updating, and scanning the developed strategies to ensure they were carried out or modified accordingly.

The mission of each task force was to identify a limited number of specific challenges that would capitalize on Fort Worth's unique strengths and overcome major weaknesses, be accomplished in a reasonable period of time with available resources, have a positive economic impact on the community, enhance the local quality of life, and have identifiable timetables and lines of responsibility. The task forces systematically grouped and prioritized numerous proposals that would address the mission statement. Each selected the four challenges that offered the highest potential for fulfilling the program's objectives and developed a series of strategies and action steps for implementation. The results of the economic development task force are summarized in Figure 2-7.

The simplicity and action emphasis of strategic planning starkly contrasts with traditional comprehensive planning, yet many planners do not know or appreciate the difference. In one scene in the movie "About Last Night," the yuppie hero is confronted with a slick-looking ornament at a bar. Liking it, he declares "It's art deco." The piece is not art deco, though it has those sleek modern lines. The joke is that the term art deco has become so degraded by the masses that it is used to describe anything vaguely stylish. In a sense, this is what has happened to comprehensive planning.

It is increasingly difficult to generalize about comprehensive planning because there are so many different opinions and approaches to this specialized area of planning. The Texas chapter of the American Planning Association attempted to develop enabling legislation for planning during the mid-1980s but finally abandoned the effort because of an inability to develop a consensus on the definition of a comprehensive plan. In a sense, comprehensive planning is like the Wampus Cat mascot for Itasca High School in north central Texas. No one knows exactly what a Wampus Cat looks like, but most people claim that it is a cross between a bobcat, a mountain lion, a panther, a tiger, and an oversized tom. No one knows if it has long ears or short, or whether its tail is one color or ringed, but the general feeling is that it's black.

Comprehensive planning also is as difficult to define as the mythical Wampus Cat, and it has generally come to be recognized that it is an impossible ideal as originally envisioned and that we need to seek better planning products.[96] Ernest Bonner, former planning director of Portland, Oregon, is a strong believer in comprehensive planning. Yet he offers the following stinging commentary:

> Comprehensive planners are like the Hare Krishna. Have you ever encountered one in the airport? They want to sell you a book. They want you to know the light. They want you to see God and Truth, and all that. If you ever walk by one of them, then you get an idea how people could walk by you as a planner.[97]

For too many years, comprehensive planning has been a product in search of a market. In many communities, the comprehensive plans funded under Section 701 of the Housing Act of 1949 were the equivalent of Ford Edsels—no one was buying. The client was the U.S. Department of Housing and Urban Development, not the local community. Plans were not designed to solve local problems, but rather to qualify for various grants or public works programs. Implementation was, at best, only a minor consideration.

It is recognized in the private sector that product development must be driven by the needs of the marketplace. Gone are the days of manufacturing a product and then asking the sales department to figure out how to sell it. As noted in *Direct Marketing: Strategy, Planning and Execution:*

> Today the emphasis has reversed, with product-development teams directed to find products or services to meet marketing opportunities. Instead of the old dictum "we make it, you (the consumer) should buy it," we now have "you want it, we'll make it."[98]

In order for planners to be more effective, we are joining the chorus of practitioners and scholars recommending that comprehensive planning should incorporate the issue-oriented, action

Figure 2–7

ECONOMIC DEVELOPMENT TASK FORCE
FORT WORTH ACTION STRATEGIES

CHALLENGE

Give priority attention to economic development in the Cultural District, the Stockyards area, the Central Business District and the Trinity River corridor

Strategy

A. Provide recommendations regarding the implementation of private and public development in the Cultural District

B. Convene Stockyards Task Force to encourage input, support, and involvement from civic groups and businesses

C. Accept primary responsibility for implementing Central Business District Sector Plan

D. Preserve urban green space while undertaking projects that make appropriate maximum use of Trinity River corridor

Responsibility

Cultural District Task Force

North Area Council of Chamber of Commerce

Downtown Fort Worth, Inc., in cooperation with Fort Worth Chamber of Commerce

City of Fort Wort, Tarrant County Water Control and Improvement District No. 1, Streams and Valleys Committee, U.S. Army Corps of Engineers

CHALLENGE

Assist existing businesses while attracting new enterprises

Strategy

A. Establish Fort Worth Center for New and Emerging Businesses to assist local enterprises in planning, managing, and financing start-ups and expansion projects

B. Develop cooperative program to systematically identify and seek solutions to problems experienced by local businesses and industry

C. Continue cooperation between Fort Worth Corporation and Fort Worth Chamber of Commerce to market Fort Worth

Figure 2–7 (Continued)

Responsibility

Fort Worth Chamber of Commerce

Fort Worth Chamber of Commerce and City of Fort Worth

Fort Worth Corporation and Chamber of Commerce

CHALLENGE

Develop strong neighborhoods and economic development at the neighborhood level

Strategy

A.   Conduct economic development education for neighborhood leaders, city officials, and developers

B.   Encourage visibility of neighborhood organizations

C.   Review and update city's zoning and planning ordinances and functions

Responsibility

City Council and city manager

City Council, city manager, city staff, other officeholders

CHALLENGE

Use educational institutions as tools in community and economic development and research efforts

Strategy

A.   Work with area colleges and universities to strengthen, upgrade and deepen research capabilities and high technology capacity

B.   Support recommendations contained in Education Task Force report

Responsibility

Businesses, foundations, city

Economic Development Task Force

Source: City of Fort Worth, Texas.

bias exhibited by strategic plans and be designed for implementation. In addition, we agree specifically with Anthony Catanese that "if planners are to be considered good managers of change and responsive to both politicians and special interest groups, they must concern themselves with only a limited number of issues that are definable, concrete, and solvable."[99] In essence, we believe that less is more.

The recent strategic planning experiences of Chicago buttress our conclusions. Robert Mier, the city's commissioner of economic development, and several of his colleagues involved in the development of the strategic plan described their successes in the *Journal of the American Planning Association.*[100] They reported that the standard strategic planning process was followed in developing the Chicago plan. Recognizing that an excessive number of goals and policies discouraged the implementation of traditional comprehensive plans, they chose to limit their plan to only five primary goals. Their approach made it easy for the local commissioners to deliver a concise and consistent message that was easily understood and accepted by the community. They reported that "direct public communication of the goals has begun to influence priorities and plans in other government departments and in non-government groups."[101]

STRATEGIC COMPREHENSIVE PLANNING

Have you ever considered how complicated things can get, what with one thing always leading to another? E.B. WHITE

It should be noted that some skeptics argue that strategic planning is only old wine in a new bottle and that it's "just an advertising gimmick to sell the old stuff in a new way."[102] We don't agree. Strategic planning clearly is not comprehensive planning, nor does comprehensive planning result in strategic decision making.

Making informed decisions about the growth and redevelopment of urban areas is no easy task. Urban areas have become centers of complex and interrelated activities. Employment and residential areas are interconnected and supported by public and private facilities such as streets, water, sewer, storm drains, parks, and services including delivery services, garbage removal, police and fire protection, medical and human services, recreation and entertainment, and personal services. Many of these facilities and services are interrelated, as are the land uses they support or serve. Fully understanding the complexity of this urban system requires a thorough understanding of all the elements that make up the system.

Today, even with all the information and modeling capabilities available, no one person can understand this complexity. But decisions that affect one aspect of this system can ripple and end up influencing the whole system. Ideally, decisions about small parts of the system should include some assessment of the system as a whole. Such consideration becomes almost an impossible task when one attempts to set long-range policy about the general future of the community. Comprehensive planning attempts to do just that. It attempts to look at a community and its urban system and assess how the system works. Such a comprehensive understanding cannot be achieved by a strategic process that narrows the scope of study.

However, this comprehensive view of the community, if carried forward to the structure of the decision-making process, can result in a bias for inaction and ineffectiveness. The complexity of the urban system is not only reflected in its process and activities, but also in the way people perceive the community. The issues and concerns people express about the future of their community can range from "Why does my street flood?" to "Why is it so hard to hire local people?" During a major community-wide review of the future of a community, so many issues can be raised that the process becomes overwhelming. In fact, the major failure of many comprehensive plans has been trying to do too much at once. In the end, those issues that were easy to address, but unimportant, got done. Those that were hard to address, but important, never got done.

Strategic planning has more of a bias for action than comprehensive planning. It focuses on the important issues and provides a clear direction. Using strategic planning to overcome the stigma of ineffective comprehensive planning is a classic example of making lemonade out of lemons.

An illustration of the reform that we are advocating and the successful transfer of strategic planning concepts to comprehensive planning is provided by Arlington, Texas. Arlington's latest comprehensive plan blends the best aspects of comprehensive planning and strategic planning. It uses traditional comprehensive planning techniques to gain a thorough understanding of the community and to identify issues and goals related to the community's future. However, it also uses strategic planning concepts to focus on the key issues and proposed actions to address those issues.

Arlington's plan, when initiated, used the standard practice of comprehensively viewing how the urban system works in the community. Through an extensive citizen participation program, all of the issues related to the future of the community were identified. Then, based on extensive goal-setting efforts, goals for what Arlington should be in the future were established. Existing conditions in Arlington were documented, and accepted standards for future development were identified.

Up to this point, what was prepared was a typical comprehensive plan: existing conditions, issues, goals, principles, and standards. But here the process deviated. Rather than preparing the traditional plan elements, such as parks, water, land use, and transportation, effort was moved back to the issues. Through a series of workshops with a variety of homeowner, business, civic, and special interest groups, all issues were discussed and assessed and thirty key issues were identified.

The thirty issues were thoroughly analyzed and the results for each issue were reported in short separate legislative briefs. The analysis included a laundry list of strategies that could be used to address the issue. In a second series of meetings with the same groups, each issue of importance was discussed and the strong and weak points of the strategies were summarized. The summary was added in a pro/con format to the issue briefs; the issue briefs became the heart of the comprehensive plan and were included in the planning document.

Another strategic plan concept that differed from traditional comprehensive planning was the use of alternative futures, or contingency planning. Arlington's comprehensive plan did not use projected population or employment as a basis for future land use. Past studies in Arlington had demonstrated that such projections were extremely difficult to make. Because Arlington is an integral part of the Dallas/Fort Worth metroplex, the factors that influence growth are numerous and complex. Past efforts at projecting population were low by 10 to 50 percent. Rather than use projections, three possible economic futures were proposed. Each future provided a possible set of short-term and long-term economic conditions, a possible regional population and employment growth rate, some indication as to which economic sectors would experience growth or decline, and a description of some economic trends that could initiate such a scenario. These scenarios were based on forecasts by several prestigious state forecasting groups. Figure 2-8 provides a summary of the three scenarios used.

Figure 2–8

Arlington Strategic Comprehensive Plan
Economic Scenarios

Scenario I - Flat Growth

National economy remains poor, oil prices remain low, defense industry and hi-tech (small business) experience moderate growth. Texas economy remains poor, Dallas experiences growth in the services (2-3%) sector and defense related areas (small business).

Employment

> **Short Term:** Stays stable, possible slight decline with an increase in unemployment and less workforce participation.
> **Long Term:** Slight growth of close to 1% to 2%.

Population

> **Short Term:** Slight increase of 1% to 2%
> **Long Term:** Slow growth of 2% to 3%

Development

> **Short Term:** Construction activity declines. Office market depressed, retail development only in unserviced areas. Very little major industrial development. Some employment growth related to defense, but little development. Some research type development. New residential sales very weak.

> **Long Term:** Construction remains stable, no growth. Office market improves but, but still weak. Retail with slow growth to match population increase. Less major retail, more small retail. New residential sales remain stable at lower levels.

Scenario II - Slow Growth

National economy improves, oil prices remain low, defense spending and hi-tech (semiconductor and services) experience moderate growth. Texas economy begins to diversify. Dallas experiences growth in trade (3-4%), non-durable goods (2-3%), durable goods (1-2%), services (4%), finance (3-4%), communications, and utilities (3-4%) sectors. Construction becomes the weakest sector.

Employment

> **Short Term:** Stays stable
> **Long Term:** Moderate increase 3 to 5%

Population

> **Short Term:** Slow growth of 2%
> **Long Term:** Moderate growth of 3 to 5%

Figure 2–8 (Continued)

Development

Short Term: Construction activity declines. Office market depressed, retail development only in unserviced areas. Very little major industrial development. Some employment growth related to defense, but little development. Some research type development. New residential sales remain stable while inventories decline, then sales decline.

Long Term: Construction activity remains stable, slight growth in residential and industrial. Office market will absorb all space in key areas, which then experience growth; other areas (North Dallas) remain weak. Retail with slow growth to match population increase. Some major retail development, growth in small retail development.

Scenario III - Fast Growth

National economy picks up, trade deficit declines, oil prices rise (maybe $20 a barrel), offshore Texas exploration increases, growth in defense sector, growth in hi-tech (semiconductor and service). Texas economy in process of diversification receives boost from higher oil prices. Dallas experiences high growth in services (6%), durable goods (4%), construction (4%), trade (5%), and finance (5%).

Employment

Short Term: Slight increase 1 to 2%, unemployment remains slightly below nation
Long Term: Increases at 5 to 6% rate

Population

Short Term: Increase at 3 to 4% rate
Long Term: Increase at 6 to 8%, with peaks as high as 10 or 11%

Development

Short Term: Construction activity declines. Office market depressed, retail development stable except in over built areas. Some major industrial development. Some employment growth related to defense, but little development. Some research type development. New residential sales remain stable, construction slows to match sales.

Long Term: Construction activity increases, with growth in residential and industrial. Office market will absorb all space and then experience growth in all areas. Access will become a key commodity. Retail experiences rapid growth to match population increase; including both major retail development as well as small retail development. New residential development will reach past highs.

Source: Arlington Planning Department, <u>Arlington Comprehensive Plan</u>, 1987.

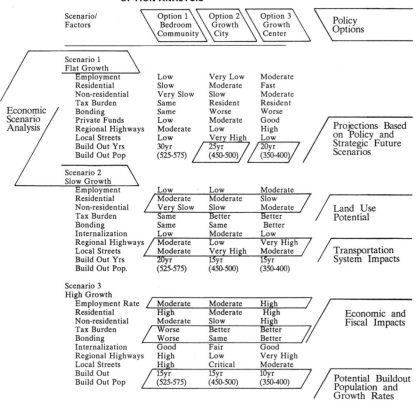

Figure 2-9
**BUILD OUT ECONOMY
OPTION ANALYSIS**

Scenario/Factors	Option 1 Bedroom Community	Option 2 Growth City	Option 3 Growth Center	Policy Options

Economic Scenario Analysis

**Scenario 1
Flat Growth**

	Option 1	Option 2	Option 3	
Employment	Low	Very Low	Moderate	
Residential	Slow	Moderate	Fast	
Non-residential	Very Slow	Slow	Moderate	
Tax Burden	Same	Resident	Resident	
Bonding	Same	Worse	Worse	
Private Funds	Low	Moderate	Good	Projections Based on Policy and Strategic Future Scenarios
Regional Highways	Moderate	Low	High	
Local Streets	Low	Very High	Low	
Build Out Yrs	30yr	25yr	20yr	
Build Out Pop	(525-575)	(450-500)	(350-400)	

**Scenario 2
Slow Growth**

Employment	Low	Low	Moderate	
Residential	Moderate	Moderate	Slow	
Non-residential	Very Slow	Slow	Moderate	Land Use Potential
Tax Burden	Same	Better	Better	
Bonding	Same	Same	Better	
Internalization	Low	Moderate	Low	
Regional Highways	Moderate	Low	Very High	
Local Streets	Moderate	Very High	Moderate	Transportation System Impacts
Build Out Yrs	20yr	15yr	15yr	
Build Out Pop.	(525-575)	(450-500)	(350-400)	

**Scenario 3
High Growth**

Employment Rate	Moderate	Moderate	High	
Residential	High	Moderate	High	Economic and Fiscal Impacts
Non-residential	Moderate	Slow	High	
Tax Burden	Worse	Better	Better	
Bonding	Worse	Same	Better	
Internalization	Good	Fair	Good	
Regional Highways	High	Low	Very High	
Local Streets	High	Critical	Moderate	
Build Out	15yr	15yr	10yr	
Build Out Pop	(525-575)	(450-500)	(350-400)	Potential Buildout Population and Growth Rates

The scenarios then were used in the analysis of the issue strategies, the question being how well specific strategies would address different issues under each of the scenarios. Strategies that were particularly strong or particularly weak under different scenarios were identified and discussed. Under one major economic issue, possible populations and growth rates were estimated for each scenario and each strategy. Figure 2-9 provides a summary of strategies by scenario.

Arlington's strategic comprehensive plan contains one last element, much different from traditional comprehensive planning: an action plan. This final component is not organized by issue or functional planning area but by the players who will be involved in implementing the plan. It lists by player the tasks that need to be carried out to implement the adopted strategies. Where possible, a time frame and budget for initiation and completion is included with each task. This component of the plan not only makes a strong statement for action, but it links action with the city's and community's resources to initiate action. It provides the opportunity to review priorities in light of available resources. It also provides a clear way to monitor and measure how the comprehensive plan is being implemented.

This depth of analysis provided Arlington's decision makers with the information to strategically plan the key steps to achieve a desired future for the city. The final "plan" part of the comprehensive plan simply identified the strategies that were recommended for action. However, all the strategies, including those not recommended, and the analysis of each were included in the plan document. Arlington's intent is to review each issue annually and to verify that the recommended strategy still is appropriate under the economic conditions that exist at that time. Any change in the local or regional economy can be quickly assessed as to its impact on adopted strategies and an appropriate response can be made.

Arlington's plan is different in several ways from traditional strategic planning. First, the thirty issues and more than 100 strategies addressed in Arlington's plan would be considered by most strategic planners as being too broad. The breadth of the issues addressed is a result of the fact that Arlington's plan has remained comprehensive. It covers most functional areas of public government, including land use, economy, transportation, public utilities, public services, human services, and urban design. However, in the process of strategic planning, just a few clearly identifiable issues have been addressed in each functional area. This approach has resulted in a comprehensive document that provides a focus on action.

Second, Arlington's plan for some issues states that no course of action should yet be adopted. In most cases, this conclusion resulted from a lack of information or analysis. Most strategic planners would consider this conclusion a transgression. Making decisions on available data is a much-touted aspect of strategic planning. However, Arlington's plan recognizes that a conscious decision to take no action is itself an action. In the public sector, some actions may be very expensive or politically difficult to alter or remedy if they prove to be wrong. If the available information on a particular issue is not adequate and essential information is forthcoming, then a conscious delay in making that decision may be warranted. In such cases, the Arlington plan recognizes this approach and identifies what must be done to reach a point where a decision can be made.

Under the appropriate circumstances, patience is an acceptable strategy for delaying decisions even in the private sector. In his classic book, *The Functions of the Executive,* Chester Barnard offered the following observations:

> The fine art of executive decision consists in not deciding questions that are not now pertinent, in not deciding prematurely, in not making decisions that cannot be made effective, and in not making decisions that others should make. In other words, patient executives know when not to decide.[103]

Though it is too early to measure the effectiveness of Arlington's approach, there are two early signs of its success. The first is the overwhelming praise accorded the format of the plan by all facets of the community. Arlington's 1979 attempt at developing a comprehensive plan failed because of a lack of consensus. Since then, comprehensive planning has been viewed dimly by many sectors of the community. For six years, Arlington had been using a land use plan that essentially was a generalized zoning map.

The second good sign is the time frame in which the plan was prepared. Following an extended period of staffing problems and changes in department priorities, the time frame for completing the plan was accelerated by the city council from nine to three months. Even under this constraint, Arlington's planning staff was able to complete a viable plan. They attribute this primarily to the strategic planning process and the willingness to act on available information.

The strategy that is developed for marketing any plan is a critical determinant of its ultimate success. In essence, the profession has the challenging situation of having to revitalize a stale product—a process akin to reopening a shut-in oil well or a played-out gold mine. We talk elsewhere about the necessity of repositioning agencies or departments in order to serve the needs of potential clients. This concept also has application to individual products, programs, and services that are developed and offered by an agency. With a traditionally ineffective product such as comprehensive planning, it may be necessary to reposition it. According to Edward Nash, president and chief executive officer of one of the leading agencies in the direct marketing field, repositioning of a product or service involves "presenting it in a different placement vis-à-vis competition, by aiming it at a different market segment, or by selling it at a different point in the buyer's decision-making process."[104] This is exactly what we mean when we emphasize the need to redefine the target market for the users of the plan and to be more aggressive in intervening at various stages in the political decision-making process that is followed in developing the plan.

Further, our concept of strategic comprehensive planning takes full advantage of existing resources. Current programs of comprehensive planning data collection and analysis need not be abandoned. Rather, these efforts can be channeled into the strategic planning process. This has a dual benefit: first, it makes use of past programs and does not require restructuring of existing programs, and second, it provides some stability in what could seem to be a drastic change in the planning process. Strategic comprehensive planning also can be more effective than traditional comprehensive planning because its strategic aspects make it possible to respond more quickly and specifically to social, economic, or political changes.

Our concept of strategic comprehensive planning gives the profession the chance to reintroduce comprehensive planning as a refined and improved product with a different focus and an orientation toward the intended user. Still, the effectiveness of the new product will depend on it having improved features with real value to the decision makers. You can't turn lemons into lemonade without some sweetener.

For a plan to be effective, individuals must see themselves represented in it. The process used to develop the plan must be representative, participatory, and responsive, and the product must be perceived to be credible, legitimate, and fair. This means, according to Hilary Silver, an assistant professor of sociology and urban studies at Brown University, and Dudley Burton, associate director of the Institute of Environmental Studies at Baylor University, that planners "must be as concerned about how a program is designed, publicized, and implemented as about the substance of the plan itself."[105]

Finally, we want to suggest that strategic planning offers a device for shifting any debate about whether or not to do planning to a discussion of how to do it better. We wholeheartedly agree with the conclusion of Anthony Tomazini, of the City and Regional Planning Department at the University of Pennsylvania, that strategic planning has the potential to revitalize public planning by invigorating planning agencies and revitalizing the interest of top

officials in planning.[106] It also has the potential to reform and rein-
vigorate the profession.

One cautionary note is in order. Robert Mier and his associates
who worked on the strategic plan for Chicago discovered a number
of limitations in their ability to engage in this kind of planning
and concluded that "local government bureaucracy is, at present,
ill-equipped to conduct and implement strategic planning."[107]
They report that to develop an effective program:

> administrative officials must address issues of staff capacity, communi-
> cation, intercultural sensitivity, cooperative intra- and intergovern-
> mental working relationships, systems for monitoring and evaluating
> progress toward performance targets, and good relationships with key
> leaders and organizations outside government.[108]

TIMELY ACTION

If not us, who—if not now, when? RONALD REAGAN

Planners must learn to value and respect the need for timely action. Donald Spaid, former planning coordinator for St. Paul, Minnesota, is convinced that "planning implementation is a product of
timing" and that "if we do not have that plan and that planning
component done the day before the decision needs to be made,
then we are at least one day too late."[109]

Beaumont, Texas, was involved in 1980 in revising and updating
its outdated comprehensive plan. The land use plan element had
just been completed and it was enthusiastically supported by the
planning commission and city council and had been formally
adopted as an official component of the comprehensive plan. Yet
behind the scenes there was controversy and debate among the
planning staff. One knowledgeable but very idealistic planner in
particular was adamant that separate elements or components of
the comprehensive plan should not be subject to piecemeal adoption. Citing T.J. Kent's views in *The Urban General Plan,* he argued
that by supporting the preparation and adoption of piecemeal
plans, the commission and council could lose interest in the other
elements and these partial plans could eventually be accepted as
the comprehensive plan. He also pointed out that fragmented
adoption would make it difficult to produce a truly unified and coherent comprehensive plan. However, the view that prevailed in
the debate was that it was better to have a bias for action, to complete each element and obtain understanding and support from
the decision makers, and to use each success to build support for

the next work program. To guard against the concerns that were raised and to ensure that the plan would be used, the adopting resolution specifically states that it is only a component of the comprehensive plan and, further, that the land use plan shall be reviewed, evaluated, and updated at least annually and be kept current and consistent with the other components of the comprehensive plan. To quote again from the observation of Fred Bair: "if we bear firmly in mind that the end objective of planning is not the production of plans, but the production of informed, intelligent, well-organized action, we won't go far wrong."[110]

In Kansas City, a planning and management process was used that tied planning and action together, according to Joseph Vitt, Jr. He described this process as "(1) deciding what to do; (2) committing ourselves to do it; (3) controlling the doing of it; (4) evaluating what we did; and (5) feeding the valuation back in to decide what we want to do the next time."[111] He emphasizes that there was commitment both to planning and to implementation.

Once planners understand and appreciate that planning is a means for getting intelligent action and not an end in itself, then it becomes obvious that a bias for immediate action is a necessary characteristic for effectiveness and excellence in planning. Planners need to be willing to enter the arena and take their best shot. If they don't, someone else will. In addition, planners need to cultivate policial and administrative leaders and the goodwill, respect, and support of the private sector. Providing technical assistance and support on current issues strengthens the visibility and influence of planners. A unique example is the Baltimore planning department, which furnishes a staff aide to each city council member. Melvin Levin, writing in the inaugural issue of "AICP Notes" pointed out that "it is not enough to do a good job. An agency must be perceived as efficient and useful by the public at large, business and civic groups, and the people who make budgetary and other decisions. Thriving planning agencies are visible and viewed as problem solvers, not problem makers."[112]

A bias for timely action doesn't depend on recklessness but rather an awareness of windows of opportunity, or what Donald Spaid calls opportunistic timing. Some windows are open and immediacy of action is required. Other windows are closed and an alternative strategy must be selected. Effectiveness depends on each agency's ability to anticipate and respond in a timely manner to opportunities as they become available.

William Lucy, in a book called *Close to Power* (soon to be published by APA), illustrates this point by describing the situation where the planning director for Utica, New York, presented a proposal to the planning commission that would have substantially revised the existing zoning ordinance. The director had failed to consult with the mayor or city council and the proposal was delivered just two months before the local election. A more experienced, sensitive, and aware planner would have recognized the potential for the proposal to generate intense opposition while attracting only limited public support. Lucy noted that "although the mayor might have been supportive in a less tense political season, and with groundwork having been laid skillfully, in the climate then prevailing the mayor had a lot to lose and nothing to gain." After the ordinance was withdrawn from consideration,

Lucy asked the planning director why he had presented the proposal before the election instead of afterwards. The director's shocking answer was that he had not thought about it.

Japanese sumo wrestlers are known for their *shinbo*. The word denotes patience in the face of adversity. Sumo wrestlers believe that if you are patient enough your opportunity will come. William Anderson, the long-time director of planning for Corpus Christi, Texas, was no sumo wrestler, but he obviously knew about *shinbo*. He believed in preparing plans, studies, and reports and keeping them until there was a political window of opportunity. At such times, the planning staff would produce its accumulated work and much of it would be accepted and used by the decision makers. Joseph Vitt, Jr., used a similar but more short-term strategy in Kansas City. He described his approach and reasoning as follows:

> In our business, turnaround time is very important, that is, if someone asks to be provided with a service, he would like to have that service right away because he desperately has that need. So what we do is try to anticipate what those needs and requests are going to be and pull those into our work program. At any time, we may be working on products that no one knows we are working on, products we think people are going to ask for in six months or a year—when they do, we can give them results very quickly.[113]

Unfortunately, many planning departments do not realize the importance of timing, and production strategies and schedules are never established or maintained. A bias for action depends on a commitment to production based on deadlines. As Peters and Waterman found, "under deadline pressure—and with manageable acts to perform—the impossible occurs regularly. . . ."[114]

Planners must be willing to harness their almost insatiable desire for more information and establish and meet production schedules that are in sync with the timing realities of the political decision-making process. In truth, if an agency does not anticipate and stockpile *useful* information and has to "start from scratch" when an issue or need arises, its effectiveness will be doubtful no matter what strategies it tries to use. Linking the pace of the planning process to the elected officials' decision-making schedule increases the potential effectiveness of the planner. A long-time observer of planning and politics in Honolulu summarized this important lesson:

> planners must recognize that they have to take a position at some point. They have to take it even though they don't have all the infor-

mation that they would like to have. There has to be a pace to the planning process comparable to that of the political decision-making pace. . . . [115]

In politics, timing can be everything. For instance, at the request of a majority of the city council in one city, the staff revised the existing sign regulations to make them more restrictive. The revision took just over a year for the off-premise signage regulations and was a very successful project. However, the simultaneous revision of the on-premise signage regulations was a lengthier and much less successful two-year project. Between the start and conclusion of the on-premise signage project, its strongest supporter on the council resigned, another advocate had died, and its final sponsor had alienated some members of the council and became less effective. The window of opportunity for meaningful reform of the sign ordinance closed before the staff could complete its work.

Regardless of the products and services that are produced and delivered, an effective planning program must be based on timely responsiveness. Randolph Forrester, city manager of Wyoming, Ohio, believes that quick, courteous, and efficient responsiveness to a resident's request is essential to the success of local governments. He concluded that "whether it is answering someone in person, returning a phone call, or replying to a letter, prompt responsiveness is an essential ingredient in municipal excellence."[116]

RISK TAKING: OPPORTUNITIES AND CONSEQUENCES
There is nothing in the middle of the road but yellow stripes and dead armadillos. JAMES HIGHTOWER

In the final analysis, it is the willingness to test and experiment and to take risks and even to fail that is the foundation of a bias for action. Successful corporations are willing to take these risks; many municipal governments are not.

A columnist for the *Chicago Tribune* tells a story about a friend who walked along a major street during the noon-hour pedestrian rush and saw a young man snatch a woman's purse and begin running down the sidewalk toward him. The friend, who had played high school football, said his mind said "tackle" but his body said "freeze" as the thief ran by and escaped. The friend offered the following observations on the experience: "I lost my appetite after the incident. I knew suddenly, in very tangible terms, that I was not a hero. I could have stopped the thief. He was much smaller than I. I am athletic; I have made tackles before. In a different situation, making a dive at someone is nothing more than a muscle-memory reflex. Second nature. But now, I had become gun-shy."[117]

Many planners have also become gun-shy over the years, but effective planning demands the willingness to take risks and to use strategies and tactics of intervention in the political process. Anthony Catanese delights in the old adage that the most effective planners "keep their bags packed."[118] Still, many planners have personally advanced in their professional careers by avoiding risks, keeping a low profile, and dodging controversial assignments. They fear challenges and have lost any instinct they might once have had for taking decisive action. One planner who probably makes it a practice to keep his bags packed, bitterly described ". . . the steady climb of the hangers-on to positions of responsibility as one of the critical problems in city planning departments."[119]

Caretaker planners are not interested in change or innovation nor do they see the need to become more effective. According to David Slater in *Management of Local Planning*, caretakers "concentrate on housekeeping or maintenance functions in the local governments they serve."[120] He has found that caretaker planners have the following questions and concerns:

> How can I avoid this potential hot potato?
>
> Since the council and manager have not made up their minds on this issue, how can I best play it safe and do nothing?
>
> Have I handled the budget and personnel procedures according to law?
>
> Is my in-basket getting too full?[121]

Ray Meyer, long-time basketball coach at DePaul University, remarked after the loss that broke his team's twenty-eight-game winning streak that, of late, they had become defensive and were not playing with the same degree of confidence, aggressiveness, and enthusiasm that had characterized their earlier victories. He suggested, on a positive note, that perhaps now his players would quit trying not to lose and go back to concentrating on winning. Meyer's experience with his team might also explain the excessively cautious and conservative attitude exhibited by some middle-aged managers of local planning agencies. Their goals have become more negative than positive—they are more interested in avoiding blame than in assuming responsibility.

The 1985–1986 roster of the members of the American Institute of Certified Planners (AICP) provided the following information about the age cohorts of planning directors and chief executive officers of planning organizations: [122]

For AICP members, the median age of planning directors and chief executives of planning organizations is nearly forty-three. Most managers of planning agencies experience the same pressures and stresses experienced by middle-aged managers in other lines of work.

Many planners have risen to positions of authority and responsibility only after decades of relentlessly struggling and pursuing advancement opportunities in a highly competitive environment. Countless friends and adversaries have been passed over, fired, moved into dead-end jobs, or gone into other professions. For many of the successful survivors, physical or psychological attrition has set in. In a sense, such an individual is at war with himself, and like Hamlet, he must flog his will to make it obey his instincts.

Most planning directors are male and we contend that there is, in fact, a difference between men and women managers and that

Table 2–1

Age of Planning Directors

Age	Number	Percent of Total
Under 25	4	.1
26-30	162	4.4
31-35	613	16.8
36-40	769	21.0
41-45	598	16.4
46-50	494	13.5
51-60	718	19.5
61-70	208	5.7
Over 70	93	2.5

Median Age 42.9

Source: "AICP Notes", <u>Planning</u>, May 1986, p. 26d.

middle-aged men are subject to unique psychological factors that can contribute to their eventual ineffectiveness as managers of planning agencies. Researchers have discovered that "a vast number of men harbor a large number of fears," and that they are "the kind of fears that cause men's palms to sweat and stomachs to churn."[123] But more importantly, as noted by Brux Austin, editor-in-chief of *Texas Business*, in a feature story on the mid-life crisis of males,

> man's greatest fear is of getting fired, getting passed over for a promotion, getting laid off. That fear has little to do with financial needs and a lot to do with ego.[124]

At a median age of forty-three, many planning directors may be having to weather a "mid-life crisis." John Horn, a University of Denver psychologist, found that "when their jobs and lives haven't turned out as they expected, you see burnout."[125] Burnout, as noted in a *Planning* magazine article on avoiding Scorch City, "can be defined as the feelings of fatigue and frustration," which Earl Finkler says can be "brought about when a job, a cause, a way of life, or a relationship fails to produce the expected results."[126] He added that burnout "can cause a host of more subtle problems: fatigue, absenteeism, loss of idealism, and a general lack of caring for one's work and one's fellow workers."[127]

The mid-life crisis may not be one's most traumatic life transition but Michael P. Nichols, professor of psychiatry at Albany (N.Y.) Medical College, says that "in some ways it may be the most important."[128] He suggested that "it is the time we do the final tune-up for the rest of our productive years."[129]

Miles F. Shore, psychiatry professor at Harvard University and director of the Massachusetts Mental Health Center in Boston, concluded that the bottom line for people in mid-life is that "they can either settle into a much more creative, realistic phase of their lives, or go 'haywire.' "[130] Shore found that "what happens depends on the extent people can turn outward toward others and on the extent they can take pleasure in their usefulness, in what they have produced. . . . "[131]

Frank Popper, planning professor at Rutgers University, New Jersey, believes that burnout is not exclusively a personal problem. "Sometimes whole divisions or departments go to Scorch City all at once," he said. "It's as if everyone had retired and didn't know it."[132]

This problem often is rooted at the head of the agency. Agencies that are managed either by hanger-oners or by once aggressive planners who may be experiencing burnout and are now trying only not to lose rather than win are a serious impediment to an effective planning program. The advice offered based on our research should have extra meaning to these individuals. Once they better understand the cause of their conservative nature, how it may have harmed the effectiveness of their agency, and how it can harm their careers, they may try adopting the strategies and tactics that produce victories. If not, Pogo was right when he said, "we have met the enemy and it is us."

Jacquelyn Ferguson, in her Career Track seminars on stress management, attributes burnout to the stress created when control is lost over the relationship between performance and outcome. She identifies five stages of burnout:

1. Confusion—a vague sense of loss of control and confusion over what is happening.

2. Frustration—frustration that performance does not seem related to outcome.

3. Sense of uncontrollability—where one has no control over outcome of events.

4. Anger—about loss of control.

5. Apathy—where one just does not care anymore.

It is no wonder that burnout is a problem for planners when so many believe they have no control over the forces that influence the outcome of planning decisions. Ferguson teaches that if burnout is to be stopped, it must be done before the anger stage and that if individuals are to regain control, they must adopt better problem-solving skills. Perhaps burnout in the planning profession could be prevented if planners were taught that they can be in control.

While the record shows many planning directors retained their positions by having their agencies concentrate on routine housekeeping functions and avoiding risks, it also is apparent that conditions, times, and expectations have changed. Nationally, there is an accelerating interest on the part of managers, elected officials, and the public—our customers—for more responsive and useful planning agencies. An agency willing to settle for the status quo will not be able to meet these rising expectations. In this new environment, passive managers are only rearranging deck chairs on the Titanic.

Many planning directors are satisfied with their personal accomplishments and current status and are unwilling to take the risks that are necessary to increase the effectiveness of their planning programs. Unfortunately, many of the aggressive, often younger planners who are obsessed with being effective and making a difference, "aren't," as noted by Clifford Weaver and Richard Babcock, "going to be far enough up the ladder or in enough of a performing position . . ."[133]

In the final analysis, a willingness to take risks is at the heart of the bias for action strategy. Norman Krumholz, former director of planning for Cleveland, Ohio, and 1986–1987 president of the American Planning Association, contends "if planners are to have significant impact . . . they must become activists."[134] He means that planners must diligently seek out opportunities to influence decision makers and "occasionally take some risks to be effective."[135] While Krumholz acknowledges that activism carries real risks, he confides that on the basis of his personal experiences "they are not nearly so great as they may appear to be."[136] Rick Counts, former planning director for Phoenix, said much the same thing when he noted that as the principal planner for zoning in Chicago, he never *really* had one of his legs broken.

Another well-known planner, Allan Jacobs, former planning director of San Francisco, wrote in *Making City Planning Work* that he was involved in politics and so are most other planners.[137] Jacobs adamantly advises planners to be prepared to "mix it up" and assume the risks associated with standing up for their points of view "if they want to be effective."[138]

Sydney Harris, a columnist for the News American Syndicate, noted that "all the decisive people in the world have made waves and sometimes they have been swamped by them." He added that if there are no waves, there is no progress. The only way to avoid mistakes is to be totally passive, which is to say, dead. People don't get any blame that way—nor do they get anything else.

The choice is clear for the planner who is committed to being an effective professional. The bottom line is simply that there must be a bias for action and a willingness to take on the risks associated with intervention in the political decision-making process.

Many planners are involved in political conflicts—some are successful and some fail. Charles Hoch surveyed planners in the Chicago area and found that victorious planners credited their individual skills and professional competence while the losers blamed their misfortune on the power of their opponents.[139]

Planners can fail because of circumstances beyond their control, but more often, planners fail because they aren't good enough—they don't meet the needs of their clients. It is important to differentiate between these two types of failures and to develop a support network to sustain those individuals who have experienced failure due to unfortunate circumstances.

In Morris West's novel *The Shoes of the Fisherman*, the pope at one point asks for an especially understanding welcome into the bosom of the church to those who have done less well "because they have dared so much more." The planning profession needs to do a better job of recognizing, sustaining, and supporting planners who are less successful because they have tried to do so much more than the rest of us.

Just because a planner has been fired from his or her job doesn't automatically mean that person is incompetent—especially if it is a senior-level management position. Richard Gould, author of *SACKED! Why Good People Get Fired and How to Avoid It*, found that "managers are not usually fired for incompetence: more often than not, the culprit is bad chemistry with a new boss."[140] He identified four kinds of boss–subordinate conflicts that can be significant enough to result in termination:

1. Differences in style or values that cause people to be natural antagonists.

2. Conflicts over where the business should go and how to get there.

3. Contrary ideas about how people should be managed.

4. Not fitting in with a boss's expectations about the subordinate's role in the organization.[141]

Hoch has expressed concern that the practitioners who have fought the good fight and lost not only receive no honor, but may become scapegoats and pariahs. His research on this subject deserves respect and support and we endorse his call for the profession to make an effective commitment to support networking. His views are summarized as follows:

> Recognizing and respecting responsible risk takers, even when they lose, will also help make networking a viable service. Who wants to participate in a network of colleagues victimized by political conflicts

if such participation brings with it the stigma of shame? Would we follow the advice of someone we do not respect? We think not, and so believe that successful networking must be tied somehow to a new respect of the unsung heroes and heroines of planning.[142]

THE POLITICS OF RISK

If you can't stand the heat then get the hell out of the kitchen. HARRY S. TRUMAN

An important factor in developing interventionist strategies is recognizing that while planners may be willing to assume more risks, public officials are not always as willing to take on the added expense and the risk and the political consequences of public failure. Hubert Humphrey said "To err is human. To blame it on someone else is politics." Richard Milbrodt, the city manager of South Lake Tahoe, California, has observed that while risk taking is an essential ingredient of excellence in the public sector, the readiness to assume risks simply does not exist. He has found that "council members (and boards of supervisors) do not get reelected by risking failure. They get reelected by continuity of existing provisions and rules."[143]

Many politicians are overly cautious and conservative by nature. They often come from the local business community or the legal profession and some community power studies suggest such individuals produce a conservative, elitist power structure. Anthony Catanese has taken exception to this generalization, but concluded that such individuals do "tend to signify a moderate political philosophy."[144]

A well-known mayor once vetoed an ordinance that attempted to use the violation of women's civil rights as a basis for banning pornography. He indicated acceptance of the argument that much pornography is degrading to women but was undecided about creating a legislative exception to the First Amendment. When another city decided to enact a similar law and was subsequently challenged in court, the mayor commented that he was "delighted that others are having to carry the burden of the litigation expense." Unfortunately, one of the major causes of inertia in local government is that unless something is absolutely proven elsewhere, many councils will not even look at it, much less implement it.

Elected officials can, however, be strong supporters of action-oriented planning. Milford Sprecher, town manager of St. Michaels, Maryland, found that while elected officials can be a limiting factor, "they can also provide much needed support for innovation."[145] Linda Dalton noted that such recent literature as *Mayors In Action: Five Approaches to Urban Government* "supports the ability of at least some mayors to be effective as entrepreneurs and initiators of policy."[146] For example, Henry Cisneros, San Antonio mayor and recipient of the 1985 Distinguished Leadership Award to an Elected Official from the American Planning Association, "seems to understand instinctively that in the entrepreneurial eighties, cities are on their own—and to survive they must plan strategically to look after their own interests."[147] The centerpiece of Cisneros's administration is "Target 90," a strategic planning document aimed at outlining the future of San Antonio, with its main emphasis on what Cisneros likes to refer to as a "bias for action."

John Lindsay, former New York City mayor, once said that while politicians "have an interest in postponing decisions about future problems," the reality is that "decisions will not wait for the next administration. . . ."[148] He advised that the future of our cities requires each elected official to "make those hard decisions we call 'planning' even with some risk to his own career."[149]

Politicians should take the heat off the city manager and staff and stand out in front for changes and for innovations that the city or county needs according to Bob Bolen, Fort Worth mayor. However, while many public officials are willing to take risks, Bolen warns that they "need to know how much risk that's going to be—from a dollar and cents standpoint, from a personnel standpoint, from a change standpoint."[150] In other words, he and other public officials want to know "Can we stand it?" Congressman and Speaker of the House James Wright points out yet another important perspective of public officials when he warns, "If you want us to be with you when you crash-land, then we have to be with you on takeoff."

Public officials clearly have mixed feelings about planning and planners. One hostile public official commented that while most planners were worthless, some did have a few positive traits. For instance, he had found that planners tended to be good with numbers, but they just lacked the personality to be accountants. Catanese pointed out that many politicians are suspicious of intellectuals, liberals, and public interest groups, while many planners are suspicious of businessmen and investors.[151] In a sense, both groups share the feelings of Kathleen Turner in the movie *Peggy Sue Got Married*. The movie opens as Peggy Sue is getting ready for her twenty-fifth high school reunion. As she puts on her makeup, her husband, Charlie, appears on the television as a Crazy Eddie-like huckster babbling about great bargains in appliances. When her daughter urges her to watch, she declines and laments that, "I have certain unresolved feelings about your father." Many planners have ambivalent feelings about public officials. Effective planners have resolved these feelings and have learned how to provide valuable services to the public officials they are supposed to be working for.

The overly cautious nature of many municipal attorneys also can seriously impede innovative planning actions. For example, in one community the planning director and several council members developed a proposal for regulating sexually oriented businesses and presented it in ordinance form to the city attorney. The conservative city attorney critically analyzed the ordinance and even though it was similar to what other cities were already doing, he offered the following chilling advice:

> To the extent the proposal contravenes settled law, the City, Mayor, Council members, City Manager, City Attorney, and employees enforcing the ordinance would be individually liable for actual, punitive, and attorney fee damages. It is conceivable that city liability insurance would not apply. The size of such damages cannot be underestimated given prior court cases and the scope of the proposal.[152]

Even when planners are able to overcome various legal and political obstacles, there is another significant impediment to action. Many planners advance in the profession because of their ability to avoid conflict, controversy, or failure, and they fear being labeled controversial. Action-oriented planners who have been involved in the successful solutions of controversial problems are sometimes hindered in their careers by administrators and elected officials who fear them. One such planner complained to a reporter about a story that referred to him as the "controversial planner." He pleaded to no avail that he was not controversial, only that his department had been involved in resolving several controversial issues. This fear of controversy is even more significant if the conclusion in a *Life* magazine article about city planning is correct in that "a city plan without controversy was probably not worth preparing."[153]

This chapter would not be complete without mentioning that a bias for action is generally supported by city managers and that there is usually dissatisfaction with planners who fail to exhibit this characteristic. In a series of interviews conducted for the book *Management of Local Planning*, various city and county managers indicated that they had encountered the following kinds of problems with planners:

1. The information they present is convoluted and obtuse.
2. Their work is too theoretical.
3. Research and reports arrive too late to be useful.
4. They are insensitive to the views and wishes of others.
5. They are dogmatic.[154]

In particular these managers expressed the major criticism of planners: that their recommendations are usually based on research that is out of date by the time it is finished.[155] In defense of the planning profession, J. Lee Rodgers, Jr., retired chairman of the Department of Urban and Regional Planning at the University of Oklahoma, contends that many of these negative observations and experiences have occurred because "managers hired young and inexperienced or poorly educated planners." In his opinion, these shortcomings have not generally been a problem for planning graduates who have practiced for several years and who are at the professional level, either directing an agency or working at upper staff levels.

There are managers who expect action from planners. Bob Blodgett, former city manager of Grand Prairie, Texas, and assistant city manager of Dallas, stated at the 1985 annual conference of the Texas Chapter of the American Planning Association that "planners should plan long-term but be impatient and have short-term solutions available and ready for use by decision makers."

Managers of local governments are growing aware of the importance of the planning function. A 1980 International City Management Association survey of city managers, chief administrative officers, county administrators, and directors of councils of governments revealed that respondents (56 percent) saw their influence in the future growing more in the area of planning and evaluation than in any other category of management activity.[156]

Of course, some city managers don't want to be exposed to the consequences of an overly aggressive planning staff. Charles Anderson, then city manager of Dallas, apologized to the City Plan Commission in 1986 because the planning staff had used "too much 'creative license' " and had sometimes been "too aggressive."[157] Shortly after his apology and public scolding of the planning staff, the planning director resigned. Less than six months later, Anderson resigned to take the chief executive position with the local transit authority.

CALCULATING RISKS

When you pass the football, three things can happen and two of them are bad. DARREL ROYALE

While we have preached that risks should be taken and not avoided, it is important for planners at all levels in local government to evaluate the risk-to-reward ratio before taking a specific action. In *The Future Executive*, Harlan Cleveland offered the following advice on taking risks:

> It would be hard to improve on Paul Appleby's prescription that an executive should, before acting, make sure he knows the answers to four questions: "Who's going to be mad? How mad? Who's going to be glad? How glad?"[158]

Medical laboratories use a therapeutic index which is the "ratio of the toxic dose of a medicinal substance to the therapeutic dose" when deciding to undertake the development and production of a new drug.[159] The higher the ratio of effectiveness to risk the greater is their interest in the product. In the public sector, it is important for planners to be aware of what has been referred to as the "squawk" potential.[160] This is simply an evaluation of the potential vocalized response to an ongoing activity or a proposed action.

Effective planners take calculated risks. They strike a balance between mad and glad and avoid high-rolling gambles. They also avoid the aversion to risk that commonly is assumed to characterize generic bureaucrats. As pointed out by William Rowe in the *Journal of the American Institute of Planners*, "risk is the degree of uncertainty of loss and this is an information measure, and, therefore, subject to research."[161] But many planners don't adequately analyze issues and related risks because, like evangelists, in David Riesman's phrase they "often mistake the righteousness of their cause for its marketability."

Several years ago a miner and his pack mules were crossing a deep gorge on a narrow natural rock bridge when they encountered a mountain lion. The miner turned and asked his mules, "How many of you want to stand on principle and how many want to turn back?" People with common sense always seem to be outnumbered by people of principle, and civic defenders of high principles don't usually want to be reconciled with the high principles held by others. The challenge for the effective manager is, in the words of Harlan Cleveland, dean of the University of Minnesota Humphrey Institute of Public Affairs, "to squash together the overriding principles, shove them through that narrow pipeline called policy, and extrude them as actions that work, decisions that stick."[162]

For planners there are many threats and unseen risks lurking on the trail leading to more effective programs. It should be painfully obvious that sticking to principle can jeopardize a planner's career. In an article on surviving as a planning director, Sylvia Lewis described how Richard Counts, planning director of Phoenix, and Calvin Hamilton, then planning director of Los Angeles, were almost fired for adhering to their principles on controversial zoning issues.[163]

Part of good management is knowing when and when not to fight to the death. Public service institutions exist to "do good" and many planners have a tendency to see their mission as a moral absolute. Peter Drucker has found that such righteousness can be a problem because:

> If one is "doing good," then there is no "better." Indeed, failure to attain objectives in the quest for a "good" only means that efforts need to be redoubled. The forces of evil must be far more powerful than expected and need to be fought even harder.[164]

Simplistic notions of the "righteousness" of our actions are no substitute for the development of a long-term strategic management plan based on the objective of maximizing effectiveness. Lewis also noted in her article that "on a day-to-day basis . . . compromise is the modus operandi of local government" and that "sticking to a principle without compromise on details can be the equivalent of sticking with a sinking ship."[165]

Calvin Hamilton says that he "fights for principle" but that he "compromises on little things."[166] Common sense dictates that career-threatening risks should not be lightly undertaken. For instance, more than one political analyst has noted that even a rudimentary assessment would have revealed that the benefits of selling arms to Iran as part of a convoluted effort to free American hostages in Lebanon could not have begun to equal the potential worldwide political damage that could result from such a high-risk gamble. If ultimate effectiveness is the bottom line for planners, then priorities and programs must be established to maximize this objective. Planners must always remember why they are taking risks.

When we worked together several years ago in Arlington, we struggled with our ineffectiveness for more than a year. Despite our stated belief that planners can influence and control their destinies, we could not bring about the changes that were needed to make us more effective. But we took pride in our ability to overcome obstacles and we persisted in our role as change agents. Finally, our various strategies and tactics produced an important victory on a major project and it was as if a dam had broken. From that point on, we were able to steadily improve the effectiveness of the planning department.

Our experience in Arlington is similar to what Gerald Zaltman and Robert Duncan described in *Strategies for Planned Change* as the concept of critical threshold. They explained that planners should expect a period during which efforts do not produce rewarding results. They added that "subsequently, however, other conditions being equal, effort expended will be well rewarded. To the extent that something of a bandwagon effect occurs, the change agent can use this phenomenon to stimulate greater acceptance of the advocated change."[167]

In all candor, we almost failed in Arlington. During that disastrous first year we resorted to increasingly riskier strategies and tactics—particularly in the area of intervention and involvement in the local political processes. Fortunately, we had a gutsy city manager who believed in us and who provided protection until we were able to achieve the essential changes that were needed.

The choices involved in the risk-taking dilemma can be illustrated by two examples from planning practice. In one medium-sized city in the Midwest, a planning department staff report recommended denial in a pending zoning case. It turned out that the property was owned by a state senator who pressured the staff to revise the report. The mayor, who was the chief executive officer of the city, also asked the staff to review and reconsider its negative findings. The planning director reviewed but did not change the report. The planning and zoning commission heard the case and by a vote of 8 to 1 recommended denial of the request. The state senator shifted his pressure to the city council; it voted overwhelmingly to approve the request. Several weeks later, the mayor, who was concerned about the staff's lack of political sensitivity and political responsiveness, asked for and received the resignation of the planning department director. Subsequently, the plan-

ning department was consolidated into the community development agency and a secretary was made head of the planning
section. The head of the combined department lacked both experience and education in planning. To add insult to injury, the senator's development deal fell through and the council eventually re-
zoned to residential the property in question.

This extreme example illustrates that even risks with very limited upside potential can produce serious adverse consequences. If
planners have a choice, they should concentrate their resources
and expend and leverage their political capital on risks with high-
return opportunities. In the case just cited, the staff had little to
gain but the losses were significant and the future of professional
planning in the community has been seriously affected. Of course
the staff may not have enjoyed the luxury of being able to choose to
avoid the risk that was present in this zoning case, but if the opportunity had been available, it should have been obvious that another strategy could have been considered. It may even have been
necessary to concede a short-term loss to establish a commitment to
planning and a more objective foundation for zoning decisions in
the community. The point is simply that if planners are to become
more effective, their risk taking must include an assessment of the
risk/reward ratio in conjunction with an evaluation of the organization's overall management strategy.

The second example involves a rapidly growing Sunbelt city
with a history of inadequate planning. The long-time city manager
used the departure of the popular planning director to reorganize
the department and to recruit a director who would emphasize
planning over zoning and be more successful in anticipating
emerging growth issues.

Months later, after several controversial commercial zoning
cases had been approved by the council in the face of negative
findings by the staff, the planning director was challenged by a
majority of the council to explain his department's opposition to
such cases. The director used this meeting with the council to shift
the issue from zoning to planning. He explained that zoning controversies were not the issue but rather a symptom of a bigger
problem, which was the failure to develop a comprehensive plan
for guiding growth and regulating development. The council initially rejected the planner's argument but weeks later, with the influential backing of the city manager, the staff was directed to ac-
celerate the development of a comprehensive plan and the council
dropped the negative staff reports issue. Today, this community

has a strong, viable planning program and an enviable commitment to planning.

While the planner and city manager in this example were confident of the "righteousness" of their commitment to comprehensive planning, they also recognized the political risks involved and were prepared to face the consequences. With an understanding of the issue's therapeutic index, planners can make informed decisions. Granted, it's not always easy to predict all the risks associated with an issue, but as planners initiate action they should be sensitive to the impact the action is having in the community. A recent article, "Turning Ideas into Action in the Municipal Environment," notes that risk can be measured by assessing feedback from others to "gauge whether it's possible to pursue the idea to success or wiser to bail out gracefully."[168] Planners who are either careless or overconfident and fail to seek out feedback take unnecessary risks and set themselves up for eventual failure.

An important point needs to be made here: Never make the mistake of assuming that there are no risks associated with a particular problem. No matter how obvious the problem is or how desirable or popular its solution may appear, planners should always learn if there are reasons or unique local circumstances that would favor maintaining the status quo. Remember the advice of William Donaldson, zoo director for Traverse City, Michigan, who warned the new city manager that "There is nothing so f----- up that it doesn't benefit someone."[169]

The city planning staff in Dallas recently learned this lesson the hard way. While developing a new zoning ordinance for the city, the staff was verbally and politically assaulted at committee hearings because it had included what it believed to be a series of routine housekeeping-type amendments to go along with the more substantive and controversial changes that had been requested by council. The resulting uproar created an environment of mistrust and complicated an already difficult issue, resulting in further delay of what already was an excessively lengthy updating process.

The status quo is attractive and appealing to many people, especially to those with real estate interests and to developers involved in the local regulatory process who understand the system and know how to live with or even manipulate it to their financial advantage. People who have development interests are fond of telling the joke that ends with the punch line "I'm from the government and here to help." At the 1986 National Association of Home

Builders' annual conference, one speaker asked the attendees if they knew how to tell the difference between a skunk and a planner when both had been run over on the highway. His answer was that "the skunk had skid marks in front of it." This joke was made in jest, but there is an almost innate distrust of government which can result in suspicion and mistrust on the part of some special interest groups about proposals from city planners—even those that might be in their own interests. Planners repeatedly told us of worthwhile public projects that were rejected by the people or groups who had the most to gain, simply because of knee-jerk opposition to the source of the propoal.

A majority of policy decisions can be explained by the interaction of special interest groups. Arthur Bentley, the first proponent of the group theory of politics in modern political science, went so far as to suggest that *all* political life could be explained by the interaction of groups and that "when the groups are adequately explained, everything is explained."[170]

Most day-to-day decisions in local government reflect an equilibrium among various special interest groups. Effective planners have learned how to build coalitions between disparate groups in order to reach a viable consensus on important issues. Tucker Gibson, a professor of political science at Trinity University in San Antonio, points out that Mayor Henry Cisneros is adept at this practice. He reports that:

> Cisneros prides himself on his ability to build consensus among disparate groups. It is not unusual in San Antonio to find wealthy real estate developers working side by side with militant neighborhood organizations in support, for example, of a proposed bond issue. Henry understands the use of mutual self-interest to create coalitions. He brings everybody in under the broad umbrella of economic development.[171]

In building the coalitions needed to deal with difficult issues, planners can minimize their risks and increase their effectiveness by serving special interest groups. These groups are clearly more effective presenting the proposals developed in conjunction with the planning staff than if the same proposals are presented by the staff alone. Planners can help these special interest groups become more sensitive to political realities and help them strengthen the legitimacy of their claims. But planners should not attempt to become the spokesmen for special groups. This is a needless risk that diminishes the groups' power and influence with the decision makers and reduces the likelihood of a favorable response. Catanese has found that "few groups can afford to risk such a dilution of their power and prefer to deal more directly with politicians."[172]

One other warning for change agents is in order. We have found, particularly in the regulatory area, that any local uniqueness or departure from traditional models or practices is a signal that some special circumstance or influence exists and that it should be identified and investigated. Rather than assuming that an oversight has occurred or that a simple, easily correctable mistake has been made, planners first should try to find out the reason for the deviation and use it to develop a better understanding of the community and its power structures.

In the long run, there is probably no substitute for maturity, experience, sound judgment, and even luck in dealing with risky planning issues. Turning ideas into meaningful action in the public sector is not easy, but it can and must be done if planners are to become more effective.

MAKING EFFECTIVE PRESENTATIONS

Good oral presentation skills involve the capacity to communicate in a way that satisfies others. DAVID W. MERRILL and ROGER H. REID

The manner in which proposed plans, projects, or services are presented to the public and decision makers has a lot to do with their success or failure. Today we are living in a communication age that is dominated by the one-minute news story and the thirty-second commercial. Most audiences are not prepared to listen to a long-winded exposition from a planner or anyone else. Too many planners are guilty of "information dump"—they tell their clients far more than anyone wants or needs to know. Rather than limiting their pitch to the aspects and features of the proposal that are in tune with their clients' needs, they are compelled to recite the whole chapter and verse. Excessive information bores and confuses clients and reduces the likelihood of gaining their understanding, commitment, and support. Instead, planners should avoid the unabridged version and concentrate on the specific things about the product that will make it attractive to their audience. An effective presentation is one that relates the product to the needs of the client.

Consider the following. We watched an extremely bright and capable planner present a well-researched and documented study on affordable housing. He held up a thick report, reviewed it in general terms, and encouraged the council to pay particular attention to the valuable information in the appendix. Several council members headed for the coffeepot and the others relaxed in their seats. They didn't have to bear down for the presentation because it was a lengthy study, it didn't require immediate action, and it was probably too complex to understand anyway. The following speaker, who chaired the task force, added his comments and emphasized that the report's priority recommendation was the development of federal legislation providing for a tax-exempt down payment savings program for first-time home purchases. The report was received politely by the council, the task force that had worked on it for almost a year was thanked, and the council went on to more pressing business.

Several simple things could have been done differently to increase the effectiveness of the presentation and to improve the likelihood of interest, acceptance, and action by the council. First, the substantive findings in the report could have been summarized in a pamphlet or brochure and presented as a series of action items requiring an immediate decision by the council. With pamphlet in hand, the planner could have announced that the implementation of the following specific actions recommended by the task force would make it possible for many of the council's family members, friends, and constituents to have access to more affordable housing.

Second, the recommendations of the task force could have been tailored to the needs and responsibilities of the council and could have been presented with a series of requested actions in areas in which the council had implementing authority. Finally, there could have been prior work behind the scenes to prime the council for action.

A recent article in *Planning* magazine suggested that the following strategies and tactics should be followed whenever possible for making effective presentations:

> Make sure that the objective of your presentation is clear and understood by the audience.
>
> The first phase of your presentation should include a comprehensive description of the problem and it should be delivered as clearly and simply as possible. Confusion or lack of clarity about the nature of the problem that is being solved will be fatal to the presentation.

In explaining the proposed solution (program, project, ordinance, etc.) to the problem provide a range of alternative options or possible solutions and indicate why the staff's proposal is preferable. While you should almost always leave an opportunity for the decision maker to select an alternative solution, make sure that you present a strong case for the staff's recommendation.

Always anticipate opposition and in your initial presentation make sure that you identify and answer all significant potential problems and concerns with staff's proposals.

Prior to your public presentation, you or a senior staff person, depending on the issue, should privately meet with several members of the group you will be speaking to in order to learn more about their perspective on the issue and, if possible, to obtain their support.

If the problem and/or the solution involve other people or organizations than you will be speaking to, then make sure that you can count on their support. Indicating such support at the time of your presentation will make it more effective.

Presentations should be kept as short as possible and you should use graphic aids and have detailed handouts for the audience.

Try to get the attention of the audience with your opening statements. A "hook" is a statement or an object used specifically to get attention. It entices, tempts, tantalizes, fascinates, captivates, attracts, etc. . . . and makes you want to stay tuned or even buy a product.

Learn from rejection. The decision makers are not wrong if they reject staff's recommendations. Don't criticize or complain about their treatment of you or your ideas. After the presentation, meet with selected individuals and try to learn about what went wrong. Correct your deficiencies and build on your strengths. Devise new strategies that will make you more effective in your next presentation.[173]

If at all possible, it is essential to give people time, even if it's just a few minutes, to become familiar and comfortable with you and you with them. Personal contact should help in understanding the audience and in selecting a strategy for increasing effectiveness.

An effective presentation depends on establishing rapport and credibility with the audience and gaining their confidence and respect. At some point during a successful presentation, you become a credible authority and the audience begins to give serious consideration to your statements. You can neither command respect nor be effective by forcing your views down people's throats. Consider a newly hired city planner who attended a public hearing conducted by the community development block grant (CDBG) staff in Butte, Montana. Eager to demonstrate his competence and technical superiority, the young planner corrected remarks of the program director and criticized statements of the advisory committee members. The response was immediate. The director cursed the planner and threatened to "punch out his lights" and after the meeting the planner's supervisor was contacted and told to never send the planner to another CDBG meeting if the supervisor wanted to maintain a good relationship between the two agencies. The young planner failed because, in his naiveté, he did not understand that a strategy of attacking and putting down your audience has little potential for success in any environment.

Successful communication depends on developing a basic understanding of the character and personality of the person or people you are trying to reach. Tom Landry, coach of the Dallas Cowboys, has a distinct conservative personality. He maintains a tight-lipped formality between himself and the players he coaches. He always has and probably always will. The veterans on the team know it and the rookies quickly learn it. The story is told of the rookie at training camp who, one day after practice, walked into the restroom. As fate would have it, Landry was standing at the next urinal. An awkward silence fell between them. Seconds crept by like hours. Finally, feeling as though he should say something and sensing the coach wasn't going to, the rookie turned to Landry who had been staring stonily, wordlessly, at the tile wall in front of him. "Tom," the young man blurted, "how long have you been bald?" Next day, the rookie was gone.

It should be noted that even experienced planners can make the mistake of failing to understand their audience. In one city, a veteran planner, hired by the city manager, reported to work as the new planning director and learned that the planning commission had scheduled a dinner that evening so they could get to know him better. At dinner, the commission members grilled the director about his views on planning and zoning. Without the chance to observe and learn his audience's views, the director was able to offend almost everyone. He never overcame the negative first impression he created with the commission members and his effectiveness was severely restricted for the two years he worked in that city.

The ability to read and evaluate reactions of the audience also is critical to making an effective presentation. Think of your presentation as tennis practice, where the objective is to keep the ball in

Learn How to Influence Them

Here are some tips from a management consultant to help you prepare to deal with a variety of people:

- **When communicating with an action-oriented person,** be brief. Emphasize practicality and focus on results. Use visual aids.

- **When communicating with a people-oriented person,** emphasize the relationship between your proposal and the people concerned. Show how the idea worked well for other people. Indicate support from others and write informally. Allow for small talk when discussing the proposal.

- **When communicating with an idea-oriented person,** work from the general to the specific. Emphasize the uniqueness of your proposal and allow enough time for discussion. Emphasize the key concepts that underlie your proposal.

- **When communicating with a process-oriented person,** present your facts in a logical order. Be precise and include choices.

From an article by Arnold M. Ruskin, adapted by special permission from CHEMICAL ENGINEERING (July 21, 1986), copyright (1987) by McGraw-Hill, Inc., New York, N.Y. 10020.

---

play and to allow you and your partner to sharpen your playing skills. Monitoring and responding to feedback is akin to keeping the ball in play. Of course, communication is a two-way street and the best presentations occur when the audience participates and provides visible feedback. Many audiences will have limited feedback skills but, just as in tennis practice, if the partner is not as skilled as we are it is still possible to have a productive session.

ETHICS

If to do were as easy as to know what were good to do, chapels had been churches, and from poor men's cottages princes' places . . . I can easier teach twenty what were good to be done, than be one of the twenty to follow mine own teaching. WILLIAM SHAKESPEARE, *THE MERCHANT OF VENICE*

"Whether or not power corrupts, the lack of power surely frustrates," and, as further pointed out by John Forester of Cornell University's City and Regional Planning Department, "planners know this all too well."[174] The preceding discussion on the lack of correlation between righteousness and effectiveness, particularly as it relates to zoning administration, raises important questions about the role of ethics in planning agency management.

During a session on the future of planning at the 1986 annual conference of the American Planning Association, Forester noted that there are serious problems and differing views involving the role of ethics in the decision-making process. He said that to some, ethics are incomprehensible, while to others they are used as window dressing for their public relations value. He warned against the "dangerous and unworkable" view that there is only one right answer and reasoned that "ethics is often only a way of arguing about what to do."

Let us illustrate part of what we think Forester was saying. An elderly woman's cat died after providing her with many years of companionship. She went to a local church and asked the preacher if he would say a few words over her cat. The preacher said, "We're taught in theology that animals don't even have souls, so we don't believe in that kind of stuff. No, I'd just rather not do it." She remarked that she had been going to give the preacher $20 for saying the words over the cat and maybe give the church $50. The preacher responded, "Well, they *could* very well have souls. Like I tell my congregation, they don't teach it anywhere that I know of, but we don't really *know*." They had a real nice service for her cat.

A more realistic illustration of the complexity of an ethics issue involving zoning was provided in a survey conducted by the International City Management Association. One of the ten theoretical questions that were asked of city managers was as follows:

A new civic plaza is in the plans to restore the downtown area of your city. The bond issue for development that was passed three years ago is already too little to assure completion of the project, because of inflation. A developer who wants to erect a high-rise office building and mall near the civic plaza offers to buy a large tract of undeveloped land in the plaza area and donate it to the city, in exchange for permission to build his proposed building higher than the present zoning restrictions will permit.

He has made this offer to you and it is up to you to decide whether to communicate the offer to the city council. Do you pass on the offer to the council?[175]

The example illustrates the basic bribe. In return for a favor from the city, the individual will make a payoff in land, yet the vast majority of managers responding to the survey answered that they would pass on the offer. Some, however, did indicate that they would recommend rejecting the offer. Our response is to compare this example to the example of the planner who was offered a bribe to issue a building permit. The planner told the individual that only the building official could issue permits and that he would not serve as a go-between on such an unethical and illegal offer. Afterwards, the building official thanked the planner for not becoming involved in the matter because he preferred dealing directly without third-party involvement in such situations.

What is ethical behavior to one person may not be considered ethical behavior by another. In Austin, sixteen different officials consisting of ex-city managers, assistant managers, city attorneys, and assorted department heads and assistant department heads have resigned their positions in recent years to work for development interests in the private sector. John Heldreth, of Texas Common Cause, contends that such behavior "is sad and it's sickening."[176] He adds that public service is no longer perceived as an end in itself and that "the idea is to get a few years of experience and training on city time, and then cash in on their contacts and expertise and strike it rich."[177]

Neil Peirce, in an article on the "revolving door syndrome" in government, reported there is growing local opposition to allowing planners and other government employees to leave their positions to work for the private sector on the same projects with which they were formally involved.[178] In addition to ethicists and government do-gooders who are concerned about the ethics of such revolving door practices, Peirce notes that the newest Austin city manager and other municipal administrators are upset about training employees and then having them "fly the coop."[179] It should, however, be noted that the current Austin city manager would not have his job unless the former manager had left for the private sector. Richard Lillie, former Austin planning director who served as director for fifteen years, was recognized as one of the most respected planners in the state. He was a champion of citizen participation in local government and compiled a lengthy record of public service. Lillie is now the chief of planning and a lobbyist for a real estate investment and development firm.

It has been said that the best revenge is living well, and it may well be that some of the opposition to revolving door activities is caused by sour grapes on the part of former employers. In the cases of Lillie and other long-term planning directors, what type of employment should they seek when they have completed their years of public service? Can the public expect such individuals to abandon their education and experience and start over in an entry-level position in a new career?

In reality, each jurisdiction has its own body of laws and accepted local customs and practices concerning ethical behavior. As noted in the January 1986 issue of *American City and County,* "the threshold for corruption is different in each municipality. There's no underlying consensus of what's right or wrong."[180] The same article suggests that guidelines are often considered more important than the actual code because they tell public servants how to apply the code to reality. In this area, the National Municipal League has developed a set of guidelines called a "Model State Conflict of Interest and Financial Disclosure Law" which are supplemented by a booklet that "was designed to allow sufficient flexibility for adaptation to particular conditions and political traditions."[181]

The following verses are from the poem "The Blind Men and the Elephant," by John Saxe, which was based on the Hindu fable about the six blind men who feel and then describe an elephant. They go a long way toward describing our views on the nebulous issue of ethics.

Each in his own opinion
Exceeding stiff and strong,
Though each was partly in the right,
And all were in the wrong!

Moral

So oft in theologic wars,
The disputants, I ween,
Rail on in utter ignorance
Of what each other mean,
And prate about an elephant
Not one of them has seen!

There is obviously a great deal of disagreement about the issue of ethics in planning. Peter Marcuse, in an article on professional ethics and values, contended that "existing ethical standards are often inherently contradictory, guild oriented, and inconsistent with the public image that the profession attempts to maintain."[182] Reviewing a number of case studies he concluded that:

> (i)n most cases, even the rules for telling right from wrong are not clear. Obligations to clients conflict with obligations to the public; following professionally accepted standards of conduct produces results repugnant to most laymen; professional integrity and democratic decision making seem to conflict; the bounds of professional concern are hazy.[183]

Much of what planners do reflects ethical choices. But as pointed out by Jerome Kaufman, "even with increased awareness of the ethical nature of our profession and greater skill in approaching the task of making ethical choices, the sorting out of what is right and wrong still entails a well-thought out moral code."[184]

In the climactic scene in *The Wizard of Oz*, Dorothy and her companions are being addressed by the wondrous but fearsome Wizard. Amid the smoke and thunderous noise, Toto pulls back the curtain and reveals a very human Frank Morgan operating the special effects machinery. A shocked and angry Dorothy tells him, "You are a very bad man." "No, my dear," says the Wizard, "I am a very good man. I am just a very bad wizard." In truth, we are more concerned with the issue of ineffective planning than we are about bad people practicing planning. Our simplistic advice on ethics is to practice the profession in accordance with the American Institute of Certified Planners' *Code of Ethics and Professional Conduct*. Carol Barrett contends that "planners' primary obligation is to the public interest" and that the code "recognizes the challenge of determining what the public interest might be in any given situation."[185] Barrett explains in debating what the public interest might entail, that a planner is to:

> focus on the interrelatedness of decisions and long-range consequences of present actions; to provide complete information and meaningful opportunities for public participation; to protect the natural environment and conserve and enhance the built environment; and to expand the choice and opportunity for all with a special responsibility for the disadvantaged.[186]

Under no circumstances does effective planning depend on unethical behavior on the part of planners. What is needed is a commitment to a bias for action that results in the meaningful, effective participation of planners in the problem-solving and decision-making process. Ethics should not be used as a crutch to justify or defend ineffectiveness. Hells bells! What's more unethical than collecting a paycheck in the guise of promoting and protecting the public interest while having no real influence or impact on anyone or anything? The best ethics are based on commitment to excellence.

3

Close to the Customer

No government program can be sustained except by the support of elected officials or by public opinion or by both. ROBERT MOSES

Theodore Levitt postulated in *The Marketing Imagination* that the purpose of a business is to create and keep a customer, and to do that you have to produce and deliver goods and services that people want and value.[1] This simple thought applies equally well to both the private and public sectors. In theory, communities grow and prosper in the same way as any business does: by adding new customers (in-migration of population) while retaining satisfied consumers (no out-migration). It may sometimes be difficult for municipalities to maintain consumer satisfaction in high growth areas because people may perceive a decline in the quality of the original product due to increased traffic, overcrowded schools, lower air quality, higher costs, or changes in the community's character.

SOLVING CLIENTS' PROBLEMS

The most common task set for planners is to solve problems and clean up messes. BRIAN J. L. BERRY

Development of a management plan and work program for a planning agency begins with asking and answering such broad questions as: What business are we in? What business do we want to be in? Why do people use or buy our products and services? Who is our competition? What are we doing right? What are we doing wrong?

Many planners cannot answer even the first question because they are not sure about their business. The value of asking these questions is that they stimulate serious thinking and prod planners to question the validity of their assumptions about agency operations.

Nan Lin and Ronald Burt, in "Differential Effect of Information Channels in the Process of Innovation Diffusion," explained that unless doctors in developing countries can help poorly educated parents to understand the germ-disease relationship and the chemistry of immunology the parents are reluctant to have their children immunized.[2] This simply illustrates that maximum effectiveness depends on an organization's ability to communicate a clear understanding of the basic concept behind its products and services. Planners have the challenge, according to Donald Spaid, former planning coordinator for St. Paul, Minnesota, of putting planning "in terms that are understandable to the political process."[3]

Terry Moore has suggested in an article in the *Journal of the American Institute of Planners* entitled "Why Allow Planners to Do What They Do?" that there is inadequate knowledge among practicing planners about why they should plan.[4] He contends that it is glaringly inadequate to assume that the goodness of planning should be accepted simply on face value. Instead, he suggests that the legitimacy of planning can be demonstrated by reliance on an economic theory of public goods. At a minimum he believes that "planners should become more familiar with the themes of political economy and the tools of economic analysis" and use this information to support and defend the legitimacy of their activities in the local community.[5]

We concur with Moore's main point that many planners and planning organizations need to do a better job of understanding and being able to explain and defend why planning is necessary. Such information and insight provides much needed guidelines for assisting planners in identifying the degree of planning that is desirable and the best method for planning in their communities. When clients understand the basic concept behind each planning product and service, planners can do a better job of meeting their needs and become much more effective service providers.

Developing a "positioning" strategy is the first step in establishing an effective management program for any planning agency wanting to become more effective. "Positioning" involves creating a niche in a complex, changing environment that is unique, important, and appropriate given the resources and capabilities of an organization.[6] Too many planning agencies have been slow to recognize the need for internal operating changes, preferring instead to whine about their hostile, nonsupportive external environment.

Some planners even view changes in the external environment as transitory and adopt the strategy of waiting for a more favorable set of events.[7] The department's official uniform becomes trendy camouflage attire which makes the wearer as nearly invisible as possible.

The manager of any public or private organization has the over-riding responsibility to communicate and explain to the staff the relevance of external environmental changes to internal operations. It is a serious mistake to assume that the staff understands and appreciates the need to be responsive to these changes.

Van Gordon Sauter, former embattled president of CBS News, was strongly criticized by his staff for failing to defend their division, like past presidents had, from the budget cuts and operational changes that were threatening their independence. Rather than responding to the severe financial problems and aggressive competition that was hurting CBS, the staff wanted a leader willing to sacrifice his position to defend their status quo. Sauter defended his actions to the *New York Times* by explaining that "no matter who was sitting in my chair, the same steps would have been necessary because of the economic woes facing CBS and the broadcasting industry in general."[8] He added that if he had failed in his leadership it was because he "did not adequately represent the forces of the outside world to the news division."[9]

One frustrated planning director told us that "sometimes you just have to shake a person and tell him 'You're failing, you're failing! You may be going home to your wife ecstatic about some memo, report, or study that you completed today—but you're failing.' "

Effective planning agencies are similar to other successful organizations in that they practice a proactive, adaptive response to changes in the external environment. They view these changes as evolutionary and accordingly adjust their operating programs and services. Repositioning becomes a fundamental strategy for protecting and promoting the organization. Warren Bennis and Bert Nanus found that internal operating environments can be changed and made more responsive and more effective by "granting or withholding funds, manpower or facilities; training and education; by selection, hiring and firing; and by deliberate efforts to design a corporate culture that develops certain values at the expense of others."[10]

Agencies have a myriad of ongoing duties and responsibilities and it is difficult to reduce existing commitments but, as a good west Texas farmer knows, you can't worry about tumbleweeds when you're being smothered by a sandstorm. To be effective, planners must make their products and services stand out in what in many local governments is a confused and saturated marketplace, and they must create a clear and positive "user-friendly" image in the minds of both administrative and elected decision makers. The most successful strategy for getting your message across in an "over-communicated society," according to Al Ries and Jack Trout in *Positioning: The Battle for Your Mind*, is to "create a position in the prospect's mind, a position that takes into consideration not only a company's own strengths and weaknesses, but those of its competitors as well."[11] It should be a position that is both unique and appealing.

What comes to people's minds in your community when they think of your planning agency? Are the images positive or negative? The development of a positive image—based on a conscious positioning strategy—is fundamental to the effectiveness and success of most agencies. The secret to positioning is "not to create something new and different," as Ries and Trout point out, "but to manipulate what's already up there in the mind, to retie the connection that already exists."[12] Further, the product must be credible. "Consumers won't buy an assertion in advertising that runs counter to what they believe," according to Rajeev Barta, assistant professor of marketing at the Columbia Graduate School of Business.[13] Consider the example of the R. T. French Company's attempt to challenge Grey Poupon Dijon for the gourmet mustard market. French launched Vive La Dijon mustard in an ornate jar but consumers recognized the French's red logo and were not impressed. Dan Cohen, an advertising executive, pointed out that the product was a mistake because "French's will always be considered a kid's ballpark mustard."[14]

What does all this mean for the typical planning agency? Planning clients—elected officials, managers, department heads, developers, and residents of a community—do not necessarily buy "things" from planners; they buy solutions to problems. As Theodore Levitt noted, "the surviving and thriving business is a business that constantly seeks better ways to help people solve their problems—functionally better, valued better and available better. To create betterness requires knowing what customers think betterness to be."[15]

Margarita McCoy, former head of the Urban and Regional Planning Department at California State Polytechnic University, views a planning education as a problem-solving education.[16] Planners, who are trained in problem-solving skills, should take this approach to serve "public" needs. Instead of just being available to help, planners need to position themselves as aggressive providers of services to decision makers. They need to actively seek out what their clients do, how their "businesses" work, and, most important, what problems they are experiencing. In an article in the *Wall Street Journal* with the intriguing title of "How to Manage the Boss," Peter Drucker suggests that it is both the subordinate's duty and in the subordinate's self-interest to go to the boss—at least once a year—and ask: "What do I do and what do my people do that helps you do your job? And what do we do that hampers *you* and makes life more difficult for *you*?"[17]

Insight about the problems and needs of the general public and other potential special-interest clients is critical to an effective positioning strategy. Communication must occur in both a formal organized fashion and in informal "one-on-one" situations. It has been suggested that the good Lord gave us two ears and one mouth and that we should use them in that proportion.

Russ Staiger, executive director of the Bismarck, North Dakota, Development Association, has urged planners to do a better job of listening and learning from the public about local problems. He suggested that planners should:

> . . . take a notepad and pencil, or a pocket tape recorder, and get out into the community and listen to what people have to say. . . . We (planners) need to get out of our little coffee coves and data procesing retreats and begin to talk with individuals—white- and blue-collar— who are struggling with survival sixteen hours a day.[18]

Effraim Garcia, planning director for Houston, Texas, provides an example of the success in planning that comes from taking a problem-solving approach to the job. Since being hired in 1982, he has been able to win support for establishing a formal planning process in Houston's hostile planning environment. In assessing his accomplishments and management style, one staff planner noted:

> He's forceful, yet he's not inflexible when it comes to working with staff or developers. Most of all, he's a problem solver. And that gets respect in this town.[19]

A thorough study in 1970 provided a review and critical evaluation of the plan-making process for thirteen planning programs located in most of the largest U.S. metropolitan areas.[20] The study revealed serious shortcomings, with one of the most important being the failure of planners to identify and sharply focus on significant problems. The study's researchers concluded that a problem-oriented approach to the plan-making process was essential for effective planning. They pointed out that "it is often the case that a good statement of the problem is not only necessary for its solution, but also leads directly to its solution."[21]

During the 1971 annual conference of the American Society of Planning Officials, Albert Waterston, formerly of the Economic Development Institute of the World Bank, spoke on making the planning process more effective. He advocated "a problem-oriented approach to planning, starting from the bottom up," and noted that the process should result in "highly specific objectives derived from the problems to be solved."[22] It was Waterston's view that a problem-finding and problem-solving approach to planning would be more effective than other conventional planning processes. He cautioned that this approach depends on planning from the bottom up with emphasis on self-help.

For too many years comprehensive planning has been ineffective because it has been a product in search of a client. Planning must address—as openly, realistically, and thoroughly as possible—the "pressing current issues" in the community and come to grips with those issues or "the plan will soon be filed and forgotten."[23] To be effective, the plan must meet the needs of its clients. Robert Herchert, former city manager of Fort Worth, offered the following relevant comment:

> The key ingredient in future planning is involvement of the public, the city council, the planning commission, and staff. Effective plans are developed when such intense involvement takes place. Most plans without such involvement are shelved.[24]

Planners can learn about the need for an action and the problem-solving and service emphasis from the experiences of city managers. Robert Kipp, former city manager of Kansas City, Missouri, contends that successful managers listen to the public and translate their ideas into action.[25] Andrea Beatty, former city manager of Bellevue, Washington, said that in her early months on the job, she wanted to identify a problem that would demonstrate her ability to take charge and "to implement a solution in a way that would inspire confidence and credibility."[26] Charles Meyer, former manager of Genesse County, New York, advises younger managers to "look for a few 'quick fixes' that can save the community money without a great deal of effort."[27] And Norman King, former city manager of Palm Springs, California, advocates a management strategy and style based on building credibility with decision makers. He and other managers have found that identifying a small problem and helping to solve it can be an important way to gain credibility and increase effectiveness.[28]

Robert Einsweiler found in his experience that helping public officials solve a problem they couldn't solve led to trust and respect for his political judgment and technical knowledge. After two successes, they were eager to listen to what he had to say; after a third victory he could count on their enthusiastic support in the community. Using low-risk strategies that concentrate on resolving simple problems or symptoms of larger problems is an acceptable initial strategy for building credibility—but the technique does not provide a long-term, workable strategy for an effective planning program.

Planners should focus their resources and energies on solving significant problems. John Friedmann, respected director of the UCLA planning program, has concluded that too many planners are "more adept at problem avoidance than at problem solving."[29] As Craig Hickman and Michael Silva have noted, "the way to create excellence is to confront problems (suffering the inevitable pain of doing so) and develop effective solutions (which takes good old-fashioned hard work)."[30]

PROBLEM-SOLVING PITFALLS

Government is not the solution, government is the problem. RONALD REAGAN

Government is neither the problem nor the solution. Government is only the government and, just like everything and everybody else, when it acts wisely and well, it solves problems; when it doesn't, it doesn't.

As a general rule, planners don't solve problems; they make it possible for others to solve problems. But in interviews with practicing planners, Howell S. Baum, associate professor at the School of Social Work and Community Planning at the University of Maryland at Baltimore, found that two-thirds regarded themselves as competent intellectual problem-solvers and that they resented the intrusion of elected officials and community organizations into decision-making processes.[31] This fundamental misconception about the problem-solving role of planners is dangerously flawed and ensures ultimate ineffectivenes and dissatisfaction with the profession. Baum concluded that many planners are academically unprepared for the real-world way in which bureaucratic planning decisions are made. Planners frequently make three *false* assumptions: (1) the problem in planning is the analytical or technical problem on which the planner works, (2) the planner "owns" the problem on which he or she works, and (3) the planner is an independent, free-lance, intellectual professional, similar to an attorney, that is employed to provide rational solutions to clients' problems.[32]

Baum noted that in reality planners "are aids to others who are, in fact, the problem solvers" and that elected officials "do not give the problem to the planners—they lend part of it and demand it back."[33] He pointed out that, most important, elected officials "do not ask planners to solve problems" but rather "they ask the planners to formulate the problem meaningfully—so that the officials can solve it."[34]

Effective planners are able to appreciate the difference between problem formulating and problem solving and understand the ways in which decisions are made in the political decision-making process. They help identify and solve problems in accordance with these constraints.

How the problem is defined often determines how or even if it is going to be solved. Dennis Rondinelli warns that "few issues are defined in the same way by all who participate in the policymaking process."[35] For example, a newly hired planning director discovered that several respected civic leaders were concerned about the lack of coordination and communication between the planning commission and the zoning commision. The planning commission thought the zoning commission was too responsive to the city council and not well versed in planning fundamentals. It also seemed that the planning commission was trying to do the zoning commission's job. The development community was concerned about the atittudes of many of the members of both commissions, but also believed that any structural changes would be detrimental to their development interests. Neither commission was aware of any public concern or dissatisfaction with its performance. Obviously, the planner who tried to tackle this problem was quickly in deep trouble.

One of the most important pitfalls to avoid is solving nonexistent problems. This is a particularly needless way to get in trouble, as illustrated by these two stories. The first concerns the experience of a baggage handler at Dallas/Fort Worth airport who found an animal-carrier containing a dead dog while unloading a plane. The airline officials, fearing an embarrassing lawsuit, notified the passenger that her dog had been sent to another destination but that it would be quickly brought back to Dallas and delivered to her house. Then a half dozen customer service employees were given pictures of the animal and sent out to find a look-alike dog. After several hours a live ringer was found and purchased for $500 and the dog was rushed to the woman's home. But when the dog was delivered the woman noticed right away that it wasn't hers. She exclaimed: "That's not my dog! My dog is dead." She had been bringing the dog home for burial.

The second story occurred in Butte, Montana. A young and eager planner excitedly advised his council that he was working on solving their flooding problems by developing a storm-water management plan and an application to make the city eligible for the federal flood insurance program. When the mayor responded that they didn't have a flooding problem, the planner asked what did they call all of the water that was overflowing the boundaries of the local creeks. The naive planner was informed that it was simply the annual spring runoff. There are any number of stories that we could have used to make this point, but the message should be clear. Planners who value their credibility and effectiveness do not propose to help solve nonexistent problems.

NICHEMANSHIP

Unlike product manufacturers, service organizations can have considerable difficulty delivering more than one "product," more than one type or level of service, at one time. JAMES L. HESKETT

Closeness to the customer does not guarantee that you understand and know how to service your market, teaches Marvin Nesbitt, director of the Small Business Development Center at Florida International University in Miami. He recommends that "you must find and exploit your niche by systematically identifying the distinct market segments into which your customers fall."[36] Many planners are familiar with the concept of needs assessments, yet according to Gerald Zaltman and Robert Duncan in *Strategies for Planned Change,* many agencies "do not monitor the knowledge, attitudes, and practices of their clientele to determine what client needs exist or are emerging." They further noted that an "agency is likely to flounder if its products are not matched with needs as perceived by the target audience or client group."[37]

Nichemanship is a term used by Peters and Waterman to define a way of "tailoring" to meet a particular niche that expands services to specific groups or segments of customers. Segmentation is the process of identifying groups of customers with enough common characteristics to make possible the design and presentation of a product or service that each group needs. By dividing the customer base into numerous segments, it is possible to tailor products and services to meet these special markets. Peters and Waterman found that five fundamental attributes are shared by those companies that are close to the customer through niche strategies: "(1) astute technology manipulation; (2) pricing skill; (3) better segmenting; (4) a problem-solving orientation; and (5) a willingness to spend in order to discriminate."[38]

This approach to niche identification and service is more one of problem solving, and less one of sales marketing. Niche masters are geared toward catering their products and services to solve specific client problems. Better results are achieved by focusing activities on those groups or individuals which have an identifiable need or desire for what you are doing, than by force-feeding a planning product or service to the widest universe of possible consumers.

An important side benefit of using a nichemanship strategy is that it removes the planner from the dilemma of having to select and serve just one primary client. Some departments are perceived as favoring homeowners, or development, or bureaucracy, and they often try to shift their alliances and services as the power shifts in the community. We believe such a chameleonlike strategy eventually results in failure. Carl Sandburg told a short story that makes our point: "There was a chameleon who got along very well, adjusting moment by moment to his environment, until one day he had to cross a scotch plaid. He died at the crossroads, heroically trying to blend with all the colors at once."[39]

In the private sector, Peters and Waterman identified Minnesota Mining and Manufacturing (3M) as a classic player of the problem-solving, niche-building game. After 3M identifies a market niche, the company immerses itself in the potential client's operations to learn the client's needs. In some cases, 3M has actually invited the chief executive officer of a targeted company to come and lecture on how 3M could serve it.[40]

A municipal planning example of this technique was found in Arlington, Texas. There, the planning department sought information from past zoning and subdivision applicants to learn how

Table 3–1

User Survey of Rezoning Applicants
Arlington, Texas

Category	Excellent	Good	Poor	Not Satisfactory
Overall Service/Efficiency	33%	60%	5%	2%
Employee Efficiency/Courtesy	53%	42%	5%	-
Employee Knowledge	37%	49%	12%	2%
Objectivity of Staff Reports	26%	47%	16%	12%
Length of Processing Time	14%	40%	33%	12%
Comparison of Our Service to Your Experience Elsewhere	26%	59%	10%	5%

Source: Planning Department, City of Arlington, Texas (1984)

their needs were met and determine how the department could better serve their future needs. In Arlington, applicants are recognized and treated as customers—not adversaries—and problem solving is the focus of the planning department's marketing efforts.

Table 3-1 provides results of the user survey the Arlington Planning department conducted. Length of processing time was the most significant negative factor revealed, which reinforced the planning department's previously initiated efforts to reduce the length of time needed to process a rezoning application.

In an effort to improve the efficiency and quality of services, the Grand Prairie, Texas, Department of Community Development initiated in 1985 a comprehensive service evaluation program. The program sought input from people who had used the services of one or more of the department's three divisions (Comprehensive Planning, Current Planning, and Building Inspections) during the first six months of the year.

A formal questionnaire was sent to every individual on record who had some form of contact with the department, such as participation in the development of a sector plan, applying for a building permit, or requesting a zoning change, subdivision plat or site plan approval. Respondents identified the division with which they had been associated, and evaluated the division and its employees on the basis of six separate criteria.

The results provided information about how actual users perceived the services provided by the department and what areas of service delivery needed the most improvement. The director used the information as the basis for the development of a series of specific recommendatins for ensuring service improvements. The recommendations were forwarded for consideration to each division head. An accompanying memo urged that "regardless of whether or not the recommendations are endorsed by practice, it is imperative that each division recognize the concern and implement whatever measures are necessary to ensure service improvement over the next period of assessment."

But no planning department can be on top of all facets of its community. The idea is simply that you aren't going to be all things to all people. You're going to be some things for some people. A major responsibility of the staff is to identify those segments of the community for which the agency can be most effective. The planner's community can be viewed as a marketplace consisting of development and real estate people, neighborhood residents, business managers, workers, special interest groups, and other public and semipublic agencies. Each potential customer has a multitude of needs. Providing each client with a broad spectrum of planning services is like trying to be all things to all people, which is impossible.

Many years ago, an attempt was made to promote Rheingold beer to the large working class market in the New York City area. A series of well made ethnic commercials was prepared featuring Italians drinking Rheingold, Irish drinking Rheingold, blacks drinking Rheingold, etc. Unfortunately for Rheingold, this advertising campaign became a classic marketing disaster because, by trying to appeal to everyone, they ended up appealing to no one.

Targeting is an essential aspect of successful marketing. If a plannng agency is going to be effective, it is essential that it focus its activities. At some point, you have to say, "Holy Toledo. How the hell are we going to do everything with the resources we've got?" Some agencies also believe that they can do everything well and that they have no technical weaknesses. They attribute any obvious shortcomings to bad luck, not lack of skill. It is a mistake to believe this. In reality, every organization has strengths and weaknesses that are specific to the collective experiences and talents of its employees. Consider the following. A friend who ran track with Jim Ryan in school noted that Ryan couldn't make his junior high school track team because the longest race was only a quarter of a mile. However, he made his high school team, ran for the University of Kansas, and represented the United States in the Olympics because he found a niche for his unique physical skills: Ryan, who couldn't compete effectively in races under a quarter mile, was one of the best "milers" and 1,500-meter runners in the world.

Part of good planning is coming to terms with limitations—your own included—and realizing that some things can't happen without undermining others. Choices must be made. Planning agencies obviously do not have unlimited financial or staff resources so marketing strategies must be developed that will maximize the impact and influence of the products and services that can be provided. John T. Howard, former head of the Department of City and Regional Planning at the Massachusetts Institute of Technology, went so far as to suggest that staff assignments and program priorities for planning agencies should be based on "methods and structures which will accomplish not necessarily as much work as possible but rather as *effective* work as possible."[41] (Emphasis added.) Again, the real danger is that planners will try to do everything for everyone and end up not doing anything very well—a prescription for ultimate ineffectiveness and failure.

Finding the time and resources to create new products and services in response to changing conditions and emerging opportunities in the marketplace requires that organizations eliminate the no-longer-productive, the obsolescent and the obsolete. Planners must be able to identify what works and what doesn't work. During good times, it is easy to become blinded by success and assume that everything is working. Waiting until times are bad to examine activities makes planners victims rather than managers of change. At all times, planners must be willing to critically examine all activities and ask, "If we were not already committed to this activity, would we decide to do it now?" If the answer is no, then find out how *fast* you can get out of it!

Effectiveness depends on concentrating resources in a few critical priority areas. Planners and local government officials, in general, must avoid the temptation of trying to overcome ineffectiveness by putting more resources and energy into becoming more efficient. It is effectiveness, not efficiency, which is the primary target. It is the failure to be doing the right things that is the primary cause of ineffectiveness in most planning organizations.

The simple truth is that no institution likes to abandon anything it does. Peter Drucker makes the following observations with respect to this point: "All service institutions are threatened by the tendencies to cling to yesterday rather than to slough it off, and to put their best and ablest people on defending what no longer makes sense or serves a purpose. Government is particularly prone to this disease."[42]

Planners is search of effectiveness must critically evaluate the linkage or lack of linkage between their products and services and the essential purpose and mission of their organizations. Blindly continuing to do something just because "it's always been done" or worse, because of an inherent belief in its righteousness, will waste valuable resources and impair the organization's effectiveness. Planners tend to believe that most of what they do is virtuous and in the public interest. Lacking the discipline that is enforced in the private sector by the marketplace, individuals in public institutions are tempted, according to Peter Drucker, "to blame the outside world for its stupidity or its reactionary resistance, and to consider lack of results a proof of one's own righteousness and a reason in itself for keeping on with the good work."[43]

Planners should be interested in efficiency, but our point is that ultimate effectiveness depends on providing specific products and services that are linked to the primary mission of the agency and service the critical needs of clients. This means that to maximize their effectiveness, planners must segment their community into a multitude of discrete clients. They must begin to deliver their products and services on a carefully selected priority basis in order to meet the specialized needs of these specific market segments. Joseph Vitt, Jr., explained that the Kansas City planning department tried "to tailor the products we develop to meet the needs of the particular clients."[44] He pointed out that this "means that no two products of the department are really ever alike because we are very sensitive to the needs of the groups in the areas in which we are operating."[45]

At this point it must be made clear that under no circumstances should the selection of program priorities be used as a basis for discrimination against or exclusion of potential clients. Truly effective planners must demonstrate a service philosophy consistent with Melvin Webber's view that a planner must be "capable of serving the interests of pluralism and diversity by aiding those he opposes."[46] All groups and views must have access to planning products and services and to maintain effectiveness the planner must enthusiastically respond to and support the needs of those segments of the market which are selected to be served.

One other note of caution is in order. In developing market segmentation strategy and deciding to deliver new products and services to unique client groups, planners must always be alert to any perception of unfair favoritism. Often there are conflicts between different constituencies and any expansion of service to one group may be construed by another group as an actual shifting of support from them to their adversaries.

One planner recognized this situation and handled it well. The planner was invited to a local neighborhood conference to explain how to fight a rezoning request. He was eager to serve the important client group and readily accepted the invitation. However, he also recognized that the development community might think that he was supporting neighborhood interests over their interests. Working through the local development community, he was able to get on the program at the annual convention of the National Association of Home Builders to speak on"How to Win at the Zoning Table." He made it a point to tell both the neighborhood and development groups about each of his speeches.

In *Strategies for Planned Change,* Gerald Zaltman and Robert Duncan pointed out that the change agent must be sensitive to undercurrents and tensions among persons and groups, especially in the context of changes in their programs, and use this information in "determining the appropriate strategies and techniques to effect a change."[47] This is valuable advice for planners who are trying to use a market segmentation strategy to serve their clients.

Most planners should have no difficulty in understanding the market segmentation strategy and using it to increase their effectiveness in delivering services. Planners have extensive experience with demographic analysis and instinctively know that age, income, educational attainment, family size, and location are just a few dimensions of possible market segments. Demographic information is available to most planners and is a relatively simple and cost-effective way to identify a target market. The real challenge for planners is learning how to adjust their products and services to take advantage of the marketing opportunities that are created by changes in local demographics.

Demographic variables reveal trends that create new market segments and service opportunities in both the public and private sectors. Most planners know how to use demographics to identify discrete groups of potential clients, but they do not necessarily understand how to tailor or develop new products or services to respond to these opportunities. Your customers are constantly changing and you must change with them if you are going to be effective.

In *Managing in the Service Economy,* Harvard Business School professor James Heskett indicated that "psychographic" information should be used to supplement demographic analysis of the marketplace. He explained that psychographics describe the way people think and the actions prompted by those thoughts.[48] This type of information explains the way people act and live. Heskett noted in particular that "one important psychographic dimension whose understanding has provided the foundation for more than one highly successful service is that of perceived risk, including perceived economic, social, legal or medical risk." The following is a summary of the most significant aspects of the risk factors associated with services from the perspective of the consumer:

> Customers associate risk more highly with the purchase of services than goods;
>
> Customers for services often feel they have less information about services than goods;
>
> Causes of perceived risk are the nonstandard nature of many services, the lack of evaluative criteria, and the absence of or difficulties with guarantees against poor performance; and persons displaying high levels of perceived risks often lack knowledge or self-confidence about a particular product or suffer from a high level of exposure. . . .[49]

The psychographic dimension of perceived risk creates important markets for planning products and services. For example, there is a growing segment of families with high levels of education, little knowledge of local government, and a basic dislike and fear of the new developments that they perceive to be threatening to the character and stability of their neighborhoods. This group, in particular, offers an attractive, influential, and profitable market for neighborhood planning products and services that have traditionally been associated with urban renewal and redevelopment areas.

A recent national survey of the directors of neighborhood planning programs revealed that slightly more than 47 percent of the respondents indicated that middle-income neighborhoods were most likely to participate in these programs; only 6 percent indicated that high-income neighborhoods were likely to participate.[50] Yet there was wide-ranging disparity in the responses to the survey and many planners indicated that the pendulum was swinging and that there was currently a shift in the geographic and client focus of their local programs.

William Rohe and Lauren Gates in their important book *Planning with Neighborhoods*, concluded that "an effective planning strategy must include a mechanism for addressing the smaller problems of residential areas."[51] They argued that neighborhood planning makes it possible to address the local problems experienced by residents on a day-to-day basis and to provide a better balance between the attention and resources focused on large-scale development and that given to small-scale neighborhood development. They recommended "that all medium-to-large-sized cities adopt a neighborhood planning program."[52]

Employing market segmentation strategies that recognize and capitalize on neighborhood service opportunities is one way to make local planning agencies more effective. An example of the application of this simple technique was provided several years ago in Forth Worth. For a variety of reasons, this city developed the Sector Planning Program as a substitute for updating the traditional comprehensive plan. Eleven separate planning sectors were delineated with each sector containing between 30,000 and 50,000 residents in an area of up to twenty square miles

Sector planning was a new and untested service, so the city plan commission chose to begin the project in a relatively affluent sector that had few pressing physical problems. The first sector included a major university and many of its residents were active in government and civic affairs. The sector was selected based on the simple belief that planning would be much more effective in this area and that the lessons to be learned from this initial experience would prepare the staff and commission for dealing with the areas with more difficult problems. The first sector plan was well received and over the next ten years plans were prepared for the remaining sectors. Those sectors most in need of planning services or where redevelopment pressures were the most intense were priority targets.

There are many other ways to successfully practice marketing segmentation/nichemanship strategies. Fort Worth has produced a series of marketing opportunity studies in brochure format to encourage and promote economic development in a selected number of designated revitalization areas. These brochures, prepared under an Economic Development Administration (EDA) grant, contained land use, zoning, infrastructure, demographic, and socioeconomic data that was considered of use to potential developers. This program was of short duration and limited to only a few areas in the community.

Another example of producing products for a specific market niche was *A Developer's Handbook* which the Multomah County, Oregon, planning department published. This popular handbook included an evaluation checklist, site development guidelines and performance standards, and a technical appendix and bibliography of other pertinent reference sources.[53] In a similar vein, a seventy-four-page developers' guide prepared by Las Cruces, New Mexico, recently received an honorable mention as an outstanding planning project from the American Planning Association. It clearly and simply provides developers with concise advice and information on subdivision regulations, zoning, annexation, building permits, and utility hookup procedures.

Earlier we pointed out that perceived risk was an important psychographic dimension that should be capitalized on when developing new products or services. Heskett noted that customers have a basic fear and dislike of being placed in the hands of an unknown, untrusted service provider. Many customers will gladly pay more for the same service if they understand and trust the process. Something as simple as the visual clues or diagrams in a development guide can help the customer get through the service maze and develop more trust in the system. Development customers' basic distrust of the local government service provider also explains why they are willing to pay a consultant for many of the same services that are freely provided at city hall.

Austin, Texas, is attempting to reduce the level of perceived risk for developers by using an ombudsman, troubleshooter or problem solver to keep projects on the processing track. They recently employed an individual with extensive experience in both the public and private sectors to serve as a process manager. His primary role is to come to the aid of applicants whose projects have stalled and to get the projects moving again.

In Fort Worth, the planning department prepared a report which analyzed the service delivery system for zoning, platting, annexation, and other regulatory processes. All the components of each possible service transaction were diagrammed and the "fail points" most likely to cause problems were identified. This type of analysis makes it possible to give special attention and support through staffing, facility layout, or checking procedures so that potential problems can be avoided or at least minimized. It also has the added benefit of enabling the service provider to see and measure the service as the customer sees it.

Another potential planning service involves training real estate agents to more effectively represent their customers on rezoning applications. One planning director teaches zoning in the real estate program at a local university and hands out a paper on winning at zoning. In Dallas, the planning department has prepared a "neighborhood notebook" as a resource and educational tool for area residents interested in improving their own neighborhood environment. "In essence, it is a 'self-help guide,' giving people information they need to know and answering questions they often ask in undertaking the revitalization, conservation, or enhancement of their own surroundings."[54] The notebook contains fifty-five leaflets that address numerous popular topics.

Aurora, Colorado, and Arlington, Texas, are attempting to improve the distribution of their public hearing information by targeting information to smaller, more responsive groups of individuals. Both cities have started neighborhood referral programs which identify a key set of individuals who represent homeowners and business groups. These groups are notified of any development application, regardless of where it is located. Enough information on each application is provided to allow each group to decide if it should be involved. Development applicants are provided with the list of local organizations and are encouraged to contact those groups that might comment on their proposal. Applicants can also request that they be informed of any comments or requests for information made by those on the contact list. The result in Aurora has been shorter and less heated public hearings, as well as shorter review times when communication between applicants and homeowners is improved.

Some planning departments, such as the one in Beaumont, Texas, actually organize neighborhood associations. In Austin, Texas, the planning department certifies neighborhood associations and notifies them about rezoning applications and capital improvement projects in their area. The planning department in one medium-sized city conducts an annual training session for neighborhood organizations that focuses on permit procedures and standards.

Land use, traffic, employment, and population projections are valuable products and information services that are provided by many planning departments. The material can be organized to meet the specific locational and specialized demographic needs of developers or public agencies such as local school authorities.

Packaging of such products is also important. The production of one document which tries to be all things to all people may fall short of meeting anyone's particular needs. Zoning information on specific cases may need to be packaged differently for the planning commission, the applicant, and adjacent landowners. The commission may be most interested in what the overall density will be, what other uses would the requested zoning district permit, and whether there is currently adequate street, water, and sewer capacity to service the proposed project. The applicant may be most interested in learning about the site plan requirements, signage regulations, and what public facilities and parking spaces will be required. The adjacent neighbors may be most interested in how much additional traffic will be generated, what the proposed project will look like, how their property values will be affected, and where and when they need to appear in order to protest. A single staff report that tries to meet all these needs may confuse everyone or be ignored because of its length. Obviously targeting staff reports to each "niche" could provide more desirable and useful data for each client. Further, the packaging or appearance of each may be different to fit with the type of material that each client is used to reviewing.

A similar approach can be used to provide current and projected demographic data as well as long-range planning information in a manner that best meets the needs of each client's "niche." Peters and Waterman point out that many successful businesses are successful not because they are the "first and foremost, leaders" in their field, but rather "their main attribute is reliable, high-value added products and services."[55] The added expense of developing products which provide targeted services can, in the long run, provide a keener focus to problem solving.

Peters and Waterman emphasize that "niche people are masters at learning about sophisticated technology in one niche, testing it with later uses, ironing out the bugs, and passing that technology along to still others."[56] These niche people use new technology to enter into a specialized market niche, where the high value of the product can bear the high cost of production, the key being the production of a high-valued product for which the client is willing to bear the higher cost. These areas—the application of new technology and pricing—are two in which planners have traditionally been behind the times.

Microcomputers, which are standard equipment in the business world, have yet to be significantly embraced by the planning profession. David Sawicki, head of the city planning program at the

Georgia Institute of Technology, questions the often heard hypothesis that there is a technological revolution taking place in planning as a result of the personal computer and believes that "few planners have attained a high level of proficiency in microcomputing."[57] In one city, the data processing manager said that he could tell when a planner had been using a computer terminal because there was Liquid Paper on the screen. We can laugh, but as noted by Dennis Waitley and Robert Tucker in their book, *Winning the Innovations Game*, "by ignoring the computer today, you risk becoming the illiterate of tomorrow."[58]

The potential of emerging technology is enormous. Microcomputers can be used to create interactive data systems which can provide easy production of targeted data products, word processing systems can be used to quickly convert canned staff reports into a variety of formats, and telecommunications, video technology, and the expanded use of cable television can be used to enhance citizen participation and education. Each of these is a technological way to provide targeted distribution of information. Each of these potential tools could be used to efficiently provide targeted services, which though perhaps more expensive, are more valuable to the client. We describe other, more innovative uses of microcomputers in planning in Chapter 4.

INVOLVING CUSTOMERS IN PLANNING

... planning which does what it is supposed to do is usually done with a maximum of local participation as it goes along, building in local understanding and support. FRED BAIR

Effectiveness requires a maximum of local participation in the planning process and planners have particular skills in promoting and managing such citizen participation and involvement. Contrary to some opinions, most people are not apathetic. They care about their community, but they often do not understand how to put their concerns and feelings into positive action.

It has been suggested by Efraim Gil and Enid Lucchesi in *The Practice of Local Government Planning* that :

> ... citizen participation occurs when there is a meeting of several factors: existing social problems; dissatisfaction with the solutions of local authorities; at least a minimum of affluence to provide the leisure time for planning for future solutions; and knowledge of government and planning.[59]

The relevant aspect of citizen participation in the context of effective planning is an understanding of the value of applying the corporate philosophy to this issue. Lew Young, editor-in-chief of *Business Week* stated that, "probably the most important management fundamental that is being ignored today is staying close to the customer to satisfy his needs and anticipate his wants. In too many companies, the customer has become a bloody nuisance whose unpredictable behavior damages carefully made strategic plans. . . ."[60]

In many communities, public officials view participating residents as a burden or nuisance that interferes with their decision-making authority. All across the country, they wonder why citizens don't support plans, projects, or zoning cases that are in the community's best interest. In Atlanta, it was opposition from the residents of Cabbagetown and Reynoldstown to Seaboard Railroad's plans to build a piggyback terminal in its Hulsey Yard beside their neighborhoods. In Arlington, Texas, it was opposition to the density and concentration of apartments. In Detroit, it was opposition to the involuntary displacement of Poletown residents for a new General Motors automobile assembly plant. In Dallas, it was opposition to continued intense commercial development in the north area already burdened by high traffic volumes and congestion. In Los Angeles, it was opposition to the extension of intensive commercial development into areas adjacent to residential neighborhoods. In Boston, it was racial violence in response to school integration. In each case, the residents involved lost confidence in public officials and reacted by becoming more demonstrably involved in the decision-making process.

Opposition to "locally undesirable land uses" (LULUs) is commonplace and easily understood. Yet regardless of the issue, meaningful citizen participation and involvement in the decision-making process is critical to obtaining public understanding, tolerance, and even support. A workshop sponsored by the Edison Electric Institute on the use of public participation in siting electric utility facilities included the following important observations:

> An effective public participation program must be instituted early in the project planning process to obtain meaningful input from interested parties. Project developers must prove to the public that their concerns and ideas will be given serious consideration.[61]

While there has often been public conflict in communities over controversial development issues, there is now growing opposition to once popular economic development programs. In many cases, these previously popular programs are receiving opposition because of a failure to obtain public understanding and support. The residents were taken for granted and it was incorrectly assumed that the community would support any economic development project that the elected officials deemed to be in the public interest.

In Corpus Christi, Texas, there was public concern about the length of leases that the city council was granting to encourage development of public property along the bay front. This concern was ignored by the council and the public's response was to initiate and approve a charter amendment to limit the length of such leases.

Port Arthur, Texas, residents became angered at their city council when it rejected a coal processing plant in favor of maintaining a commitment to recreational-based development on Pleasure Island. This decision was based on a well-thought out economic development plan but the plan was not understood or supported by the community.

In New Orleans, Louisiana, the 1984 World's Fair was intended to promote local economic growth and development. The project did not receive the necessary commitment and support of the community and it was a failure. Peter Spurney, executive director of the fair, warned other organizers of such major projects that "it is important that all segments of the community have a blood oath, early on, to commit total resources to the project." This type of commitment requires massive public participation and involvement in the planning of such projects to achieve necessary public understanding and support.

An excellent illustration of this need for full participation and support was described in a *National Civic Review* article about goals for Corpus Christi.[62] The article noted that the president of the Corpus Christi chamber of commerce sponsored a luncheon in 1974 for thirty-nine community leaders to determine the desirability of developing a local goals program. The consensus was that there was a need to involve the entire community in the local decision-making process and that a goals program would be the way to obtain that involvement. The Goals for Corpus Christi Program was imaginative and innovative. During its two years, the $151,000 program achieved an outstanding rate of community participation. The heart of the program was a series of televised documentary films, the publication and distribution of a book, and newspaper supplements that proposed several alternative solutions to the major issues in the community. Ballots were available to interested participants and more than 12,000 were received from a community with a total population of 220,000.

Goals for Corpus Christi technically was a successful project; however it failed in one significant area. A comprehensive citizen participation program will require support and commitment from all segments of the community: leaders, average citizens, businesses, local government officials, and the local print and broadcast media. A weak link anywhere can damage the effectiveness of the program.

In Corpus Christi, the weak links were the mayor and city manager who disagreed on almost everything except for their opposition to the local goals program. These strong independent leaders were not interested in sharing their decision-making authority with the public. They contended that the ballot responses to the goals program did not truly reflect the goals of the community and that the manager and city council, in a republic form of government, were better qualified to set goals and establish policies and priorities.

One of the reasons why Robert Moses, legendary chairman of the New York City planning commission and noted critic of the planning profession, was so effective according to Mark Gelfand, associate professor of history at Boston College, was "because he had a knack for knowing the public's desires."[63] In a 1952 article in *The Atlantic Monthly,* Moses rhetorically asked, "Do most professional planners in fact know what people think and want?" He then derided planners who he believed "to be oblivious to the needs of the average citizen to make a living and to his preferences, immediate concerns, and troubles."[64]

In truth, despite all the lip service that is given to citizen participation by planners and public officials, the resident customer is still either being ignored or considered a nuisance in most communities. In contrast, Peters and Waterman were amazed at the extent and the intensity with which customers intrude into every nook and cranny of the business-sales, manufacturing, research, and accounting operations of successful businesses. They discovered that the scale and intensity of customer involvement in operations was one of the best-kept secrets in American business. A summary of their research concluded that "the excellent companies really are close to their customers. That's it. Other companies talk about it; the excellent companies do it."[65]

Customer satisfaction and the quality of service is an obsession with successful businesses. Dinah Nemeroff of Citibank reported in 1980 that there were three principal themes in an effective service orientation: (1) intensive, active involvement on the part of senior management; (2) a remarkable people orientation; and (3) a high-intensity of measurement and feedback.[66]

William Drew, commissioner of city development in Milwaukee, Wisconsin, reported his department developed a socioeconomic demand/need index that was used to identify areas suited to various types of programs. More importantly, the index allowed them to monitor the effectiveness of these programs over time.[67] Obviously a key component of any successful market segmentation strategy is the monitoring and evaluating of feedback from the clients being served.

Everyone in the organization should understand the importance of marketing and have a contributing role in the marketing and selling process. The DuPont Company wants all of its employees to be aware of the value and importance of marketing and to have an awareness of customer needs. The company encourages such awareness by trying to make every employee a salesperson.

For example, DuPont "enlisted 500 stenographers, factory workers, and clerks in its all-volunteer 'Antron Army' to sell a consumer-credit plan to retailers of its antron-fiber carpets."[68]

Every person in the organization needs to be aware of the importance of selling the products and services being produced. Chuck Sussman, a recognized authority on marketing and selling, notes that "a great salesman always thinks that the product he's selling is a great product" and "when you are really, genuinely enthusiastic about a product, it's catching."[69] The bottom line in both the public and private sectors is that a product or service is no good if it can't be sold.

The selling of planning, in general, and of the products and services of the planning department, in particular, is a responsibility of the entire professional staff in Arlington, Texas. Planners are expected to make frequent presentations to citizen groups, civic clubs, neighborhood associations, real estate groups, development associations, and local schools. This type of promotional activity builds public understanding and support for planning while contributing to the development of speaking skills that individual planners will need for their own professional advancement. It also makes the planning staff more aware of the market for planning products and services and encourages them to be more conscious of the ultimate users during the planner's participation in and involvement with different projects.

Unsuccessful planning agencies are reluctant to let citizens in on their internal operations except on a marginal, superficial basis. In contrast, successful planners use the public's growing interest in volunteerism, self-help, and coproduction to obtain what Nathan Glazer refers to in "Toward a Self-Service Society" in the Winter 1983 issue of *The Public Interest* as "mechanisms for a more continuous day-to-day involvement for individuals and neighborhoods in govenment."[70] The devolution of service responsibilities to citizens is a natural result of efforts by employees and users to share more service and decision-making responsibilities.

COPRODUCTION

While there are local government service areas for which self-help would not be suitable as an alternative service delivery mechanism, a surprisingly large proportion of service delivery could include a self-help component.
ICMA MUNICIPAL YEAR BOOK: 1983

One of the most effective techniques for making citizens an integral part of the service delivery process is through coproduction. A standard definition of coproduction is "the joint provision of public services by public agencies and service consumers."[71] The most common coproduction activities involve citizens either volunteering their time to aid public sector agencies in providing services or providing private goods and services which substitute for those publicly provided. Coproduction is seen as a mechanism for developing "more responsive citizens; more responsive political processes; increased use of neighborhood groups; a humanistic political process; and more *effective* service delivery."[72]

Coproduction in the development and delivery of products and services by planning agencies has become more widespread; however, this sharing of responsibility is occurring primarily in response to budget pressures. We suggest that planners take advantage of the public's interest in coproduction and use this technique to more effectively involve citizens in the internal operations of their agencies. Integrative experiences often lead to a broader perspective and greater appreciation for the agency's production and delivery process. Support, respect, and loyalty for the agency are additional characteristics that can be nurtured through this process. It should be noted, however, that no matter how desirable and tempting these secondary benefits might be, the real value of coproduction is the integration of the customer into internal agency operations.

There are numerous examples of communities where citizens have either taken or been given the opportunity to assume total or shared responsibility for the development or delivery of planning products or services. In Dallas, the residents of the Oaklawn area formed the Oaklawn Forum for the purpose of taking over the local planning responsibilities for their neighborhood. The residents were dissatisfied with the level of service and support they had been receiving from the city's planning department. Funds were raised and a consultant was hired to assist the residents in developing plans for the protection and controlled redevelopment of their neighborhood.

A more recent example of voluntary coproduction from Dallas involves the Lakewood Country Club Estates area. In this case, the city's planning staff had been actively working with these residents to provide them with specialized products and services. To help in the development of plans for the area, the planning staff asked the residents to hire an architectural historian. This consultant provided valuable technical assistance to a planning staff that lacked both the time and technical expertise to do the work. The results of the consultant's work were incorporated into the agency's plans for the area and used to justify designating the area as a conservation district.

Planners in Arlington engaged in an aspect of coproduction when they added the name and phone number of rezoning applicants to the public notification signs that are posted on property proposed for rezoning. Adding the information to the sign was designed to obtain the applicant's involvement in providing information to the public. In essence, the applicant becomes a coproducer of this planning service. The level of service has been improved because affected property owners have expanded access to information and the applicants are more effective in their negotiations and presentations at public hearings.

In Grand Prairie, Texas, the planning staff introduced a fast-track procedure for the processing of subdivision plats. The applicants could shave up to two weeks off the processing time simply by circulating the plat to the various review departments and agencies and obtaining their evaluations and comments themselves. As coproducers of the plat-processing service, the applicants save time and money and learn more about the review requirements and procedures. An improvement in both the quality of the plats and the effectiveness of the planning department resulted.

Like many cities, Fort Worth, Texas, has a record of successfully involving citizens in planning for their neighborhoods. But it solved its difficulty in generating citizen participation in comprehensive planning and dissatisfaction with the level of local involvement in the planning process with the development of the neighborhood-based Sector Planning program.[73] As discussed earlier, the sector plan represented market segmentation strategies, capitalized on neighborhood service opportunities, and made the planning department more effective. Here the sector plan demonstrates its contribution to generating long-term public interest in the planning process.

A sector strategy committee consisting of a group of citizen leaders was appointed to help the city plan commission and staff in the establishment of a sector planning council. The mission of the committee was to make the initial organizational arrangements, motivate sector residents to serve on their sector planning councils, conduct a publicity campaign, and select a temporary chairperson and officers. The sector planning council provided the overall coordinating umbrella for each area's individual sector planning council.

The series of sector plans that were produced and still are updated were basically traditional general plans. However, the rapport that developed between the planning staff and local residents was far more than traditional. The program showed that citizens were willing to devote long hours to study, discussion, and debate and were not apathetic when given a real opportunity to participate in a meaningful planning process.

A city report noted that sector planning was more demanding of the citizens in terms of time and effort and more costly to the local government. Sector planning required more than twice the staffing than necessary for preparing the comprehensive plan. But the city reported that the higher costs and the increase in preparation time were justified by the higher levels of citizen involvement that resulted from the sector planning process. Also, very important but less quantifiable benefits were derived from the valuable information that was eagerly supplied to sector planners by residents, business owners, employees and employers, developers, land owners, religious congregations, and neighborhood associations in a wide range of settings across the city. The significance of Fort Worth's local sector planning program was recognized in 1978 when it received the merit award for outstanding contributions to the field of professional planning from the Texas chapter of the American Planning Association.

Ernest Bonner, former planning director of Portland, Oregon, believes that planners should place a priority on "developing a set of services by which people could help themselves."[74] Chris Argyrs, in *Intervention Theory and Method*, went so far as to suggest that change agents should "assist a system to become more effective in problem solving, decision making and decision implementation in such a way that the system can continue to be increasingly effective in these activities and have a decreasing need for the intervenor."[75] Thus, in theory, it may be that the goal of the planning staff in the coproduction process is to enable the consumer to assume ultimate responsibility for the delivery of the product or service being produced. It would appear that one of the primary objectives of coproduction should be to shift as much authority, autonomy, and responsibility to the consumer as possible.

SERVING THE PUBLIC
. . . success in the service industries belongs to managers and employees who can share the excitement of working with people and who insure that even the most menial of services are performed well, even seeing no more tangible a result than a customer's smile. JAMES L. HESKETT

Howell Baum's survey of planners in Maryland found that "most planners prefer to have limited contact with citizens" and that they "regard work with citizens as generally unrewarding."[76] We have worked in a number of different planning organizations around the country and generally found that most planners understand the importance of working *with* people. But we also have encountered several glaring exceptions to this rule. We were particularly distressed by a sign in one planner's office that read: "This is not Burger King. You don't get it your way. You take it my way, or you don't get the son of a bitch."

Equally offensive and ineffective attitudes were found in several other planning organizations and, surprisingly enough, these individuals appeared to take great pride in their hostility and wanted everyone to know about it. Not only did they resent it when citizens happened to venture into their offices and interfere with their so-called work, but they also advertised their attitudes with a proliferation of sayings on their walls. One noted that,

---

A Homecoming Lament

To a returning American grown accustomed to the civility and efficiency of modern Japan, the U.S. seems to have become a quagmire of bureaucracy, ineptitude, mean spirit and lackadaisy.   In Los Angeles, New York, Miami and other cities, the repatriate is appalled and depressed by the lack of efficiency and simple courtesy and caring....

The sign in the lobby of the West Los Angeles city hall says the planning department opens at 8 a.m.   On a recent morning a clerk finally shows up at 9, without apology. As the petitioner pays the application fee for home improvement permits, the clerk says the process will take 75 to 120 days.   It is 132 days and still counting....

To an American old enough to remember American competence, work well done and pride in fine service swiftly rendered, it is jarring to realize how much Americans have forgotten, and how quickly.

"Public service doesn't mean private service," another said, "The masses are asses," and one even cautioned, "Not responsible for people who are ate up with the dumb ass." Even if you are not familiar with this latter Cajun expression, you probably intuitively grasp its meaning and the attitude that it conveys.

In contrast, William Kirchhoff, city manager of Arlington, is one outspoken advocate of corporate management concepts and has clearly demonstrated an awareness of the importance of the service function in local government. The corporate city of Arlington is like many businesses in that it devotes an explicit part of its mission statement to excellence in service. The city manager personally meets with all city employees and discusses the following statement:

> The mission of the Arlington City Corporation is to provide excellent service delivery programs to the citizens of Arlington. The organization exists for the single purpose of providing the best possible services to the people who reside in this community.[77]

Arlington employees who have any contact with citizens must attend a three-hour program on excellence in customer service. Personal contact with government employees is one of the most important ways citizens shape their attitudes toward their local government. The planning department is one of the primary sources for citizen interaction with local government; citizens who have a favorable and pleasant contact will have a positive attitude toward planning and city government in general. Citizens appreciate a friendly smile, a pleasant greeting, and a helpful attitude in face-to-face contacts. Citizens deserve and expect courtesy and competence when dealing with city government. Arlington employees are given the following guidelines for helping establish good relations with local citizens:

1. The citizen's problem, complaint or request for information deserves your undivided attention, interest and concern. Be sure to listen carefully and ask questions.

2. Citizens need to have their questions answered clearly and in a language they can understand. This means elimination of complicated technical jargon or slang whenever possible.

3. Citizens expect to receive accurate, thorough, and complete information in a timely fashion. (An employee may not like to admit that he/she "doesn't know," but this is preferable to giving a wrong or incomplete answer.)

4. Citizens deserve a prompt response to their questions or requests. Nothing is worse than "passing the buck." If you do not know the answer, you should accept responsibility for finding the person who does. Whenever possible, obtain the information for the citizen by making a call or talking to another employee in person. Refer citizens to another City employee only if you do not know the answer and are positive that the employe you are referrring the person to will be able to solve their problem.

5. Citizens expect courteous treatment. Not everyone an employee meets in the course of their duties will be courteous, but a part of your job is to maintain good relations in spite of these difficult situations. Do not make an issue a personal matter, maintain a professional attitude, and keep the conversation on the facts.

6. Citizens should feel that every attempt has been made to assist them by the time they leave the City building.[78]

Nemeroff would describe Kirchhoff's personal actions and commitment to "excellence in customer service" as "service statesmanship." It starts with a commitment to a company philosophy and is implemented by senior executives who exercise such statesmanship through personal example.

Public Management reported that in Luverne, Minnesota, the city administrator has a citizen hotline that rings only in his office. William Hansell, executive director of the International City Management Association, concluded "that's getting about as close to the citizens and customers as you can!"[79]

Albuquerque, New Mexico, uses a full range of techniques to get close to its customers. According to Joel Wooldridge, assistant chief of advanced planning, the city has a 24-hour turnaround response time to all citizen correspondence, holds bi-weekly press conferences, gives an annual televised state-of-the-city address, has more than fifty boards and commissions, conducts monthly town meetings, uses a speaker's bureau, and includes promotional and informational material and questionnaires in the bills that are mailed to utility customers. Mayor Ken Schultz warns that each method of communication has certain limitations and advises that "cities must always continue to look for good communication tools."[80]

A final service example comes from the city of Blacksburg, Virginia. In 1985, this city instituted an extensive customer relations training program for its employees. City administrators and a private consultant developed a program consisting of ten half-day training sessions, a manual with tips on customer relations (including how to deal with angry people), and a series of small group discussions covering the personal meaning of good relations and the rewards of treating citizens well. This successful program received the 1985 human development achievement award from the Virginia Municipal League.[81]

Peters and Waterman observed that with such a heavy emphasis on service, "almost every one of our service-oriented institutions does 'overspend' on service, quality and reliability."[82] Unfortunately, how many planning departments and local governments can say that they "overspend" on getting to know their local consumers?

SURVEYING THE COMMUNITY

Planning is 90 percent people and working with them. And you don't work with one town like you do with another. MARVIN SPRINGER

Dayton, Ohio, stands out among local governments for its budgetary emphasis on service quality and for its commitment to getting close to its customers. One way the city is able to get closer is through an annual public opinion survey, described in the 1983 *Dayton Program Strategies* document:

> Each year, we ask about 1,100 Dayton residents to evaluate services which they experience on a frequent basis. We have conducted such an annual survey for 12 years and can use the results to identify either City-wide or neighborhood trends.[83]

Dayton uses the customer evaluations in conjunction with performance/efficiency data generated internally by each service provider to identify and differentiate between performance problems and perception problems. This process provides an early warning of service problems and is an invaluable aid in developing service provision strategies.

In 1979, local government in Galveston, Texas, was stunned by the passage of a series of charter amendments that resulted in significant mandatory reductions in tax revenue and budget levels. This public expression of customer dissatisfaction with the cost, level, and quality of local government services generated management's support for the planning department's proposal to convert the budgeting process from a line-item budget to a program/performance-based budget that was supported by an inexpensive citywide opinion survey. As reported in the 1979–1980 annual budget, the survey asked residents to indicate: (1) how they felt the city's funds should be allocated for each city service; (2) how well they felt services were being performed; (3) how they felt the city should finance its services; (4) what were the important problems in their neighborhood; and (5) how they felt in general about the future of their neighborhood.[84]

There was a 12 percent response to the citywide survey and that year significant budgetary changes were made in the allocations for various programs and services. The budget message stated that "the resident, who is the ultimate consumer and recipient of public services, is clearly a source for information concerning the needs of the community" and a commitment was made to an annual citizen survey.[85] Interestingly, both the city manager and planning director accepted professional advancement opportunities in larger communities in the following year and subsequently both the survey and program budget were dropped. Two years later, a civic group asked voters to rescind the fiscally restrictive charter provisions, but the customers still weren't buying the municipal product and the rescission effort was resoundingly rejected.

Many local governments use survey techniques to learn more about the needs of their communities. Each has strengths and weaknesses. Some communities use relatively simple techniques, such as the "tell us" system in Traverse City, Michigan, that polls residents visiting city hall, while others use expensive, sophisticated public opinion polling techniques.[86] The point is that there seems to be a growing commitment on the part of local governments to listen and become closer to their citizens/customers.

QUALITY AND VALUE

It's a whole new ball game. A city no longer needs a natural harbor, a surplus of labor, and lots of sunshine in order to prosper. It needs quality universities, quality workplace, quality airport and telecommunications systems, and yes even quality government. DAVID L. BIRCH

We debated using the familiar adage, "It's good enough for government work" for the introductory quote to this section but decided to use instead the quote from David Birch, director of MIT's program on Neighborhood and Regional Change, author of *Job Creation in America*, and a columnist for *Inc.* magazine. His view reflects a shift in the private sector away from the philosophy that "the cities that govern least, govern best" to one that demands quality services from local government.

One of the serious limitations of giving advice in a book is that you often must generalize, oversimplify, and resort to extremes to get your primary message across. Our concern is that there are almost always exceptions to every rule and that it is important that readers pick up the significant nuances. The issue of quality is one of those areas. Let us explain why and how.

During the 1986 National League of Cities' City Innovations Conference, Bill Evans, vice president and director of public sector services from Cresap, McCormick and Paget, advised the participants that "it is very important to remember that it is more important to be doing the right things than it is to be doing things right."[87] The following story demonstrates this important point. During the 1929 Rose Bowl game between the University of California and Georgia Tech, Roy Reigels of California got the football and with 70,000 fans standing and screaming, he ran until tackled at the one-yard line. He had run well but his coach and the fans from Berkeley were incensed. Not because he was tackled just short of the goal line but because he had run in the wrong direction. He had failed to keep his eyes on the right goal.

We agree with Bill Evans and other respected management authorities about the importance of doing the right thing and have emphasized the importance of focusing and prioritizing activities. However, this does not mean that interest in quality can be abandoned. It only means that it should be secondary to finding out and deciding what it is that the organization should be doing (i.e., which direction to be running in). Once focusing and prioritizing has been completed, then energies should be directed toward achieving maximum feasible quality.

One of the important objectives of any manager, according to Philip Crosby, should be "getting people to do better all the worthwhile things they ought to be doing anyway."[88] In discussing quality, we are really dealing with people and their performance. And just as performance can be measured, so too can quality. Philip Crosby points out that "requirements must be clearly stated so that they can be understood," and "measurements are then taken continually to determine conformance to those requirements."[89]

Quality comes from people who care and who are committed. It comes from the knowledge and belief that anything we make or do can be done better. It's built on the belief that everybody in the organization has the ability and responsibility to contribute to improving what we do. Tom Peters and Nancy Austin warned in *A*

Passion for Excellence that "attention to quality can become the organization's mind set only if *all* of its managers—indeed, all of its people—live it."[90] A person can't allow typos in internal memos and then demand perfection in reports. Part-time conscientiousness is not a foundation for excellence—it is a full-time job.

Daniel O'Connell, policy coordinator for the growth management coordination unit of the State of Florida, reported that the Florida legislative body is committed to raising the quality of local government planning in that state. He told us that the Omnibus Growth Management Law in Florida actually directs the department of community affairs to set minimum quality standards for all the elements in local comprehensive plans and that in a few areas, the legislature has already developed its own quality standards. O'Connell believes that quality planning can be legislatively mandated and successfully achieved. He notes that it will be difficult, time-consuming, and expensive and that it will require persistence in administration, implementation, and enforcement, but that it can be done. Success will depend on the development of model quality planning standards. His message to planners and public officials in local government is that "the quality of our planning can no longer be considered a luxury, it is a dire necessity." He adds that "we must demand excellence from ourselves and begin producing 'good plans,' maybe even some great ones."

Joseph Vitt, Jr., is typical of many successful public agency managers in his commitment to quality. He reported that his Kansas City agency "focused on producing high-quality professional products."[91] A similar commitment was expressed by Donald Spaid, former planning coordinator for St. Paul, who said that because of the high quality of government in Minnesota, "we do things well in the St. Paul planning department . . . and I mean it!"[92]

The penalty for the lack of quality planning in local government can be fiscally enormous and potentially life-threatening. A growing number of local government officials are recognizing the value and importance of quality and are demanding it from their organizations. Allen Colman, Fresno County administrative officer in Fresno, California, contends that with service needs rising and funds declining, his organization is "reducing services to maintain quality."[93]

Increasing production costs in order to provide a quality, higher valued, and more useful product is one way to maintain or raise quality but it creates a dilemma for planners. Many planners believe that planning products and services should be provided at no extra cost to the customer, which means that the cost is borne by the taxpaying public as a whole. But many planning agencies are faced with dwindling budgets and find it difficult to provide even minimum basic services and providing higher cost services appears out of their reach. However, if these new targeted services can be provided in a value-added manner and priced at a market rate value, it is possible that agencies can even make a "profit" on such services.

Never underestimate the value and importance of quality. An increasingly popular acronym in business is SOQ NOP which stands for "sell on quality, not on price." Superior quality *is* valued by planning clients. Recently we formed a consulting team called Code Technology Group and submitted a proposal to provide planning services to a small community. Our firm initially emphasized that we could provide more service at a lower cost than could our more well-known competitors. The city's selection team narrowed the list of consultants to two firms but could not agree on a final selection. Both firms were asked to make presentations to the full city council. At the second presentation, we changed our approach and emphasized that our staff had superior knowledge and expertise and that we would produce a higher quality product. The council voted to select our firm for the assignment.

Our firm was selected for two primary reasons: (1) the council was convinced that we were the most knowledgeable firm, and (2) our proposal contained a provision for after-market service. We proposed to monitor the results of our work for one year at no additional cost. We clearly demonstrated an extended commitment to customer satisfaction that was not exhibited by the other firms. Customers are willing to pay a premium for products that solve problems and are well serviced.

Some planning agencies have begun to supplement their declining budget allocations with revenues generated from new services. More specifically, a regional agency in New Hampshire, and planners in Baltimore, and Portland, Oregon, have begun to generate new revenues by selling consultant services to the private sector. In Butte, Montana, the autonomous planning commission competitively contracted with the city's renewal authority to provide technical planning services. San Francisco and Phoenix have increased their user fees and product costs, and have been able to generate revenues amounting to more than half of their total budgets. Phoenix has also expanded its services to include fiscal planning analysis of proposed annexations, data for municipal bond underwriters, and consulting services to the private sector on fiscal issues. Even in Houston, where public planning has taken a back seat to private development efforts, development practices clearly emphasize the market value of services that were traditionally provided by a public agency. In that city, many residential and business areas have turned to business and homeowners associations to obtain needed planning services. These "clients" bear a cost over and above their public cost in order to ensure that they will have adequate public facilities and services and a planned neighborhood.

Many of the "planned residential neighborhoods" in Houston are planned by the developer, in part because of the lack of local public planning. The cost of this planning is reflected in higher development and housing costs. These plannng services are high value services for which the "client" is willing to bear the higher cost. Developers are willing to pay these costs because in addition to the improved marketability that results from developing a planned neighborhood, there are significant direct cost savings. Richard Peiser conducted research which contrasted the various costs associated with development of a 7,500-acre tract in Houston in both planned and unplanned neighborhoods. Peiser found that:

> (t)he net present value of the developer's total cost, including profit, is $115.6 million in the planned community as compared to $117.5 million in the unplanned community—a $1.8 million savings in the planned community over the project life. Transportation costs (net present value) are $182.7 million per year in the planned community versus $188.8 million per year in the unplanned community—a $50 million savings to residents and workers in the planned community over the project life.[94]

The examples cited from Houston and the other cities mentioned clearly demonstrate that traditional planning functions do have a direct market value to the private sector. The values are tapped by astute market-based pricing of products and services. After all, Pubilus Syrus wrote more than two thousand years ago in his Maxim 847 that "everything is worth what its purchaser will pay for it."

A planner told us this story: He and his best friend had gone to college together. He got straight *A*s and went to graduate school while his friend got Cs and Ds, dropped out, and went to work in private industry. They lost contact and when they met again years later the planner had a respectable position in a local government agency but his friend had his own company and was obviously wealthy. The planner asked him how he had become so successful. The businessman explained that he made a product that costs $2 to make and he sells it for $5. He noted that you "can make a lot of money with a 3 percent profit margin."

Paul Zucker, one of the nation's most experienced and highly regarded planning managers, recommended in the *Management Idea Book* that planners, too, should look at their profit margins and do the following: "examine all fees for services. Raise old fees to full cost recovery and begin to charge for traditionally free services. In particular, look at fees for uncontrolled expenditures, such as preapplication conferences. Consider the first fifteen minutes free, for example, with a charge thereafter."[95]

There is both a cost and value associated with planning products and services. In Atlanta, a League of Women Voters position paper supported the preparation of complete impact statements so the county commission could properly evaluate and act on rezoning applications.[96] The same paper also noted that the existing overworked planning staff could not do complete impact statements if they were required. In response to a similar need and problem, the planning department in New York City hired planning consultants to prepare individual staff reports on a large backlog of pending rezoning applications. The city recognized that this was a special service and that it was proper that the applicants using this service should pay for it.

In *Managing with Less*, there is a chapter on "Improving Effectiveness: Responsive Public Services" that profiled a unique municipal program developed by Savannah, Georgia. The simple market segmentation concept reflected in the particular program was that:

> the level of services being provided uniformly throughout the community is not adequate for some neighborhoods. . . . This will mean that some neighborhoods will have to be supplied with a higher level of service than others if we are to achieve and maintain an acceptable quality of life in these neighborhoods.[97]

A key component of the Savannah program was a user survey for each planning unit designed to obtain citizens' opinions about the services and recommendations for improvements. In combination with a series of indicators, the neighborhoods were rated by their degree of relative deviation from the norm in order to identify specific problem conditions. The survey findings had a major impact on city operations and planning with a result being that "planning units with significant problems were targeted for projects and programs to upgrade the services delivered by the city government to those particular neighborhoods."[98]

LISTENING TO THE CUSTOMER
Someone with roots in the community and common sense had better be around to listen to the people and help direct the community's planning and growth toward where they want to go. ALBERT SOLNIT

In completing this section on being close to the customer, it should be emphasized that Peters and Waterman found that the "excellent companies are not only better on service, quality, reliability, and finding a niche . . . they are also better listeners" and that the best companies are "pushed around by their customers, and they love it."[99]

Belding, Michigan, has a unique and truly extraordinary commitment to seeking out and listening to its citizens. One of the particularly innovative aspects of their "tell it to the city" program is that "the city has a regular representative available for two hours one Saturday morning each month at the downtown shopping mall. Either the mayor or a council member will sit at a table set up in the main concourse of the mall. City staff provide the elected officials with information on projects they might wish to discuss with the public at the same time."[100]

When we asked good planners what it takes to make the planning process successful, we heard one theme repeated over and over: You can't plan successfully unless you are able to involve the community in the process. Typical was the comment of Mark Stephens, project planner for the consulting firm of TRA/Farr in Anchorage, who said that "in short, one needs to be prepared to spend time in the community and do a good deal of listening and learning before acting."[101]

Planners and decision makers must understand that their success in planning will depend on their ability to identify common goals and shared values and a willingness to share their power and authority with their customers—the residents of the community. Norman Tufford, long-time executive director of the Northwestern Indiana Regional Planning Commission, found that the real threats to effective planning "come from people who don't want to work together, wanting the 'power' for themselves."[102]

Cleveland, Ohio, is one community that has recently made a commitment to sharing and pubic involvement. *Nation's Cities Weekly* reported that a two-day goal setting conference was held on what Mayor George Voinovich called Cleveland's "Civic Vision"—a visionary concept plan for charting the city's course over the next ten to twelve years. The article noted that:

> (t)he decision to give citizens such an important vote in planning for the city's future stemmed from the feeling among city officials, including Voinovich, "that a long-range development plan requires the understanding, support and participation of the people."[103]

Every person residing in the community is a potential customer and each should be given the opportunity to become involved in the planning process. Unlike the business community, local governments are not driven by the profit motive but instead by the primary goal of customer satisfaction. The ultimate measure of success in local government is customer satisfaction and this is easily measured—especially at election time. In 1979, New Orleans Mayor Moon Landrieu, who became the secretary of the United States Department of Housing and Urban Development (HUD), spoke at the annual conference of the American Planning Association. He advised the planners that reelection was his primary goal and that he expected his city planners to approach their work with this objective in mind. The bottom line in politics, after all, is what gets counted on election day.

In *Urban Politics and Public Policy*, Robert Lineberry and Ira Sharkansky pointedly illustrated the critical relationship and direct linkage between the actions of public sector service providers and the corresponding impact on elected officials. They observed that:

> (c)itizens who find that contacts and requests for service get immediate results are likely to return incumbents to office; citizens met with sullen, "bureaucratic," and delayed responses are a power to be reckoned with in the next election.[104]

Successful elected officials have an ability to get close to the customer and Moon Landrieu noted there is a simple test—elections— that measures their perceived effectiveness. As Voltaire wrote many years ago, "I am a leader, therefore I must follow." Most politicians instinctively know that it is easier to lead the community in the direction that it wants to go. Walter Lippman cynically suggested in *The Phantom Public* that:

> We must abandon the notion that the people govern. Instead we must adopt the theory that, by their occasional mobilization as a majority, people support or oppose individuals who actually govern.[105]

President Lyndon Johnson once observed that the most difficult problem with decision making was to know what was right, not to do what was right. Similarly, Lineberry and Sharkansky concluded that in public policymaking the "problem of knowledge is in the long run more important than the problem of money."[106] Peters and Waterman also found that in the bottom line-conscious private sector "the excellent companies tend to be driven more by closer-to-the-customer attributes than by either technology or cost."[107]

For local governments there are many citizen participation techniques that can be used to get close to the customers, including citizen advisory committees, attitude surveys, neighborhood planning councils, referendums, field offices, and outreach and neighborhood referral programs. An excellent source of introductory information on these techniques is provided in the chapter on "Citizen Participation in Planning" in *The Practice of Local Government Planning*.[108]

The citizen advisory committee is one of the most effective techniques for getting closer to the customer. As noted in *Citizen Committees: A Guide to Their Use in Local Government*, a wide variety of benefits have been ascribed to the employment of citizen committees including the following:

> Use of citizen committees should *increase public access* to the decision-making process, thereby expanding interest in and understanding of public issues. This broadening of public knowledge should improve the ability of the community to equitably distribute power and public resources. Self-determinism in local affairs should be strengthened;

> Committees serve as effective informational and education channels to "grass-roots" constituencies. A greater citizen consciousness of public programs and plans should result, and in turn, *provide feedback* that would permit public programs to reflect sensitivity to individual and local needs;

> A greater involvement of knowledgeable citizens should *generate new ideas* and *increase innovation and creativity* in developing and implementing public programs;

Citizen committee efforts often make the exercise of political power more visible and bring issues into sharper focus. This increased public deliberation may result in the polarization of opinions and *force decisions,* thereby *reducing lethargy in official actions;*

A committee may establish a forum where *ideas and concepts can be tested* and where ligitimate differences of opinion can be resolved.[109]

There you have it. As emphasized by the italics, citizen committees increase customer access to the decision-making process, provide customer feedback, generate new ideas, increase innovation and creativity, force decisions, and test ideas and concepts. These are obviously beneficial and desirable objectives which should encourage and promote excellence in city planning and many other aspects of local government.

ZONING IS NOT A SUBSTITUTE FOR PLANNING
There's always an easy solution to every human problem—neat, plausible, and wrong. H. L. MENCKEN

As noted earlier, there are not enough resources for planners to be all things to all people. Unfortunately, zoning, more often than not, is the tail that wags the dog in many planning agencies. Too often, planners put aside their current priority projects to respond to requests for special zoning studies. For example, in one city an application to rezone a portion of a block from residential to industrial was denied because it was clearly premature, still, the staff was also directed to do a special zoning study of the area. The long-range plan for the area proposed an eventual transition from residential to industrial. The tough question was just when and how the transformation would occur. The planning staff promised it would get right on the study and quickly bring it back to the commission. The urgency of the problem was not related to the ripeness of the area for redevelopment but rather the impatience of a zoning speculator. The quick response of the staff resulted in a rearrangement of the department's work program and delayed the completion of two other projects.

We have reported that effective planning organizations do a better job of listening to their clients, but the previous case illustrates an inappropriate application of this principle. If the planning department has already listened to its many clients and developed a work program that has been understood and endorsed by the chief executive or other decision makers such as the planning commission or city council, then requests that would alter the priorities require careful evaluation before the program is amended. Consultation with the supporters of the original work program is an essential step in maintaining respect for the staff. It may or may not turn out that a reordering of priorities is appropriate.

In the example cited, the staff's quick response served to indicate that zoning was the most important activity of the department and that the staff probably doesn't have enough to do. The request by the commission was an indication of a lack of respect for staff time and the approved work program for the planning department. By being responsive, in this situation, the focus of the department and some of its effectiveness was lost.

The director of the department or agency has the responsibility to promote the value and importance of the planning program. If zoning dominates the department's agenda it is doubtful if it has an effective work program. Zoning controversies are usually a symptom of a failure to plan. Zoning is not an acceptable substitute for planning.

Downtown decay, flooding, the need for economic diversity and growth, the rising cost of housing, transit subsidies, traffic congestion, noise and visual pollution, air and water quality problems, and the deterioration of neighborhoods are but a few of the common urban planning problems that communities often try to resolve with zoning regulations. However, the solution to such planning problems is not zoning but more and better planning in the form of a comprehensive plan.

Confusion often exists as to the difference between a comprehensive plan and a zoning ordinance. According to the International City Management Association, "much of the confusion has arisen out of the fact that many cities adopted zoning ordinances before embarking on full-scale planning. Consequently, persons outside the planning profession have not always understood the logical connection between the two concepts."[110]

The use of zoning in the absence of a current viable comprehensive plan is contrary to the basis on which zoning has received most of its legal justification. It is the traditional view of legal historians that the presentation made by Alfred Bettman on the planning justification for zoning was responsible for the U.S. Supreme Court's upholding of the constitutionality of zoning in the 1926 landmark case of the *Village of Euclid v. Ambler Realty Company.*[111] Bettman indicated that zoning was directly related to planning and the comprehensive plan. In theory, there could be no proper zoning without such planning.

The Standard State Zoning Enabling Act prepared by the U.S. Department of Commerce in 1926 as a model for state zoning enabling legislation recognized that relationship between planning and zoning when it contained the requirement that zoning regulations were to be made in accordance with a comprehensive plan. The zoning enabling legislation of forty states requires zoning to be in accordance with a comprehensive plan.

Despite this almost universal requirement, most cities have zoned without benefit of such a plan and the courts have tended to uphold these zoning ordinances. However, recently there has been a growing awareness on the part of both legislative and judicial bodies about the need to more clearly relate zoning to the implementation of a local comprehensive plan. A number of states have indicated that comprehensive planning and the zoning ordinance are not the same and that for zoning decisions to be valid they must be based on and be consistent with the policies of the comprehensive plan.

But while the comprehensive plan guides zoning administration, the zoning map does not immediately duplicate the comprehensive plan map. The comprehensive plan provides long-range guidance for controlling and directing growth and development while the zoning ordinance gradually moves the community toward compliance with the long-range plan. The comprehensive plan proposes eventual objectives which will be met in the future while the zoning ordinance regulates existing conditions. In a simplified sense, the comprehensive plan proposes "what" and "where" and the zoning ordinance controls "where and when." The zoning district designation of a piece of property should indicate that the property is currently suitable for development as zoned. Property should not be zoned for a future use shown in the comprehensive plan if, at the current time, the site is unready or incapable of supporting the proposed use.

In 1980, the California Office of Planning and Research issued a draft version of guidelines for comprehensive plans. The guidelines were advisory and offered for use by the courts, elected officials, and citizens for use as a standard for assessing and evaluating the adequacy of local comprehensive plans. The guidelines discussed three dimensions that should be taken into account with respect to the requirement that zoning be consistent and in accordance with the comprehensive plan:

> The first is "consistency of standards and uses" (the text of the zoning ordinance must be adequate to implement the plan). The second is "spatial consistency" (uses should be similarly distributed on both the zoning map and the plan diagram). The third is "timing" (plans are "long-range" documents, whereas zoning responds to shorter term needs. Zoning in most cases only gradually fulfills the "prescriptions" of the plan).[112]

Zoning is not the same thing as planning. Zoning is a tool used in implementing planning goals, objectives, and policies and is not, in itself, planning. The design of a comprehensive plan, coordinating and properly interrelating the various major land use elements, is an essential precondition to the drafting of zoning regulations. When zoning is based on a comprehensive plan, it is recognized, both technically and judicially, as legitimate zoning. Zoning laws enacted without regard to accepted goals, policies, and planning principles may be considered unreasonable, arbitrary, or capricious when subjected to legal test.

Planning is a process for resolving problems and achieving goals. A measure of the success or value of planning and the comprehensive plan is how well the problems are solved and the goals are achieved. The logic is simply that it is wise to look ahead, to anticipate rather than react, to coordinate rather than to compete, and to make decisions that are based on shared community goals and objectives. Zoning cannot provide a comprehensive, coordinated approach to solving urban problems and it cannot be allowed to substitute for more and better planning.

DECENTRALIZATION

Decentralization creates more centers. That means more opportunities and more choices for individuals. JOHN NAISBITT

Planning on the basis of the problem-identification and problem-solving approach advocated by our research findings requires that the planning process be decentralized. As noted by John Naisbitt in *Megatrends,* "in the city or the country, decentralization empowers you to tackle problems and create change at the local level."[113]

Decentralization of planning and zoning functions to the neighborhood level is a recent development that promises to grow in value and importance. As reported by Efraim Gil in a report on neighborhood zoning, a number of cities throughout the United States have already initiated a process of decentralizing their zoning function.[114]

A national survey and study by the U.S. League of Women Voters identified the political, social, and administrative justifications for governmental decentralization in general and neighborhood zoning commissions in particular. In the twenty-six cities that were surveyed, the respondents agreed on the following relevant points with respect to neighborhood zoning programs:

There was a definite increase in citizen participation;

The program resulted in increased influence of neighborhood residents, and many were able to implement some of their own ideas in regard to changes and development in their neighborhoods;

As a result of the programs the attitudes of neighborhood residents toward city officials improved;

The programs produced an increased flow of information between neighborhood residents and city officials;

Zoning practices changed as a result of increased information about neighborhood needs;

Relations between neighborhood residents and city officials improved as a result of the program; and

There was no noticeable change in the workloads of either planning commissions or zoning boards of adjustments as a result of decentralization programs.[115]

Some states, such as Texas, have enabling legislation which specifically authorizes neighborhood zoning commissions.[116] It is debatable in other states whether specific enabling legislation for neighborhood zoning commissions is required before local governments can decentralize the zoning function. In fact, the decentralization of the planning and zoning function is a logical, natural response to the natural trend toward decentralization of our institutions and a growing self-help philosophy on the part of individuals and neighborhoods.[117]

The basic rezoning process in many communities is complicated by the late injection of citizen input into the decision-making process. The developer's plans have been solidified, the hearing is held, and there uninformed citizens hear for the first time the actual details of the proposed project. There naturally is conflict and opposition and frequently it is suggested that the request should be tabled either for further study or to work out a compromise. *Zoning News* reported that in response to this recurring situation and to reduce friction between developers and neighborhood residents while also opening up communication channels, Lakewood, Colorado, has instituted an innovative neighborhood referral program:

> The referral program requires developers to give written notification to property owners within 300 feet of a proposed development and special notification to registered neighborhood organizations (e.g., homeowners associations). The developer must hold at least one neighborhood meeting to discuss the preliminary proposal and to learn about neighborhood concerns. Only after this can the developer apply for the rezoning or special permit."[118]

It is important that planners listen, hear, and appreciate what their customers are saying. Effective planning depends on planning *with* people not *for* people. Successful private sector businesses that are driven by the marketplace have discovered that being close to their customers takes care of the bottom line. In contrast, the public sector does not generally appear to have the same intensity of commitment to understanding their customers and solving their problems.

DOING MORE WITH LESS

The main challenge confronting managers who must cope with the squeeze between rising demand and costs and stable or declining budgets and work forces is how to maintain organizational effectiveness. CHARLES H. LEVINE

Across the nation, planners in local government are finding that their activities are being significantly affected by adverse fiscal factors. Charles Levine, a senior specialist in American national government and public administration at the Congressional Research Service with the Library of Congress, has predicted that in the future local government decision makers will increasingly be characterized by a cutback management philosophy. More specifically, he believes that:

> (i)t will be a period of hard times for government managers that will require them to manage cutbacks, tradeoffs, reallocations, organization contractions, program terminations, sacrifice, and the unfreezing and freeing up of grants and privileges that have come to be required as unnegotiable rights, entitlements, and contracts.[119]

The difficult challenge for many planners is how to reduce resource consumption while at the same time using the strategies and tactics that are essential to a more effective program. Levine has found that under cutback management, "creativity diminishes, innovation and risk taking decline, and the sense of excitement that comes from doing new things disappears."[120] Simply put, the characteristics that are essential for an effective planning agency are sometimes more difficult to create or sustain in a cutback environment.

In the opening chapter, we indicated that planners control the critical factors that determine their effectiveness to a far greater extent than realized. Some planners faced with the need to reduce their budgets might disagree with our view. However, while cutback management is a challenge, it also is an important motivator. It provides an incentive for planners and agency managers to reexamine their mix of products and services, to eliminate wasteful and unproductive activities, and to shift resources to more fruitful areas. In truth, no matter what their financial circumstances are, agencies are more effective when they focus and constantly prioritize the maintenance, development, and delivery of products and services. Regardless of the circumstances, new kinds of strategic choices will need to be made in order to become more effective. For the static organization, budget cuts can provide the catalyst that is needed to get the agency moving again.

An effective agency will not decide to share the pain of cuts by allocating them across the board. Cuts must always be targeted. The sixty-four-dollar question for many managers is how to target. The first step in the process is to survey your staff and ask each member to provide answers to the following basic questions:

- What are the things that you "must" do?
- What things can you stop doing?
- What things can you get others to do?
- What things can you do more efficiently?
- Where can you substitute capital for labor?
- Where can you ration services or reduce demand?

The results of these questions will help provide the foundation that is needed to organize the focusing process. Guidelines that should be followed in the focusing exercise are provided in Figure 3-1 and a summary of alternative strategies and tactics for either resisting cuts or for accommodating reductions are provided in

Figure 3–1

Focusing Guidelines

	Stop Doing?	Get Others To Do?	Do More Efficiently?	Low Cost or No Cost Labor?	Substitute Capital For Labor?
Examine Organizational Missions:	■	■	■	■	■
■ What are the organizational "musts" and mandates?			■	■	■
■ What are present non-mandated organizational functions?		■	■		
■ What are activities the organization does well?			■		
■ What are the activities the organization does poorly?		■	■		
■ What are the traditional organizational functions that have not undergone close scrutiny in recent years?		■	■	■	
Examine Marginal Investments	■	■	■	■	■
■ What programs have high unit costs?	■	■	■	■	■
■ What units serve small or isolated clientele?		■	■		
■ What programs provide services available from other organizations, public or private?		■			
■ What programs have consistently fallen below their goals and expectations?		■		■	
■ What programs, if cut back, would have long-term pressures and greater future costs?			■	■	
■ What immediate reductions will lead to long-term pressures and greater future costs?			■	■	■

Charles H. Levine, PTI Workshop in Fort Worth Texas (1986).

Figure 3-2. Both of these tables were prepared from information developed by Public Technology, Inc.

Many of the planning directors we interviewed had experienced cutbacks at one time or another and they indicated that they had become more effective managers as a result. They now are able to apply many of the strategies and tactics they had learned in a period of decline to make their agencies more effective.

Figure 3-2

Management Strategies and Tactics
for Resisting or Accommodating Cutbacks

Resisting Cuts	Accommodating Cuts

Problem Depletion

■ Diversify programs, clients, and constraints ■ Improve legislative liaison ■ Educate the public about the agency's mission ■ Mobilize dependent clients ■ Become "captured" by a powerful interest group or legislator ■ Threaten to cut vital or popular programs ■ Cut a visible and widespread service a little to demonstrate client dependence	■ Make peace with competing agencies ■ Cut low prestige programs ■ Cut programs to politically weak clients ■ Sell and lend expertise to other agencies ■ Share problems with other agencies

Environmental Entropy

■ Find a wider and richer revenue base (e.g., metropolitan reorganization) ■ Develop incentives to prevent disinvestment ■ Seek foundation support ■ Lure new public and private sector investment ■ Adopt user charges for services where possible	■ Improve targeting on problems ■ Plan with preservative objectives ■ Cut losses by distinguishing between capital investments and sunk costs ■ Yield concessions to taxpayers and employers to retain them

Political Vulnerability

■ Issue symbolic responses like forming study commissions and task forces ■ "Circle the wagons," i.e., develop a siege mentality to retain esprit de corps ■ Strengthen expertise	■ Change leadership at each stage in the decline process ■ Reorganize at each stage ■ Cut programs run by weak subunits ■ Shift programs to another agency ■ Get temporary exemptions from personnel and budgetary regulations which limit discretion

Organization Atrophy

■ Increase hierarchical control ■ Improve productivity ■ Experiment with less costly service delivery systems ■ Automate ■ Stockpile and ration resources	■ Renegotiate long term-contracts to regain flexibility ■ Install rational choice techniques like zero-base budgeting and evaluation research ■ Ask employees to make voluntary sacrifices like taking early retirements and deferring raises ■ Reassign surplus facilities to other uses

Source: Levine, "Organizational Decline and Cultural Management", <u>Public Administration Review</u>, American Society for Public Administration, July-August, 1978.

The natural response to minor short-term budget problems is for agency managers to employ a strategy of decrementalism—that is, make small short-term adjustments in the operating budgets that will produce some cost savings without causing a corresponding loss of visible operating effectiveness. Traditional tactics include hiring freezes, minor across-the-board cuts, reductions by attrition, deferred maintenance, and freezing or rationing operating expenses.

Some managers persist in using short-term tactics even when it becomes apparent that their fiscal problems are the result of long-term structural changes in the local economy and the political environment. In our opinion, such a short-sighted, nonadaptive approach will eventually produce an agency or department that is not only smaller and cheaper but also less vital and much less effective.

The preferred response to long-term resource scarcity is to develop and promote a clear understanding of the agency's mission and essential core services, to prioritize accordingly, and to put in place an effective service delivery system. As mentioned earlier, it is essential that there be a common, agreed-upon vision that identifies the agency's purpose, plans, programs, size, and resources—in essence, what it will be doing and how it will be doing it.

Some planners become discouraged by having to operate in a cutback environment. Aggressive and enthusiastic planners thrive on the chance to develop or be involved in dynamic and innovative projects and activities. They commonly believe that there are no opportunities for them in a hostile budget environment. Yet it is the pressure created by the cutback environment which makes it possible to get rid of the obsolete and ineffective programs that local government tends to perpetuate and to free resources for use in developing innovative products and services. Thus while there will be fewer opportunities available for innovation during periods of fiscal contraction, they do not totally disappear. Budget problems close some windows of opportunity for innovation, but also open others. Barbara Reynolds, inquiry page editor for *USA Today*, moderated a management panel at the 1986 Congress of Cities and noted that "fiscal constraints have created a heyday for innovative management programs."[121] In particular we have found that innovative proposals that either generate new revenues or promise to produce savings will often find receptive audiences during periods of fiscal contraction.

Administrators who are searching for ways to respond to unrelenting fiscal pressures are particularly open to ideas that strengthen their ability to understand and manage their operations. Warren Walker and Jan Chaiken, in "Local Government Initiatives in a Climate of Uncertainty," identified the five types of management innovations that appear likely to succeed in times of fiscal constraint. They are:

> *Low-cost innovations:* Innovations that have low continuing cost and yield substantial improvements in efficiency will . . . be likely to gain sufficient support for implementation.

> *Revenue generation:* Innovations that promise to generate revenues are likely to gain ready acceptance. Such innovations include computer software packages that facilitate collecting revenue such as fines, parking tickets, and user fees.

> *Effective budgeting tools:* Innovations likely to be implemented give clear answers to questions like: How much will be saved by a specific budget cut? Who will be affected? What will the consequences be?

> *Resource allocation packages:* Innovations that rationally allocate resources by need or demand (such as patrol allocation models and call screening schemes), are likely to be found attractive during periods of resource contraction.

> *Innovations that confer relative advantage on an agency:* Innovations that convey advantage to an agency in budget battles and other turf struggles are likely to meet acceptance. Such innovations provide meaningful management information about productivity, work loads, and priorities that allow a department with well-documented charts and graphs to fare better in relative budget allocations than agencies whose demands are undocumented.[122]

The planning director of Galveston during the late 1970s was able to introduce and complete several innovative projects during a time when a charter amendment had literally gutted the available fiscal resource base for the city. Consistent with the findings of Walker and Chaiken, the city manager was particularly receptive to proposals and projects that could produce new revenue or that could provide information useful in the budget allocation process.

The pressures from fiscal constraints can have a powerful positive influence on agency operations. If it only causes the planning staff to focus attention on alternative service delivery options then this, in itself, is an important benefit. Peter Colby, with the University of Central Florida, has extensively analyzed public sector management practices. He has found that too often public administrators have narrowly focused on the "one best way" to provide services—that is, "through a public bureaucracy staffed by professionally trained, merit-selected, and protected employees, accountable through a rigid hierarchy to elected officials who in turn are accountable through the electoral process to citizens."[123] Richard Musgrave, professor emeritus of political economy at Harvard and a leading authority on American public finance theory, has concluded that "there are good reasons government should see to it that services are provided—garbage pickup and road construction, say—but there is no logical reason government must do it itself."[124]

John Naisbitt, in *The Year Ahead 1986: Ten Powerful Trends Shaping Your Future*, made the following observation:

> Whether pro or con, virtually all political observers agree that in transferring public services to private control, local governments are redefining their role. They're making a distinction between setting policy—including minimum level of service—and actually providing services. In effect, governments are telling constituents that they can't be everything to everybody—that their responsibility is to see that services are made available, but not to provide them."[125]

There is an important question that all service providers should be asking: Is there another way of delivering the service that would be either more effective or cost less? Some of the alternative service delivery options that should be considered include contracting for services, user fees, self-help, and coproduction. James Ferris and Elizabeth Graddy, associate professors of public administration at the University of Southern California, found in their research that "when financially squeezed local governments reexamine their methods of delivering services, contracting is usually the first option considered."[126] In a recent issue of *Forbes*, it was noted that the New York Privatization Council estimated a total of $100 billion was spent last year by state and local governments to buy services from the private sector—up from $27 billion in 1975.[127] The following are a few of the more innovative contracting ideas that were described in the same article: Chandler, Arizona, buys wastewater treatment services from a $22 million plant built and operated by Parsons Corporation at its own financial risk. Kansas City, Missouri, contracts with the Wackenhut Corporation for fire protection and rescue services at Kansas City International Airport, and Los Angeles County uses a private firm to supply food services at the USC Medical Center.

An extraordinary example of commitment to privatization is provided by Marvin Andrews, city manager of Phoenix, Arizona. He reports, "Phoenix officials feel very strongly that they have an obligation to provide needed municipal services to citizens in the most economical, yet effective, manner."[128] In Phoenix, city government is willing to compete with private business and it is driven by the marketplace to reduce costs while maintaining and even improving services. George Latimer, St. Paul mayor, also contends that private sector competition forces public agencies to become more efficient and enhances the accountability of local government. Specifically, he has found in St. Paul that "private contacts act as a good discipline on our own operations."[129]

Despite the example of Phoenix and other communities, and despite the estimate by one conservative think tank in Dallas that most cities could cut their budgets 50 percent by contracting to private firms, we found from our experience and research that planners were more likely to contract out for work when demand exceeded their ability to produce or deliver products or service. We discovered few instances where staff levels were reduced and outside vendors were hired to do their regular work tasks. Of course, many planning agencies are understaffed and it is not uncommon for consultants to be employed on special projects in order to avoid hiring more in-house planners. We observed that the most common response by planners to budget pressures was an increased reliance on the coproduction of products and services.

When making the adjustments necessary to operate in a cutback management environment, it is essential that increased emphasis be placed on communication. Lakewood, Colorado, provides a good example of what we mean. In the early 1980s, Lakewood was suffering from a severe revenue shortage and drooping employee morale. The city manager's response was to formulate a resource retrenchment program and to use two stratagems of communication between management and those who would be affected by budget cuts. The first involved the development of a clear and illustrative series of slide shows, each designed for a particular audience, such as the city council, the public, and city employees. The second stratagem was a personalized approach used to present the city's financial dilemma and the solution to the affected groups.

The slide presentations made Lakewood's situation abhorrently clear—a picture was worth a thousand words. A veteran councilman, after viewing the presentation, stated, "I've been hearing about our financial problems for years; now I really understand them." Even the local press, which had been traditionally anticity, not only understood Lakewood's plight but began to actively support management's attempts to cope with the many problems inherent in a budget reduction program.

The personal selling of the program by the city manager and department heads involved countless small and large group meetings. In each case, the city manager delivered the same message—the city was on the brink of a financial crisis, but it was solvable if an aggressive cutback management program were immediately implemented. The personalized presentations resulted in an unusually high level of support by city employees and the press.

The communications effort was successful because the city manager and department heads met frequently with the employees in small groups in their offices or work areas rather than convening large impersonal meetings. An enormous amount of time was devoted to personal and direct interaction with the employees. The effect of meeting directly with employees, particularly those such as police officers and mechanics who work the late night and early morning shifts, had a great deal to do with convincing employees that not only was the problem real, but that management cared about them.

The initiation and completion of a positive resource retrenchment program in Lakewood, against an unusually trying set of circumstances, resulted in a city government that as an organization emerged stronger and more credible than ever within the community. Because of the personal efforts made by management, the retrenchment program was successful. It earned accolades from the local press and the city manager received the local chamber of commerce businessperson of the year award and the award for outstanding contribution to financial management from the Denver federal executive board.

Whether you develop a sophisticated strategic directions program like the Lakewood resource retrenchment program or simply shift your organization's focus and priorities, it is the responsibility of the manager to develop an effective communications stratagem for selling the concept of doing more with less. And as noted by William Kirchhoff, "Since no one rings the leper's bell quite so loud as the manager responsible for a retrenchment program, it is important that the selling program be personalized." In situations where inoculation from the economic vagaries is virtually impossible and the weight of organizational leadership is further exacerbated, the loyalty and commitment of the top staff is absolutely essential to any successful program.

We want to close this section by returning to the opening theme of this chapter: An effective response to fiscal constraints depends on developing a clear vision of the agency's mission and the prioritization of essential services. This, in turn, provides a foundation for the operating strategy that sets forth the way the service concept will be successfully achieved by the agency. Professor James Heskett has noted that "focused operating strategies are found at the heart of successful operations in all service industries."[130] We have found that city planning is no exception.

4

Autonomy,
Enterpreneurship,
and Innovation

Public-service institutions such as government agencies . . . need to be entrepreneurial and innovative fully as much as any business does. Indeed, they may need it more. The rapid changes in today's society, technology, and economy are simultaneously an even greater threat to them and an even greater opportunity. PETER DRUCKER

Many critics of government would argue that the very concept of decentralized entrepreneurial government is a contradiction of terms and that government, by its very nature, is inefficient, unwieldy, and bureaucratic—the absolute antithesis of entrepreneurial behavior. Obviously there must be some fundamental shift in the political philosophy of local government to introduce the administrative changes that are needed to create an environment for excellence. Ted Gaebler, former city manager of San Rafael, California, and a noted advocate of entrepreneurial government, stressed that:

> . . . government officials must learn to take risks and seek profits, "think outside the box," avoid paperwork and regulations. Managers must be given autonomy and encouraged to continually rethink their product mix."[1]

As advocated by Gaebler and other innovative managers, a commitment to decentralization, autonomy, and entrepreneurship is a fundamental requirement for success and excellence in planning. Growth and prosperity of the planning profession and university planning programs depend on the extent to which these characteristics are emulated. David Sawicki, director of the city planning program at the Georgia Institute of Technology, recognized the importance of such characteristics when he wrote that:

154

... the basis for action in city and regional planning is undergoing a fundamental change. Whereas a key component of that paradigm was once the planner as social critic, the key has now become the planner as entrepreneur.[2]

This does not mean that planners must become pushy peddlers of growth or even planning. That is not entrepreneurship. *Webster's* defines an entrepreneur as "a person who organizes and manages a business undertaking, assuming the risk for the sake of the profit."[3] Some critics argue that planners—or any other public official for that matter—cannot be entrepreneurs because there are no profits involved. The question becomes why should one take risks if there is no opportunity for personal gain? It is true that there usually is no direct financial gain, but the reward of "public" entrepreneurship is effective problem solving. Our experience is that when planners are effective problem solvers, they eventually earn some form of gain, whether it is personal or departmental. So there are rewards, but the bottom line is effectiveness. And in this respect, we don't believe there is that much difference between the public and private sectors.

One of the great myths of entrepreneurial behavior is that the hope of obtaining financial rewards plays the critical role in stimulating innovativeness in the private sector. Rosabeth Moss Kanter, in *The Change Masters*, reached the following contrary conclusions about rewards and innovation in the private sector:

> People tackle innovative projects because they have finally received the go-ahead for a pet idea they have always wanted to try, or they feel honored by the organization's trust in them implied in such a big assignment, or they simply want to solve a problem that will remove a roadblock to something else they want to do, or they take pride in their company and cannot sit still while a problem continues. They do *not* take on this kind of effort because a trinket is dangled in front of them that they can win.[4]

Planners can emulate the entrepreneur's tools of the trade and become more effective. Their profit is effectiveness with emphasis on the right results. It is simply management for performance. Entrepreneurs in the public or private sector are risk takers seeking success. And as noted by Dennis Waitley and Robert Tucker in *Winning the Innovation Game*, "success in the new era is heavily dependent upon innovation, creativity, and the solving of problems for which there are no precedents."[5]

OVERCOMING BIGNESS

In the physical world, one cannot increase the size or quantity of anything without changing its quality. PAUL VALERY

Peters and Waterman observed that innovation was responsible for the creation of big successful corporations but that largeness itself discourages continued innovation. In essence, their very success lays the foundation for stagnation and failure. A National Science Foundation study in the April 1981 issue of *Inc.* reported that, "small firms produced about four times as many innovations per research and development dollar as medium-sized firms and about twenty-four times as many as large firms."[6]

But Peters and Waterman noted that there are large firms that continue to innovate because they have "an ability to be big and yet to act small at the same time."[7] These firms are able to encourage an entrepreneurial spirit among their employees through decentralization and autonomy in management and product development.

In *Innovation and Entrepreneurship,* Peter Drucker pointed out that innovation is directly related to size and proximity to the environment and that:

> almost by definition, it has to be decentralized, ad hoc, autonomous, specific, and microeconomic. It had better start small, tentative, flexible. Indeed, the opportunities for innovation are found, on the whole, only way down and close to events. They are not found in the massive aggregates with which the planner deals of necessity. . . .[8]

Recognizing the need for closeness and small-area awareness, the planning department of Arlington, Texas, divided that city of one hundred square miles and 230,000 persons into three districts and staffed each area with a complete planning team. Each team was an autonomous unit responsible and accountable for handling both the planning and administration of the land use regulations. Friendly competition was encouraged, innovation and productivity were rewarded, and management skills were developed. Arlington planners successfully used the team approach for almost five years before reorganizing the department to undertake the development of the comprehensive strategic plan discussed in Chapter 2.

Several planners have asked why we changed something that was working so well. Our response was that as conditions changed in Arlington, new priorities and opportunities emerged and that the planning department changed to take advantage of them. We were also keenly aware that a success that outlives its usefulness may in the end be more damaging than failure. Stopping what always has been done and doing something new or different is one of the most difficult things for local governments to do.

Innovative and entrepreneurial activities are not always neat and clean. In both local government and the business community, decentralization, the creation of autonomy, and the encouragement of entrepreneurial spirit often results in overlapping jurisdictions and responsibilities, duplication, and personnel conflicts. Peters and Waterman found that successful corporations were:

> creating almost radical decentralization and autonomy with its attendant overlap, messiness around the edges, lack of coordination, internal competition, and somewhat chaotic conditions, in order to breed the entrepreneural spirit.[9]

Unfortunately there is not much public tolerance for duplication, competition, or overlapping jurisdictions in local government. This is often perceived by the public as wasteful and chaotic mismanagement of tax dollars. Innovation and entrepreneurship is generally not expected from government, so there is little reason for the public to accept the untidiness which is required to produce such benefits.

Yet there is growing awareness and support of the need to improve the efficiency and effectiveness of service delivery by local governments. The International City Management Association "Green Books," published in the Municipal Management Series, stress the management and implementation of new or more efficient programs and the use of innovative technologies to increase effectiveness and productivity. The difficulty of applying management techniques of successful business to the planning function in local government is illustrated by a recent situation in Atlanta, Georgia. There, three separate public agencies at city hall—the Department of Community Development, the Office of Economic Development, and the Atlanta Economic Development Corporation—oversee economic development. Critics have argued that the public and even commercial developers are confused about just who runs the economic development function of the city and that there is too much confusion and overlapping of responsibilities. The *Atlanta Constitution* reported that:

> (i)n one way, Young (Mayor) has encouraged confusion by promoting a competitive spirit between Stogner, Martin, and Turpeau (the directors of each agency). He has often assigned the same development projects to different departments.

Mrs. Franklin (the city's chief administrative officer) said the mayor supported having three separate offices with three high-level officials heading each agency. Young encourages competition to prevent lethargy, she added.[10]

Perhaps Young should have cited the book *In Search of Excellence* and explained that he encouraged autonomy and competition to breed entrepreneural spirit and innovation in planning and to promote economic development. In any event, a subsequent editorial in *The Atlanta Constitution* chided the mayor's support for "a dose of competition in the bureaucracy" and stated that:

> teamwork is more important—especially in the field of economic development, where Atlanta has plenty of competition from without. . . . The case for consolidation seems overwhelming.[11]

The Atlanta Constitution recognizes the value of external competition but cannot see the merit and value of internal competition. In contrast, Peters and Waterman noted that at Proctor and Gamble, management decided that internal competition was "the only way to keep from becoming too clumsy."[12] They noted that managers are encouraged to compete at Proctor and Gamble and also at Bloomingdales, and that General Motors has aggressively moved to restore the old spirit of internal competition at the direction of its chairman, Roger Smith.[13]

In summary, Peters and Waterman conclude that, "internal competition as a substitute for formal, rule- and committee-driven behavior permeates the excellent companies. It entails high costs of duplication-cannibalization, overlapping products, overlapping divisions, multiple development projects, lost development dollars when the sales force won't buy a marketer's fancy. Yet the benefits, though less measurable, are manifold, especially in terms of commitment, innovation, and a focus on the revenue line."[14]

CHAMPIONS

The only time I feel really alive is when I'm walking the tightrope. KARL WALLENDA

While decentralization and autonomy are of critical importance, they don't automatically produce innovation or success. Even in a decentralized environment, you can not instruct employees to be creative and expect innovation to occur. Peters and Waterman discovered that "champions and a tolerance of failure were additional requirements for innovation and success.[15] In the same vein, Edward Schon, of the Massachusetts Institute of Technology, noted that "the new idea either finds a champion or dies" and that "champions of new inventions display persistence and encouragement of heroic quality."[16]

Peters and Waterman reported that Texas Instruments (TI) conducted a survey of its last fifty successful and unsuccessful new products and discovered that one factor was characteristic of every failure: without exception the failed project did not have a *volunteer* champion. The presence of a zealous, volunteer champion is now the top criterion used by TI in deciding on investments in new product development. "After that comes market potential and project economics in a distant second and third."[17]

In 1977, Galveston, Texas, hired a young planning director and let him create a new planning department. The director called the chairs of several graduate planning schools and asked them to identify the most creative, innovative, aggressive, and enthusiastic students in their programs. The director was able to hire the top student from each school despite the low salaries he offered because he promised a work environment in which they would be able to use and develop their initiative and extraordinary technical skills.

The team of young planners developed and implemented a series of innovative planning projects, including the preparation and implementation of a dune and beach management program which received the 1980 outstanding achievement in planning award from the Texas chapter of the American Planning Association. The program became the model for several other programs the Texas Energy and Natural Resources Advisory Council developed to help coastal communities protect and manage their coastal environments. Another winning project was an energy conservation notebook that was developed as part of Galveston's neighborhood planning program. The notebook simply communicated energy conservation strategies that were most applicable to a neighborhood's particular housing styles and socioeconomic status. This project was selected for inclusion in International City Management Association's annual innovative municipal projects publication.

It is not always simple or easy to employ the best personnel in local government. Civil service rules and regulations and personnel departments can be an impediment to hiring the planners a planning director wants and needs in order to be successful. In theory, personnel departments are service agencies that should be assisting the planning department; in reality, they often function in a restrictive, regulatory manner. For instance, the planning director of one mid-sized southwestern city hired a planner who was uniquely appropriate for his program but he was told by the personnel department during processing that the planner did not meet all of the technical requirements for the position. As a result, the director was not able to offer the planner the position or salary that had been agreed to.

It is commonly accepted that because local governments are not profit oriented, employers have no incentive to hire the best personnel and regulations and personnel departments are needed to prevent abuses in the employment process. Yet effective employers must be able to hire the best planners and to achieve that goal they must learn to manipulate the personnel system. Unfortunately, in our interviews, the number of examples of the personnel system being abused for unethical gain seemed to greatly exceed the situations of the system being manipulated to hire the best person for the job.

Some of the most successful schools in the nation today are headed by "outlaw principals" who sidestep rules to meet their school needs, according to Bruce Hasalam, director of the U.S. Department of Education's Secondary School Recognition Program.[18] He called them outlaws because "they operate on the fringes of school district policy. These principals are successful at getting the teachers they want and marshaling the community resources that are needed."[19]

Hasalam said these successful principals frequently violated district policies in recruiting their own teachers because they needed the best teachers they could find in order to provide a quality education. He recommended that ". . . school districts reexamine their policies and give more autonomy to the . . . principals."[20]

Some successful planning directors would fit Hasalam's description of "outlaw principals." These directors are committed to hiring creative and innovative planners and are able to obtain the resources and support of the community for planning programs, products, and services. More aggressive recruitment is time-consuming and often is not pursued because "we just need a body in there fast!" But careful and aggressive recruitment can result in returns much larger than the investment.

During preparation of its strategic comprehensive plan, the Arlington planning department experienced a severe turnover in staff and its top candidate to head the project rejected the planning department's offer. Even though no higher salary could be offered, rather than reconsidering their list of other candidates, the department began an intensive marketing compaign. A local real estate broker was solicited to make several contacts and give the candidate some idea of the local housing market. Several employers were asked to call the candidate's spouse to report on the local employment market. Information about the local school district was forwarded. The planners emphasized to the candidate that he was the best person for the position, and because they were at the leading edge of the planning profession, they needed the best. It was enough to tip the balance, and he accepted. The playoff came five months later when Arlington's draft plan was delivered to the planning commission three months ahead of schedule after a six-month staffing delay. An aggressive recruitment program had produced a champion.

Creativity involves thinking up new things while innovation is doing new things. Obviously, ideas are useless unless used and the proof of their value is only in their implementation. There is no shortage of creative planners, but there is a shortage of successful planning innovators. Planners must learn to become effective, successful innovators and refuse to accept being only creative. As noted by Peters and Waterman, "the scarce people are the ones who have the know-how, energy, daring, and staying power to implement ideas . . . ."[21]

Many planning departments are either unaware of the benefits of hiring potential champions or, worse, they deliberately avoid such individuals. One planning department in a large southwestern city traditionally avoided hiring graduates from the local university's recognized graduate planning program and did not advertise vacant positions in state or national planning publications. The planning director was politically astute and was successful in keeping the planning department out of controversy but local planners had little visibility or influence with decision makers. Upon his retirement, the city hired an aggressive planning director who established as his first priority the recruitment of champion planners. Today, planning is in the forefront in that community and local planners are highly visible and influential.

But even in the business community where there is so much agreement that champions are pivotal to the innovation process, there is a reluctance to hire such individuals. The reasons include that their working style conflicts with the way most businesses are managed and that they are apt to be loners, egotistical, cranky, or fanatic in the work. James Brian Quinn stated that "the champion is obnoxious, impatient, egotistical, and perhaps a bit irrational in organizational terms. As a consequence, he is not hired. If hired, he is not promoted or rewarded. He is regarded as 'not a serious person,' 'embarrassing' or 'disruptive.' "[22]

One high-profile planner in the Southwest who had a reputation as an aggressive advocate of planning was characterized as a maverick by one city manager. The word *maverick* was coined in the 1800s in Texas and used in cattle-raising regions to refer to a stray cow without an owner's brand. Its origin has been traced to Samuel Maverick, a nineteenth century Texas rancher who neglected to brand his cattle. Stray cows without brands were thus called mavericks. Today, it is used to described an independent individual who refuses to conform with his group. Being labeled a maverick is not a goal of most professional planners. In fact, it could be quipped that being called a maverick is a planner's second most favorite objective, with the first being gaining a reputation for being controversial.

Management's tolerance for champions with mavericklike characteristics expands in direct proportion to each individual's ability to contribute to the well-being of the organization. For example, football is a team sport and as Darrell Royal, the retired University of Texas coach, once said: "When the ball gets inside our five-yard line, I don't want somebody running around trying to be different." Royal did not believe there was any room for individuals on his team. When potential superstar Bill Bradley returned for his sophomore season, Mike Campbell, the chief assistant, reported to Royal that "he's got sideburns down to here!" Royal replied, "Well, I guess we better have him cut 'em off." Campbell thought for a moment. "Either that," said Campbell, "or grow some ourselves."

Champions are an invaluable asset and they can be team players. In fact, most superstars are team players or they wouldn't be superstars. It may well be that planning agencies should be letting their sideburns grow in the sense that they should be expecting their employees to emulate the traits and characteristics of their most effective planners rather than wanting the staff to conform to the lowest common denominator. Sameness in the guise of team building is not conducive to a more effective agency.

Champion planners, be they mavericks or controversial, grow and flourish only in a supportive environment. Without such an environment, most planners run from controversy like prairie dogs taking to their holes. Champions are pioneers and history has taught us the pioneer is often the guy with an arrow in his back and his face in the mud. Peters and Waterman reviewed numerous schemes describing systems of champions and found that they "all came down to the same thing—some form of primary champion plus some form of protection."[23] The protection usually comes from an older exchampion who knows firsthand how difficult it is to overcome the formal bureaucratic tendencies toward negation during the product development process. As noted by Peters and Waterman, without support systems, there are no champions. And without champions, there are no innovations.[24]

The application of innovative technology designed to increase operational and transactional productivity can result in efficient and effective service delivery within the various planning, zoning, subdivision, building permit, and engineering bureaucracies. Perhaps the best-kept planning secret in the United States today is the entrepreneurial and innovative "skunkworks" project carried out by Norman Standerfer's superstar planners in Austin, Texas.

Formation of Austin's Department of Planning and Growth Management (PGM) in 1984 included a mission requirement and responsibility for developing and maintaining automated information technologies. The city manager was committed to the introduction of such technology and Standerfer accepted the director's position in September 1984 predominately because of management's commitment to maintaining PGM's leadership role in developing such innovative technology. Immediately targeting this window of opportunity, Standerfer recruited two of his Broward County, Florida, automation superstars to join him in Austin as deputy director and planning systems division director in Austin: James Rider and Pat Brown.

In September 1985, the fledgling department's automation consisted of two word processing terminals and the planning systems division included two staff and eight vacant positions. In January 1987, the planning systems division was managing and operating a unified, five-department network of interactive, shared data base computers and graphic and mapping work stations. Following the installation of the land-based information system (LBIS), James Rider successfully designed and implemented a citywide program of "departmental computing" and office automation culminating in the award of a $5.5 million systems contract.

Austin, under the entrepreneurial leadership of its city manager reflecting a commitment to technological innovation and using the talents represented through Standerfer and his two champion planners, planned, designed, bid, and awarded contracts totaling $7.5 million, with 56 percent of those dollars representing effective reuse of existing monetary resources. The net cost impact of these systems is less than $400,000 a year in terms of additional system costs over a four-year period. The information systems department's system of multidepartmental, decentralized computing technology operates with fifteen fewer positions at a savings of almost $600,000 a year.

This all was accomplished in less than two years—less time than many large cities spend with major outside consultants in "systems design" for comparable installations—and without the hundreds of thousands of dollars of consultants costs. The entrepreneurial leadership and bias for action represented by this Austin "skunkworks" project is evidence of a supportive environment and of leadership committed to excellence.

The concept of a champion and a champion protector has significant precedence in the history of planning. For example, the McMillan Plan for Washington, D.C., was completed in 1902 and as the nation's first comprehensive city plan, it had tremendous influence on planning in many other cities.[25] Daniel Burnham, the chairman of the committee responsible for preparing the plan, was a champion and catalyst for the project. It was reported that the committee exceeded its instructions and the resulting plan "possessed ... extraordinary breadth and complexity for its day ... largely because of its chairman. ... "[26] The committee was able to set its own goals because of the boldness, persistence, and inspirational leadership of Daniel Burnham. But while Burnham was a visionary champion of the plan, Senator McMillan played the equally important role of supporter and protector. In the absence of McMillan's support and protection, the final plan would not have been innovative and imaginative and it would not have captured the interests of both its clients and the nation.

The experiences of the noted planner Rexford G. Tugwell, first chairman of the New York City planning commission, again provide a sharp contrast and a valuable lesson for planners. Tugwell possessed all of the characteristics of a champion and his "affinity for controversy . . . outspokenness and restless energy aroused intense opposition . . . ."[27] But Mayor La Guardia did not provide the support that a champion such as Tugwell required to be effective and Tugwell resigned after four years with a tenure "marked by frustration and defeat."[28]

THE DARK SIDE OF ENTREPRENEURSHIP

And everything he touched turned to gold. THE STORY OF KING MIDAS

The traits that make champions and entrepreneurs successful can also lead to organizational problems. Entreprenuers seem to have a mystique for achievement. They enjoy taking responsibility, making decisions, getting things done. Creative entrepreneurs seem to be able to consistently maintain a high level of energy and dedication. These qualities, when combined with the willingness to take risks, are the forces that fuel innovation and effectiveness. Such people can, just by their personal charisma, inspire others to succeed and create an atmosphere that gives an organization momentum and leadership.

But along with the mystique can come personality quirks that may not be appreciated within a particular organization. Some entrepreneurs, caught up in a high-energy creative process, may throw out dozens of ideas as they weigh the possibilities. This may frustrate or confuse those who need just a simple answer, not a realm of possibilities. Some may interpret an entrepreneur's strong bias for action as thoughtless and uncaring behavior. Others may react personally when the entrepreneur shuts out the world to think. Others may find an entreprenuer's unwillingness to let go of a project as the creative process ends and daily implementation begins stifling; it also can be inefficient use of the entrepreneur's time.

Entrepreneurs present other problems to managers. Manfred Kets de Vries, a professor of management at INSEAD in Fontainebleau, France, offered the following warning based on extensive observations and interviews with thirty-eight entrepreneurs operating in a wide range of organizations in North America:

> Most entrepreneurs have their internal visions in tune with reality so that they act in the real world in a way that other people can understand. For some entrepreneurs, however, things are not so easy. For these people, the high degree of energy necessary to achieve a dream has desires and needs behind it that, if let loose, can wreak havoc on an organization.[29]

Entrepreneurs have unique personal traits and characteristics, according to Professor Kets de Vries, but they do not have any more personal problems or personality disorders than other people. More importantly, it is the *mix* of irrational and creative behavior that makes them tick, which accounts for their positive influences.[30]

When trying to create a "loose/tight" atmosphere to sponsor creativity and innovation, one needs to be aware that the tight is as important as the loose. There are several traits of the individual entrepreneur—including need for control, sense of distrust, desire for applause, and defensiveness—that can hurt the overall organization if allowed to get out of control.[31]

Organizational structures must give entrepreneurs the freedom to be in charge of the creative process. They work best under loosely designed management, but entrepreneurs may need help to know when to let go or when to delegate. Upper management, if forewarned, can try to build an open relationship based on trust so that the two can talk frankly on a regular basis.

Organizations need to make sure entrepreneurs are in an environment where they can be rewarded directly for their successes. Entrepreneurs are not interested in being paid or recognized for how long they last, but for what they do. Performance pay or office perks are appropriate, as is allowing them credit from their peers. Managers can let them "sign their work," speak at conferences and workshops, or hold training sessions for the staff. Managers also can try to avoid matching them with contrary personalities. Making entrepreneurs work with people who have opposite work styles will cause them a great deal of stress. Such matches also may drive slow, methodic workers crazy.

CONSTRAINTS TO ENTREPRENEURSHIP AND INNOVATION

There is nothing more difficult to take in hand, more perilous to conduct, than to take a lead in the introduction of a new order of things, because the innovation has for enemies all those who have done well under the old conditions and lukewarm defenders in those who may do well under the new.
MACHIAVELLI

The difficulty in introducing innovation in public planning agencies cannot be overestimated. Some of the more significant impediments to innovation include these factors:

- Government decisions are subject to review and evaluation by the electorate.

- The electorate tends to be intolerant and unforgiving of failures by elected officials.

- Civil service systems often make it difficult to hire the best employees.

- Government no longer attracts the brightest and best employees.

- Government moves too slowly for real entrepreneurs.

- Government officials are reluctant to take risks and to initiate new ideas unless they have been absolutely proven to work in some other similar community.

- Traditional horizontal hierarchial structures in local government promote "segmentalism" and insulate organizations against change.

- The accumulated years of wisdom within the typical organization is convinced that innovation and new ideas won't work.

- A basic inertia exists in government that generally discourages innovation and change.

- The public doesn't expect innovation and entrepreneural behavior from local government.

- Decisions are made on the basis of public interest considerations rather than on bottom line factors.

- Many municipal attorneys have conservative and cautionary natures.

Some planning agencies are incapable of innovation, some lack resources, but a lot more simply do not have the time or ambition. Effective planning agencies find ways to overcome obstacles and impediments to innovation. They know how to turn problems, whether they be personnel or fiscal, into opportunities.

Deadwood is a legendary mining town located in the Black Hills of South Dakota. It also is the dry plant fiber from which the vital sap has gone. Bowlers use the word to refer to the pins that have been knocked down but remain on the alley lane. The word deadwood also is used to describe personnel who stay on too long and outlive the usefulness and worth they once had.

Many planning agencies have at least one person who can be described as deadwood. For whatever reason, the vitality is gone and only a shell of a person remains. We have known several planners, including agency directors, who retired but didn't leave the job. Deadwood, at any level in a planning agency, is a serious detriment to innovation and entrepreneural behavior. Consider an assessment of the Office of Policy Planning (OPP) in Seattle, which found that influential staff members were trained in fields such as law and architecture but were inexperienced in planning. In explaining the ineffectiveness of this planning agency, the citizens panel on executive department reorganization concluded that "OPP is not as good technically as it should be."[32]

Civil service procedures can make it difficult to hire the most qualified planner or to remove and replace unproductive staff members. Yet Sylvia Lewis, in an article on surviving as a big city planning director, noted that every planning director she interviewed agreed that technical competence was critical to the effectiveness and success of their agencies.[33] Separately, Joseph Vitt, Jr., former director of the City Development Department of Kansas City, Missouri, stated that in building an effective planning program you "start with developing a competent staff. Talent is the basis for the organization."[34] Under Vitt's direction, Kansas City had a strong recruiting program and a strong in-house professional development program.

Calvin Hamilton, former planning director of Los Angeles, always prided himself on his technical knowledge and the international reputation for innovative, state-of-the-art planning that his agency enjoyed. He estimated that he spent 40 percent of his time on the technical aspects of planning.[35]

In *Making City Planning Work*, Allan Jacobs, former San Francisco planning director, explained that his commitment to the development of a competent staff was based on the premise that knowledge is transferable to power and effectiveness.[36] Unfortunately his efforts to improve the competency of his staff were often thwarted by the San Francisco civil service commission.

One of the many benefits associated with budget reduction exercises is the opportunity to prune the deadwood that has sometimes been allowed to accumulate in an agency. In west Texas, we know that a rattlesnake sheds its skin each year in order to grow and be stronger. Similarly, creative management of a budget crisis and the shedding or pruning of less productive personnel can actually result in a strong and more innovative agency. At a minimum, removing deadwood clears away obstacles to increased effectiveness and makes it possible to focus and concentrate the remaining resources on the most productive and innovative personnel.

Peter Drucker stated that not too many years ago "government was the place where the ideas were, the innovation, the new things." Unfortunately Drucker has found that Japan is the only country where government is respected and able to attract top people. In his opinion, "the basic problem of American government today is that it no longer attracts good people."[37]

It is often argued that governments cannot attract the brightest and best employees, but Terry Culler, former associate director for work force effectiveness and development for the U.S. Office of Personnel Management, has advanced the rather novel view that the taxpaying public does not want a more capable government. According to Culler, "Encouraging the most highly talented people to take up government as a career will encourage more of the misguided entrepreneurial government that has saddled us with a massive debt and a high bureaucracy while denying those skills to the private sector."[38]

Unfortunately for those who share Culler's view, we have found that there are many capable and truly outstanding individuals in planning and in other professions in local government. Our experiences and opinions on this subject are shared by many others. For example, Peter Drucker concluded in *Management: Tasks, Responsibilities, Practices* that "there is no reason to believe that the people who staff the managerial positions in our (public) service institutions are any less qualified, any less competent or honest, or any less hard-working than the men who manage businesses."[39]

Yet it is not always easy for local government to attract and keep the best and brightest people. In one city, the planning director sadly announced that one of his best planners had resigned to take a similar position in other city. The chairman of the planning commission later confided that the loss was beneficial because "that planner always showed too much initiative." Unfortunately, protection of champions is not always enough to ensure innovative production. The hostile environment created by the planning commission discouraged that champion and he moved to a more challenging and rewarding environment.

A similar situation occurred in Corpus Christi. There, a senior planner had successfully directed the development of a new comprehensive plan which had been reviewed and praised by several noted national planning authorities for its innovative approach to visually linking goals and objectives to development policies and proposals. The planning director had encouraged and protected the senior planner from a hostile city manager who had allowed the plan to be prepared only because it was funded by a federal grant. When the funds had been expended, the manager halted the project and ordered that all copies of the plan be boxed and placed in a storage room. Several months later, the senior planner resigned and accepted a position as the director of planning for another city. When the planning director told the manager, the manager responded that he never trusted the planner and was pleased about his departure. Fearful that the boxed plans might be discovered, the manager later directed that they be burned.

Richard Snelling, former Vermont governor, concluded that "politicians are the least entrepreneural group of people" that he'd ever known and that "they go where the road goes." He found during his experience that "government totally lacks the ability to forge new paths, to take big risks."[40] Yet one reason that it is difficult for public officials to encourage and support innovation in local government is that most business interests prefer a stable, predictable government environment. Edward Banfield and James Wilson noted in *City Politics* that "businesssmen have usually had a principal say about the civic agenda and sometimes they have *the* principal one."[41] Such individuals tend to use their political influence to prevent any distrubance of the status quo that might adversely affect them financially. Yet Banfield and Wilson also point out business people are also interested in civic improvements, especially from a public relations standpoint. They often find it is " 'fun' to work up grandiose schemes for civic improvement and to pull strings to get them accepted."[42]

Some communities have found that they can overcome the business community's fear and opposition to innovation and change in local government by leveraging public sector investments to promote private sector investments that are in the public interest. Three communities that have been particularly effective in this area are San Antonio, Texas, and Minneapolis and St. Paul, Minnesota. As a general rule, however, it is obviously more difficult to introduce innovation in the public sector than in the private sector.

Many examples are available to illustrate the political difficulty in introducing innovation into planning agency management. For instance, the planning director in one medium-sized city approached his planning commission and city council with an idea for developing a new comprehensive plan. He described an innovative and visionary plan that promised to be of more benefit and value to them and the community than the rather limited, ineffective, and seldom-used existing plan. The commission and council reacted negatively to the idea and become visibly angry and defensive, ostensibly because the proposal implied criticism of the existing plan, which they had developed several years earlier. Their publicly stated opposition to the idea of preparing a new and more effective plan masked their real motivation, as explained by our friend and colleague George Raymond, former chairman of the consulting firm of Raymond, Parish, Pine and Weiner, Inc.: "Local government officials cherish their freedom to respond to pressures for land use changes."[43] He has found "they cherish it so much that they would rather not give their communities the advantage of guided growth in accordance with a carefully developed plan."[44] This means that many public officials will oppose the development of plans or make sure that the ones that are developed are the kind that will gather dust on the shelf.

INSTITUTIONALIZING INNOVATION

Individuals can make a difference, but they need the tools and the opportunity to use them. They need to work in settings where they are valued and supported, their intelligence given a chance to blossom. They need to have the power to be able to take the initiative to innovate. ROSABETH MOSS KANTER

The internal organization structure of a planning agency can either encourage or discourage innovation. Peter Drucker has concluded after thirty to forty years of research and study on introducing innovation into businesses that ". . . existing units have been found to be capable mainly of extending, modifying, and adopting what already is in existence. The new belongs elsewhere."[45]

Often the problem is that the existing work loads and omnipresent brushfires can overwhelm staff and preclude pursuit of new ideas—even when the existing responsibilities do not deserve their priority treatment from the staff. Still, it is always tempting to continue current activities, no matter how insignificant or ineffective they are, while the new, innovative, and unproven continue to be neglected. The proper response for local government, according to Peter Drucker, is not that "whatever we do, we'll do forever" but that "whatever we do today will, in all likelihood, be a candidate for abandonment within a fairly short period of years."[46]

To be capable of innovation, an existing entity must create a structure that requires its staff to abandon outmoded priorities and to be innovative and entrepreneural in pursuit of activities, products, and services that meet current and future priorities. According to Peters and Waterman, successful companies virtually institutionalize innovation. They cite IBM's "Fellow" program that gives a free rein and the role of shaking up the system to a limited number of "dreamers, heretics, gadflies, mavericks, and geniuses," and noted that Texas Instruments' individual contribution program and 3M's new business ventures division are "analogous forcing devices."[47] At Bechtel, project managers are urged to spend 20 percent of their time experimenting with new technologies.[48] All these efforts are intended to force innovation into the organization.

One large international engineering and planning firm based in New York City recently instituted a major program to encourage innovation and motivation within the firm. Specifically, Parsons Brinckerhoff Quade and Douglas, Inc. created the William Barclay Parsons Fellowship (named for the founder of the firm) which awards employees the time and budget to pursue a firm-related interest for one year. The firm's career development committee evaluates the entries and first fellowship was won in 1985 by an urban planner for his new approach to planning and designing pedestrian facilities. The winner, who is a member of both the American Planning Association and the American Institute of Certified Planners, developed particularly useful designs for subway platforms for mass transit systems.

Innovation and entrepreneural behavior must be linked to the problem-solving emphasis referred to earlier. A particularly interesting application of this philosophy, as proposed by John Beane, real estate manager of Visalia, California, is to take a problem and figure out how much money can be made by solving it.[49] Entrepreneurs understand why the Chinese word for crisis means both "danger" and "opportunity." In our research, we have found that successful planners have emphasized opportunity while unsuccessful planners have focused on the danger. In essence, problems really are opportunities in disguise.

This approach to problem-solving is illustrated by Galveston's handling in the 1970s of its dual problem of environmental degradation and deterioration in housing in an area adjacent to the public golf course and Offats Bayou. For years, the city had leased at low prices the prime public lands adjacent to the golf course and bayou. Some lessors made substantial capital investments but the majority provided only the minimum improvements necessary to take advantage of the scenic environment. Water quality was suffering and structural maintenance was increasingly neglected. The area obviously was not being used or developed for its highest and best use.

The local planning department studied the problem and proposed an entrepreneural solution. The staff recommended that the city should not renew the expiring leases but instead enter into the land development business. The staff proposed consolidation and platting of the properties, redesign of the street system, and provision of public water and sewerage to maximize lot yields and development potential. The results would include resolving growing environmental problems and producing significant net revenues and a phenomenal return on the city's capital investment. The losers would be the lessors who had already enjoyed the use of public property at bargain prices for many years while the winners would be the general public which would benefit from improved water quality, and local taxpayers, investors, builders, and residents who would be able to purchase the properties.

Unfortunately, the city council decided that the lessors' interests were paramount to all other concerns; the decision was made to lease or sell the property by metes and bounds as the leases expired. One member of the Galveston council who was a successful businessman explained that he usually advocated the free enterprise system and running government like a business, but in this instance he advocated compassion and respect for the investments of the lessors.

While innovative problem solving did not prevail in this case, other opportunities can be found in analyzing and evaluating the products and services the planning agency produces. Visalia, California, uses what it calls an enterprise accounting system for some departments, "treating them as businesses responsible for generating enough revenue to cover their own costs."[50] In Texas, the cities of Arlington and Austin require their planning and regulatory activities to be self-supporting by the fees that each department generates. Fairfield and Visalia, California, also use a system in which each department is allocated the same budget amount each year, with adjustments for inflation and population growth. The departments can retain budget savings from one year to the next and Arne Croce, former Visalia assistant city manager, noted that "with this system, the departments had an incentive to carefully check their service levels."[51]

There are other, simpler techniques for encouraging critical reviews of program services and products and for stimulating the development of ideas for new activities. For starters, planners should be encouraged and allowed to set aside blocks of time for independent thought and research. One planning department gives reading assignments to its planners and expects them to present written and oral reviews of the potential for applying the concepts contained in the material to the department's products and services. This simple technique can be remarkably useful. In one agency, a senior-level planner involved in zoning explained that this was the only city she had ever worked in and that she was unaware of any ways to improve on the existing staff reports. She subsequently was given a reading assignment in *A Planner's Guide to Land Use Law* and at the next staff meeting described eight factors, derived from her reading, that should be taken into account when evaluating a rezoning application. She pointed out that the planning staff was only including two of these factors in their current reports and that they should look at expanding their analysis to include these additional factors.

The planning departments in two cities encourage an interest in innovation by requiring that all planners who attend conferences or workshops prepare a report for distribution to other planners. One department requires its planners to continue their academic education, even if they have graduate degrees, as a condition of advancement in salary or position.

If Peter Drucker is right in that the new belongs elsewhere and that it should "be organized separately from the old and existing," then what responses and options are available to planning agency managers? In Fort Worth, the response was to create and staff a separate division to develop an innovative growth management program. This approach has been productive, but the effectiveness of the new division was diminished because most of the planners who were shifted to the division had to retain many of their past duties.

In contrast, Austin split its planning department into two separate agencies and substantially expanded the staffing levels for both in order to place increased emphasis on planning and growth management. Two new directors were selected and the director of the planning and growth management department was able to recruit a large number of planners skilled and experienced in growth management. Today this department is recognized for its innovative approaches to growth mangement. The companion agency, the land development services department, used the chunking concept to introduce substantive reforms into its regulatory processes. Five of the department's planners were selected to work with an attorney and another employee from the building inspection division on a special task force that was isolated and kept in an incubator environment. Members on this task force were relieved of all other responsibilities and their time was freed-up so that they could work exclusively on the project. The chair of this task force reported directly to the department director, keeping with Peter Drucker's suggestion that the staff assigned to develop innovative products "should never report to line managers charged with responsibility for ongoing operations."[52]

TOLERANCE FOR FAILURE

Whenever I make a bum decision, I just go out and make another one.
HARRY S. TRUMAN

A tolerance for failure is the remaining trait that must be present if autonomy and entrepreneurship are to result in innovation. Peters and Waterman found that a "tolerance for failure is a very specific part of the excellent company culture—and that lesson comes directly from the top.[53] Their quotes from the chief executive officers of major successful companies in support of this finding include "You've got to be willing to fail," "If I wasn't making mistakes, I wasn't making decisions," and "You need the ability to fail. You cannot innovate unless you are willing to accept mistakes."[54]

Voters are not sympathetic of failure and tend not to forgive at the ballot box. Until the public and the media can be educated to support the corporate innovation process and risk-taking philosophy in municipal government, it will be difficult to achieve innovation in the public sector.

Innovation success is a numbers game and, as a rule, the greater the number of new initiatives, the greater the number of successes. Planners should start with low-risk innovations and work up to more speculative projects as they build a reputation and gain respect. Still, one can never be completely certain when assessing the probability of risk. One planner introduced what he thought were simple organizational and graphic changes to the zoning staff reports to improve their clarity, professionalism, and ease of use. He had introduced similar changes in two other communities and had received only compliments and praise. In this particular community, however, the planning commission was angered by the revisions and instructed the planner not to make any other changes in the department. They resorted to the typical response that "if something's not broke, don't fix it." Obviously, this type of reception has a chilling impact on further innovation.

Several years ago, the International City Management Association established a "Fabulous Flops" award program that, in their words, "provides a different perspective on a very important subject in local government: the need to take risks and to try new ideas."[55] The association believed it was important to acknowledge that there was much to be learned from failures or what they referred to as "almost innovations" and that the program would help promote a needed tolerance for risk taking in local government. ICMA reports that the response to this program has been overwhelmingly positive and that both "flops" and innovative successes are made possible by "a bias for action and the creation of a culture that accepts the willingness to risk and to fail."[56]

The advice that Arne Croce, city manager of Los Altos, California, gives people who made mistakes is, "Don't quit!" She suggests

A GROUP OF MANAGERS CANDIDLY
DISCUSS THEIR FABULOUS FLOPS

that "if you get stung by an idea, learn from it, but don't let it deter you."[57] The courage to try new ideas and to be willing to make a mistake and pay the price for seeking excellence is an essential characteristic of effective planners. Our position is summed up by William Hansell who warned that "we must adopt the attitude and ideal of constantly moving and changing to succeed, always ingesting new ideas and technologies and growing from the results—positive or negative."[58]

PLANNING FOR FAILURE

Treat failure as just another problem to be solved rather than as a cause for punishment. EDWIN A. LOCKE and GARY P. LATHAM

One last and very useful concluding principle on innovation should be emphasized at this point. The decision to implement an innovative idea should always include an awareness of the possible difficulty of correcting the situation if the idea fails to produce the anticipated results. More than thirty years ago, Peter Drucker wrote in *The Practice of Management* that ". . . the importance of a decision is not the money involved but, rather, how fast the decision can be reversed if it is wrong."[59]

The Coca-Cola Company recently illustrated this principle. On April 23, 1985, Coca-Cola announced it was changing the ninety-nine-year-old secret flavoring formula of the world's most popular soft drink, Coca-Cola, to give it a smoother taste. The news of Coke's reformulation generated both surprise and skepticism from marketing consultants. One market researcher, Leo Shapiro, cautioned that "whenever you change the formula or package for a familiar product, people who really like it will immediately notice the change and be hesitant to buy it."[60]

In fact, the subsequent market reaction was very negative and within weeks the original Coca-Cola was reintroduced as "Classic" Coke. Arlington, Texas, can provide a similar example in municipal planning. Planners there decided to replace the public rezoning notification signs that are posted on property prior to public hearings. The new signs were to be more colorful, contain more information, be more visible, and cost less to produce. The planners also reduced the size of the new signs to comply with production constraints, and the public perceived the resulting signs as less visible. The original signs were immediately reintroduced in combination with the new signs and the staff worked to correct the problem.

The effects of the law of unintended consequences must always be considered. One watermelon farmer got so fed up with thieves that he injected a watermelon with cyanide and posted a hand-lettered sign that said, "Warning! One of these melons is poisoned!" This tactic worked for about two weeks until the farmer noticed the sign had been altered to read, "Warning! *Two* of these melons is poisoned!"

Perhaps it is in the area of innovative growth management that planners have had to struggle the most with the results of unintended consequences. For instance, Douglas Porter, director of development policy research at the Urban Land Institute, has pointed out that "Ramapo's program, designed to pace growth to the availability of infrastructure, achieved a certain ironic status when it managed to provide no infrastructure capacity and scared away all growth, finally closing for lack of business in 1982."[61] This is a shockingly close parallel to the watermelon story.

Some failures can't be avoided and some failures eventually lead to greater professional success. William Hansell, executive director of the International City Management Association, reported that in his experience with local government, "managers often fail their way to success."[62] But successful managers understand an important management principle. As explained by Barry Staw, of the University of California at Berkeley, and Jerry Ross, of Carnegie-Mellon University, "good management consists of knowing when to call it quits."[63]

There probably is no substitute for confidence and self-respect when it comes to making the decision to cut your losses on an unsuccessful project, program, or service. Gerald Zaltman and Robert Duncan, in *Strategies for Planned Change*, concluded that the person making such management decisions must have "that optimal level of security in his status and abilities that permits him to be open to suggestion and willing to act on advice as well as to admit mistakes."[64] They suggested that positive answers to the following questions would be a good indication of an individual's emotional maturity and ability to succeed:

Does he take good advice when it is given, without regarding this as a threat or an affront?

Does he admit to mistakes candidly, without indulging in elaborate excuses or rationalizations?

Is he reasonably relaxed about his dignity and status, and about exacting his just due in amenities and respect?[65]

An important characteristic of effective planners is their ability to understand the linkage between actions and results and to anticipate and plan for potential positive or negative consequences. Effective planners are not infallible, they just do a better job of planning, monitoring, and responding to change.

OPPORTUNITIES FOR INNOVATION

Entrepreneurs need to search purposefully for the source of innovation, the changes and their symptoms that indicate opportunities for successful innovation. PETER F. DRUCKER

Innovation isn't a mysterious activity and it does not depend on a special class of geniuses in order to occur. The economist David Ricardo concluded that "profits are not made by differential cleverness, but by differential stupidity." Peter Drucker reached almost the same conclusion when he found that strategies for innovative products or services "work, not because they are clever, but because most suppliers—of goods as well as of services, businesses as well as public-service institutions—do not think." Drucker points out that it is possible to achieve innovation simply by systematically, purposely pursing opportunities. He suggested that purposeful innovation simply means monitoring seven sources of opportunity: (1) The unexpected—unexpected successes, failures or outside events, (2) the incongruous—differences between the world as it is and as it ought to be, (3) a process need—a better way to do a familiar job, (4) unpredicted changes in an industry or market structure, (5) demographics—population changes, (6) changes in perception, mood, meaning, and (7) new knowledge.[66]

Planners traditionally have been skilled at using incongruence as a tool for innovation, and are skilled at finding better ways to do a familiar job. Early in planning history, planners were particularly good at looking at the world as it was and envisioning how it should be. This occurred because initially most planners came from a design background. This rich tradition has been carried forward by some of today's professional planners, but often is lacking in today's planning officials who frequently have a difficult time seeing beyond how things look today. Professional planners also have a good understanding of the urban system as a whole, so they often can see relationships other cannot. This also helps them to find new and innovative ways to approach old familiar problems.

To illustrate, we consider a leadership group in Arlington, Texas, that was frustrated in its efforts to get local officials to see that long-term goals needed planning actions today. To make it easier to see beyond the present they sponsored an economic awards banquet and invited, for a fee, a host of community officials and leaders. The name of the awards banquet was "The 2010 Annual Economic Development Awards Banquet," and at the banquet, the group pretended that it was the year 2010. Economic development awards were given to public officials for specific actions of the late 1980s and early 1990s. They described what action had been taken and how that resulted in the development today, today being 2010. The awards and stories were fictitious, but it helped people to see the link between the present and the future.

One of Peter Drucker's opportunities for innovation deals with taking advantage of unexpected change—changes in mood, ethics, demographic changes, industry, or market structure. Planners who monitor such changes seemingly should be able to take advantage of them, but in reality more often than not are just dragged along. Planning's traditional tools and processes seem to experience major changes in large fits, instead of regular adjustment to current conditions. Many cities have ignored changes in family structure, mobility, and free time and still use the traditional public hearing process to solicit public comment. Then they wonder why every one complains about a new street or a particular project. Other planning agencies fail to respond quickly to changes in market demand and are slow to introduce regulatory reforms. Most frequently, it is the developers beating at the public official's door complaining about inflexible standards and restrictive requirements.

This lag in response to change comes from two sources: general resistance to change, and the timeliness of data sources. There are those who find a good way to do something and stick with it. Unfortunately, many do not realize something no longer works until they are hit over the head with it. Planners spend so much of their time planning that they often fail to investigate if their planning does or doesn't work. This sometimes puts planners in a position of reacting instead of acting.

Lag in response also is due to many of the traditional data sources that planners use to monitor change—they just are not timely enough. For example, Texas went from being a major importer of people to a major exporter of people in only two years. Such rapid changes are difficult to monitor and, in this particular situation, it is likely that planning agencies will not respond to this change for several years. By then the trend may have reversed itself.

TECHNOLOGY REVOLUTION

Technology assessment introduces a new value structure about the human adventure and requires, to support it, a new, broader frame of analysis for leadership decisions. HARLAN CLEVELAND

Planing, by its nature, is an information-driven process. Planners and policymakers traditionally have used what little information was available to make decisions on a timely basis. More often than not there was not enough information, so planners relied on their experience and foresight to help policymakers make the best decisions. Microcomputers, and the information age they represent, will bring this scenario to a grinding halt. In fact, over the next ten years it is going to peg the pendulum to the opposite wall.

A by-product of the information and technology age is that planners and policymakers are beginning to find themselves inundated with more information than they know what to do with. It will get worse and planners need to prepare themselves to shift gears. They will need to find ways to digest the mountains of available data and transform it into simple, short messages that policymakers can understand and act on. Planners will have to respond to policy needs more quickly because information is now available sooner and they will have to be discriminating about the quality and validity of the expanding amount and sources of data avilable. Some of the data is good "clean" data, and some is highly inaccurate. Planners also will have to decide which of ten sources is best for the problem at hand, accurately condense it into mangeable form, and present it to policymakers in a simple understandable form. Those planners who can do so will be most effective and have the greatest impact on the decision-making process.

There are six skills planners can hone to take advantage of the new tools and data of the information age:

1. *Learn about the data sources.* Planners need to learn where they can go for inexpensive but reasonably accurate data, or expensive but great data when they need it. One of the biggest mistakes a planner could make would be to go before a city council with a recommendation on sewer extensions based on population projections that turn out to be ten years off. Eventually, data will be a commodity. Much of what is free now will be available only at a cost. Planning agencies will need to anticipate and start including the cost of data in their budgets. Planning agencies can offset these costs to some extent by packaging and marketing for sale their own internally generated data.

2. Begin to learn management analysis tools that are not traditional to planning. Management science is a well-established and fast-growing academic area. Managers in the business community, particularly those involved in finance or securities, have long been inundated with data. Over the last several years, management science techniques have become common tools in the business community. Though many of these tools are designed specifically to digest a log of data into a more focused analysis of a trend or condition and are geared toward financial issues, many could be applied to resource management issues in which planners are involved. Cash flow analysis can be used to assess the short-term and long-term effects of public/private partnerships as well as the potential for impact and development fees. Cost-benefit analysis is useful for examining the fiscal impacts of growth. Marketing analysis can be used in examining the need for commercial and industrial development. Advanced regression techniques could further refine gravity models or examine the impacts of resources on growth patterns. These are examples of only some of the simpler techniques currently in use by planners.

The Rice Center in Houston, Texas, which is the designated Joint Center for Urban Mobility Research, frequently uses a cash flow model to evaluate the potential for joint public/private development around transit stations. This technique has been used in a number of cities as a tool for estimating the funding potential for mass transit systems.

3. Do not be afraid to invent a new analysis tool. Urban issues will frequently pose problems not easily translated into a private sector management issue or a traditional planning issue. Planners need to begin developing new unique tools for analysis. Planners are fortunate in that they have the special sense of how our communities function as a complex system of support services and facilities. Until recently, it was difficult to quantify most of these relationships. But much data is now available to make such connections. An understanding of these relationships can often lead to a clearer picture of some urban issues.

4. Begin to think of planning as the study of a complex interrelated urban system. Consider the following example. In Arlington, Texas, apartment development was a much complained about subject by both homeowners and policymakers. Many in the community believed that there were just too many apartments, and that the city needed to stop approving new apartment zoning and reduce densities to help solve the problem. However, using data available through the city's geoprocessing system and a simple geographic overlay technique, the planning department was able to diagnosis several interrelated causes of the problem. It was determined that the existing densities and the single-family to multi-family ratio were the same as they had been ten years earlier but that apartments had begun changing the character of several key areas that originally were mostly single-family developments. It was also discovered that reducing densities by as much as 20 or 30 percent would have only a 5 percent effect on overall densities because development was already lower than permitted. Further, it was determined that apartments no longer served a market of people waiting to buy homes; there now was a market of people who preferred these higher density, lower maintenance housing options. This information focused the planning department's current efforts on the quality and appearance of apartment development and on targeting areas where the existing zoning is higher than current development and there is above-average potential for adverse impact. Using a nontraditional approach to the problem, the city is now headed toward a more effective solution.

5. *Keep things simple and direct.* Planners now can quote a whole gamit of data to emphasize a particular trend of use. Those who make public policy generally are not experts at understanding the urban system, and in fact frequently have very little depth of knowledge on the topic. They seek simple explanations of complex problems, preferably with suggestions for simple solutions. If a city is experiencing a decline in population, the planner could quote, to name just a few, the changes in water and electrical connections, postal deliveries, building permits, completion certificates, tax delinquencies, school enrollment, vehicle registrations, vacancy rates, home sales, traffic patterns, and sales tax. But bombarding a public official with such data is not likely lead to action. Instead, the planner should summarize the key trends and simply define the problem.

6. *At the least, become knowledgeable of the technology used for information management.* Changes in technology, particularly evidenced by microcomputers, have resulted in major changes in how the business community conducts and manages business. There will be an equal impact on city management and the planning profession, though likely at a slower rate. Planners traditionally have been good at seeing new and better ways to do their jobs,

but planning as a profession has been show in assimilating new knowledge and technology in its problem-solving processes. The techniques planners use tend to be behind those used by the business community. For example, a survey in 1983 by the International City Management Association revealed that only about 13 percent of the cities surveyed owned or leased a microcomputer. The study also found that use of microcomputers for planning processes fell behind use for public safety, engineering, and public finance.[67]

We believe this needed revolution in the planning profession lags behind business for three major reasons: (1) lack of equipment, (2) resistance to computers, and (3) lack of analysis skills and intuition.

Use of microcomputers proliferated in the business community because of their effect on business's bottom line. If used properly, microcomputers can result in significant savings in management, operation, and production costs and in significant improvements in quality for the same or less cost. Unfortunately for planners, it is harder in the public than in the private sector to justify a $5,000 to $15,000 purchase that may or may not result in budget savings next year. This can make the cost of initial equipment purchase a barrier to microcomputer use in the public sector.

Additionally, we have found that many planners are fearful or apprehensive about microcomputers, either because of lack of exposure to the technology or because of a negative or unproductive experience with a computer system in the past. Planning schools and the continuing education programs can help planners develop a minimum level of skills and comfort with microcomputers that will improve efficiency and quality of work. APA's, UMTA's and DOT's current efforts at information exchange are an important first step, but more hands-on training and publicized demonstration programs are needed.

Microcomputers offer a powerful personal tool for data analysis. But any tool, no matter how sophisticated, is only as good as the person using it. Many of the benefits are due to the skill of the craftsman. Another point is that in a field like planning—where the answers that are right today may be wrong tomorrow—planners need additional skills. Scientific theory is one of the most fundamental concepts lacking in many urban planning programs today. The concept of hypothesizing, testing *and* validating often is not used in planning because the information, tools, or time to test and validate just aren't available. The micrcomputer opens a whole new realm of possibilities, allowing the personal "what if" analysis that can begin to ingrain hypothesizing, testing, and validating into planning programs. Applying scientific theory to urban research and planning allocation could greatly improve the effectiveness of planning decisions.

There are major technological advances in store for the planning profession. Planners looking for the leading edge of planning-related technology can search in a variety of areas. Four areas that have a significant potential to have a major impact include: (1) computer-based geographic information and mapping systems, (2) land use, population, and financial modeling, (3) video production, and (4) expert systems.

Computer-based geoprocessing and base mapping systems are rapidly becoming common. Planners now can quickly generate a base map of all or any part of a city. If they overlay such a map with a variety of socioeconomic conditions, tax information, land use, zoning, ownership, street systems, utilities, and other geographic-based information they will be able to produce formerly time- and cost-prohibitive information. As digitizing technology advances, a planner could sketch out a new street plan, have the computer scan it, and overlay it on the existing property ownership, then print out a list of all the property owners affected and the value of their property. Such technology exists today on a limited basis, but it is expensive. Base mapping and geoprocessing systems already are being introduced that run on microcomputers, with price tags of tens of thousands of dollars. As prices drop, even planning staffs in smaller cities will be able to afford such a system, or lease time on a county system. Such tools open up the doors of imagination.

Land use, population, and financial models have been traditionally used by planners. However, until recently, such tools were either crude or resident on large computers and conducted by state transportation offices, regional agencies, or universities. In general, these models were only practical over larger planning areas. Information about smaller areas and local conditions was not available. Often the statistical technique being used did not use a large enough set of variables to account for variations at a smaller geography. Even with a larger geography, run times were often lengthly and costly. However, much of this is now beginning to change. Data are now much more readily available, and computer costs have dropped. Modeling systems such as transportation network allocation models are now available on microcomputer. Local agencies are beginning to use these systems to model local conditions. Their knowledge and access to data allow them to fine tune the model to their area and cover a smaller geography. Transportation planners can now test local street proposals in terms of their impact on the citywide system, without relying on a state or regional agency. Hydraulic, storm water, and water quality models are also becoming available on microcomputers. Many of the models used by the EPA and the Army Corps of Engineers (HEC1 and HEC2) can now be run on micros, as can air pollution and wind models.

Fiscal impact models are becoming readily available, too. Many communities, particularly those in Florida, California, and Texas, are developing local fiscal impact modeling systems. Planners can begin to measure the fiscal impact on the local community from major land use and development issues. Land use allocation models have yet to make a significant appearance on the scene, but will likely arise as demand increases.

Computer-generated land use, population, and fiscal impact models are extremely useful tools. But they can also be abused. As such tools become cheaper and more readily available, more people will use them. Misuse of models by those untrained or unfamiliar with their use and limitations is likely to increase. Public, private, and citizen planners will need to learn how to better scrutinize model results and their application.

Other advances in technology can also be applied to the planning profession. Video production is quickly becoming an excellent public participation and education tool. Many cities may have in-house video capabilities. Also most local cable franchises have community service facilities available for use. Video taping of presentations makes an efficient medium for contacting neighborhood groups. During the production of the comprehensive plan, planners in Arlington, Texas, were asked to conduct a wide series of meetings with neighborhood groups. To avoid overextending the staff, an introductory video tape was prepared which examined the process and issues involved in the city's comprehensive plan. Copies were distributed to homeowner groups which met to view the tape and discuss the issues.

One planning application now in its infancy is expert systems. Expert systems now are widely used by businesses in their problem-solving efforts. Expert systems, one of the more exciting results of current artificial intelligence research, are developed by condensing knowledge about a particular subject into a computer data base of rules or conditional facts. This data base can be very much like a decision tree. The expert system can infer conclusions to questions and problems by quickly searching the data base of rules and facts. The familiar bird identification book is an example of an expert system. The question is, "What kind of bird is that?" The answer is found by answering a series of questions about the bird. Each question narrows the search until there is only one type of bird that can fit the description. The major difference between the bird book and an expert system is the speed at which the expert system can look a rules and facts. Expert systems are essentially a method to capture the expertise of one or more individuals on a very specific subject. Other, less knowledgeable people can either ask the expert system questions or pose a problem and let the expert system provide one or more solutions. Expert systems are used in a variety of capacities. For example, a brewery whose head brewer was retiring developed with him a system to help train apprentice brewers. Expert systems are not designed to replace experts; rather they are designed to help experts solve problems faster.

We are developing an expert system which is designed to assist planners in analyzing zoning and land use cases. The planner indicates the use being requested and the surrounding uses. The expert system asks a series of questions about the proposed use and surrounding uses. It then indicates whether the uses are compatible, or what measures could be taken to make the uses compatible. The expert system will also suggest alternative uses for the site that are compatible with surrounding uses. The current goal of the system is only to help planners be consistent in their analysis of cases. However, future uses could include helping developers decide what action is needed to make uses compatible, or the expert system could be linked to zoning ordinances to analyze conflicting uses in common zoning districts.

We have been critical here of the planning profession's ability to quickly assimilate technological advances. We have tried to present an insight into the bright future such technologies can provide. Like many other professions, planners must begin to more rapidly cope with the fundamental change in our economy and society. We are becoming an information society. These changes can provide planners with tremendous opportunities for increased effectiveness, but if they are not prepared, the information age can also lead to pitfalls and ineffectiveness.

Innovation can be replicated and, at least according to Peter Drucker, a discipline can be made of it. In *Innovation and Entrepreneurship*, he asserts that "any one or any organization can be an entrepreneur—individual, small business, big business or government institution."[68]

While managing for innovation is a recognized business principle, Thomas Peters has concluded that other traits and characteristics dominate the process.[69] He suggests that innovation is often unpredictable and uncertain and "moreover, it is always messy."[70] He summarizes his findings:

> Breakthrough. Optimization. Systems analysis. Technology plan. Such terms are part and parcel of the usual approach to innovation management. Yet from innovative companies we hear instead about persistence (passion and obsession!), lots of tries, perverse and unusual users, five- to 25-person skunkworks sequestered in dingy warehouses for 90 days, plans gone awry, inventions from the wrong industry at the wrong time for the wrong reason, specs for complex systems on the backs of envelopes.[71]

We have concluded that much of the innovation in planning involves a systems analysis approach (planning process) to problem solving mixed with the often messy and unpredictable behavior of the citizens and decision makers who are participating in the process. But one thing is clear: Local planning agencies, if they are going to be effective, can and must be innovative and entrepreneurial in providing products and services. And most importantly, prosperity and growth comes only for those individual public or private sector businesses that systematically find and exploit their potential.

5

Integrating Management and Leadership

. . . planning needs to be relegitimatized in the eyes of the public. ALAN RABINOWITZ

In a recent "Viewpoint" column in *Planning* magazine, Alan Rabinowitz, professor of urban planning at the University of Washington in Seattle, lamented the lack of heroic figures in planning.[1] He noted that in the past Robert Moses, Edward Logue, William Levitt, and a few others provided the heroic image that legitimatized modern-day planning, even though some of them were not actually members of the profession. Anthony Catanese pointedly observed that while Robert Moses, Edward Logue, and Edmund Bacon were not traditional planners they were, in fact, the most successful planners in their time.[2]

In the context used by Rabinowitz, a hero is a person admired for his or her achievements and qualities. It is clear that leadership is often a factor in the equation, also. Alan Rabinowitz has identified the need in the planning profession for the "heroic figure who can speak for the rest of us" and painfully reminds us that "most of us would be hard pressed to come up with an example when asked for the name of a nationally known planner."[3] It may be the time for planners to emulate the business community which appears to have a cornucopia of heroic figures and learn more about developing the leadership skills and characteristics which are so essential for success and recognition.

Many young, competent planners are aggressively seeking to advance to supervisory and managerial positions. Many of their résumés cite becoming planning director in a large city as their ultimate career goal. They are impatient for the opportunity to manage and direct a staff of support planners and eager to assume the mantle of authority. But neither their résumés nor their comments during job interviews indicate that they understand or appreciate the

leadership responsibilities that are connected with such management positions. They blindly aspire for an imaginary management
role where they can serve out their careers and live happily ever
after like they have seen in one of the films on the late show. Little
do they realize that it's more likely they will become a main course
on the dinner menu of *Creature Features*.

Many younger planners are steady and relentless in their progression from one planning position to the next. Norman Krumholz, former planning director of Cleveland and past president of
the American Planning Association, contends that "the curse of
the profession—and why planning is called ineffective—is that
the model is to stay for a couple of years, look for your chance, and
move up."[4] Adding to the problem is the movement of competent
public sector leaders into the private sector or from the planning
profession into more financially rewarding fields, such as public
administration or law.

One of the biggest obstacles for younger planners to overcome
in their efforts to rise to the top is the lack of preparation for becoming a manager. Most graduate-level planning programs do not
include courses on management and leadership. Many planners
move up the ladder simply because someone believes they are doing a good job. Once made a manager, they often are removed from
the situations for which they were trained and are placed in a new,
unfamiliar position—without adequate education, knowledge, or
understanding where, according to Professor J. Lee Rodgers, of the
University of Oklahoma, "they haven't the foggiest idea of what to
do." Professor Rodgers has suggested that planning educators
should recognize this defiencey and amend planning curriculums
to place more emphasis on the development of management skills.

Other planning authorities contend that graduate planning
programs should adjust their curriculums and provide training in a
broad inventory of management skills that will meet career advancement needs and "will appeal to more planning students for
careers in both business and local government."[5] Allan Hodges,
professional associate and planning department manager of Parsons Brinckerhoff Quade and Douglas Inc., Boston, and former
vice-chairman of the American Institute of Certified Planners
Commission, notes that some of the top management jobs in planning do go to nonplanners who have management skills, but that

> advancement . . . does occur when planners show evidence of skills in
> areas besides urban and regional planning—communication; business
> management; getting things done quickly; making decisions; financial

feasibility analysis; budgeting; personnel management; understanding what computers can and cannot do; fund raising; and dealing competently with professionals in other fields, such as law, engineering and politics.[6]

Critical to the complete education of planning students is an introduction to strategy. Jerome Kaufman, chairman of the Department of Urban and Regional Planning at the University of Wisconsin at Madison, states that the typical planning curriculum is not generally designed to teach strategies for successful intervention in the decision-making process. He believes that "coursework in decision theory, organization behavor, small group dynamics, conflict resolution, coalition management and communication theory would seem helpful."[7]

In addition to the educational disadvantages, there is a final significant obstacle to the development of leadership in the planning profession: the selection and hiring practices of some city managers. We indicated earlier that some city managers hire planners who are not qualified by education or by experience to successfully take on a leadership role for the planning department. Joseph Vitt, Jr., former director of the City Development Department in Kansas City, Missouri, reported that before his tenure, no director had stayed longer than a year and a half and that most had been public administrators, not degreed planners. He noted that "they were actually moving on to other jobs, but they happened to be heading this department while they were in a holding pattern."[8] Vitt believes the frequent changes in directors and their lack of knowledge of planning was one of the factors that had historically limited the effectiveness of the Kansas City department.

Many city managers appear indifferent about the need to employ knowledgeable planning directors with administrative and leadership skills; others want to weaken the influence and effectiveness of the planning department. More than one city manager has feared the influence of an established planning director and arranged for the individual's dismissal and replacement.

This latter situation was clearly illustrated in a city in the southwest during the early 1970s. The long-time planning director for that city was a respected and influential leader in his community and in the profession. A young, dynamic city manager who wanted to concentrate power and authority in the manager's office was able to force his retirement. A nonplanner from an unrelated department was transferred into the position of planning director and became a loyal and supportive subject of the city manager. The planning director was an excellent manager and eventually was promoted to assistant city manager, but he did not provide the leadership that was needed to maintain the historic effectiveness of the local planning program.

UNDERLED AND OVERMANAGED

Managers focus on doing things right; leaders focus on doing the right things. WARREN BENNIS

Warren Bennis, professor of management and organization at the University of Southern California at Los Angeles, has concluded that "for many years, American organizations have been underled and overmanaged."[9] United Technologies Corporation once used the following advertisement in the *Wall Street Journal* to capitalize on the growing interest in the issue of management versus leadership:

> Let's get rid of Management. People don't want to be managed. They want to be led. Whoever heard of a World Manager? World Leader, yes. Educational leader, political leader, religious leader, scout leader, community leader, labor leader, business leader—they lead; they don't manage. The carrot always wins over the stick. Ask your horse—you can lead your horse to water, but you can't manage him to drink. If you want to manage somebody, manage yourself. Do that well, and you'll be ready to stop managing.[10]

In his experience, Herbert Kelleher, president and chairman of the board of Southwest Airlines, has found that while we have "a lot of good managers—who are really needed . . . there is a paucity of leaders."[11] The sixty-four-dollar question is just what is the real difference between management and leadership.

In their recent book, *Leaders: The Strategies for Taking Charge*, Warren Bennis and Bert Nanus explore the theme that managers do things right, but leaders do the right thing.[12] Managers tend to work within the context of things as they are and make things function in accordance with rules and organization manuals. Herbert Kelleher illustrates this distinction between managers and leaders by pointing out that the leader is willing to step in and say, "Hey! This is unfair," whereas the manager tends to say, "Well, this is the way the organization works—I'm sorry that it happened this way."[13]

Expanding on this definitional issue, Sally Reed, county executive for Santa Clara County, California, suggests that in addition to doing the right thing, "a leader has a very strong, almost spiritual, sense of what is right for that individual."[14] In the public sector—where elected officials are responsible for setting policy and managers and department heads are charged with managing its day-to-day implementation—planners are challenged with having to develop collaborative roles in policy-making that will provide for both external and internal organizational leadership opportunities.

Reed contends that managers in public sector organizations are moving from management to leadership philosophies because "management failed us when it came to running local government." She argues that "particularly in government that monitoring didn't work, that work studies and time studies didn't work," and that even "management by objectives (MBO) didn't help us."[15] It is interesting to note that James McManus, respected owner of Marketing Corporation of America, contends that "the greatest disservice that the Harvard Business School has ever played on corporate American is management by objective."[16] McManus explained his concern with MBO by using the sports analogy of a football coach telling his team to win by a score of 21 to 7 and then having the players come back after the game to get paid based on whether they did better or worse than that. Fundamentally, he questions why the guy on the sidelines even gets to say what the score should be.[17]

Work program objectives that typically appear in many planning departments' annual budgets include the processing of a certain number of rezoning applications or completing a study or series of reports. In reality, the achievement of these objectives may be a useful indicator of service levels but it says nothing about the quality or the actual influence that such products and services have on the community. Measurement and quantification of various products and services is a poor substitute for the more significant indicators of effectiveness.

Another important distinction between management and leadership involves motivation responsibilities. Sally Reed has suggested that the popular phrase of "management by walking around" should by changed to "motivation by walking around."[18] Some of her further thoughts on this subject include:

> We aren't out managing; we're out leading. We're out talking to people, sharing our values with them, letting them get to know us, getting to know them in return. If there's anything that it's not, in my opinion, it's not management—it's motivation.[19]

There is a big difference between leadership and management, according to Bob Bolen, mayor of Fort Worth, Texas, but he also believes that success depends on having part of both. He contends that leaders often can envision something in the future that many people cannot see, but, "you have to have very good managers to maintain an operation once it is in force."[20]

STRATEGIES FOR EFFECTIVE LEADERSHIP

Leadership means vision, cheerleading, enthusiasm, love, trust, verve, passion, obsession, consistency, the use of symbols, paying attention as illustrated by the content of one's calendar, out-and-out drama (and the management thereof), creating heroes at all levels, coaching, effectively wandering around and numerous other things. TOM PETERS and NANCY AUSTIN

In their book *Creating Excellence*, Craig Hickman and Michael Silva state that "great businesses, government and nonprofit organizations owe their greatness to a few individuals who mastered leaderships skills" and, most importantly, who "passed those skills on to succeeding generations of executives and managers."[21] In their opinion, and in the opinion of most respected authorities, the record is clear and convincing: leadership can be learned by anyone and taught to everyone.

What makes a leader? Bennis and Nanus attempted to identify leadership characteristics by selecting and interviewing sixty corporate leaders and thirty public sector administrators who had clearly demonstrated leadership ability. They were careful to select leaders, not just managers. The surprising conclusion of their research efforts was that all ninety subjects had four leadership traits or characreristics in common which were classified into the following four strategies for effective leadership: Strategy I: attention through vision; Strategy II: meaning through communication; Strategy III: trust through positioning; and Strategy IV: the deployment of self-thought (1) positive self-regard and (2) the Wallenda Factor.[22]

VISION, VALUES, AND COMMUNICATION

President Reagan's success in the White House, like that of Franklin Roosevelt and John F. Kennedy, comes from his clear vision for the country and an ability to communicate it to voters. ARTHUR SCHLESINGER, JR.

The strategy of management of attention by vision involves the creating of focus, the development of an agenda, and an unparalleled concern with outcome. Bennis and Nanus found that leaders are results oriented and that results get attention. The intensity and commitment of the leaders serves as a magnet that draws others to their influence.

Abraham Zaleznick, professor at Harvard Business School, points out that leaders "are often obsessed by their ideas, which appear visionary, and excite, stimulate and drive other people to work hard and create reality out of fantasy."[23] Fort Worth Mayor Bolen contends that "vision is the one ingredient that separates managers from leaders."[24] *City and State* reported that San Antonio Mayor Henry Cisneros has focused his efforts on a program that provides a future vision of that city and that the program reflects a community consensus that what San Antonio needs is development. "The tenet of development," according to Cisneros, "has become a 'rallying theme' for the people of San Antonio."[25] In 1986, Cisneros was named to *City and State*'s first "All-Pro City Management Team." The judges—chosen from the private sector—were asked to select officials who were sensitive to the concerns of running a public entity but manage their responsibilities in much the same way that individuals in the private sector run the best-managed corporations. The judges were most impressed that Cisneros had a vision for the future of San Antonio and a coherent plan for bringing that vision alive.[26]

Vision is a mental journey from the known to the unknown, creating the future from a montage of current facts, hopes, dreams, dangers, and opportunities. True visionary leaders tend to see opportunities before they see threats. According to the research of Hickman and Silva, the visionary leader also:

- Searches for ideas, concepts, and ways of thinking until clear vision crystallizes.
- Persuades employees to embrace the vision by setting an example of hard work.
- Acts in a supportive, expressive way that says, "We are all in this together."
- Relates the vision to the cares and concerns of individuals.
- Concentrates on those strengths within the organization that will ensure the success of the vision.
- Remains at the center of the vision, as its prime shaper.
- Looks for ways to develop further the corporate vision by taking note of changes inside and outside the organization.
- Measures the success of the organization in terms of its ability to fulfill the vision.

- Articulates the vision into an easy-to-grasp philosophy that integrates strategic direction and cultural values.[27]

While the importance of vision and an orientation toward the future have always been valued by planners, there is a growing awareness of its value by managers in the private sector. Samuel Goldwyn, founder of MGM, is reputed to have said, "If I want to send a message, I'll call Western Union," but in *A Passion for Excellence—The Leadership Difference*, Tom Peters and Nancy Austin conclude that vision is the first step in leadership and that it must be communicated consistently and with fervor.[28] Bill Moore, president of Recognition Equipment in Dallas, Texas, thought that it would be rare to ask the question, "What are you trying to do in this company?" and get the same answer from all the employees. However, he suggested that "if you keep it simple and direct, you have a chance to achieve that consistent understanding."[29]

In *Corporate Pathfinders*, Harold Leavitt insisted that American business was founded by people who dared to dream, to create, to find a new path, and that pathfinding means creative leadership based upon vision, values, and determination. He found that pathfinding is the homeland of the visionary, the dreamer, the innovator, the creator, the entrepreneur and the charismatic leader.[30]

Edmund Bacon, the long-time director of planning for Philadelphia, was an effective developer and implementor of brilliant plans. Bacon taught many the values of commitment and dedication to visions.[31] He was proud of his influence and he attributed it to the power of his ideas and the correctness of his visions. In further explanation of his successes, he stated that:

> I always dealt with the future beyond the view of the mayor's cabinet, and, when they got there, they found me in possession; they found I had staked out the territory. By the time they became concerned with a problem, I had already developed a proposal.[32]

Michael Milken, recognized by *Forbes* magazine as one of the wealthiest and most powerful men in America, contends that "the scarcest resource today is management, knowledge, vision, dealing with change, recognizing what people want and need in the future, and the ability to work together."[33] Milken's opinion should be of particular interest to the planning profession because the management characteristics he values and believes to be in such short supply are, in fact, the characteristics exhibited by most successful planners. Effective planners have technical knowledge, vision, and an ability to deal with change. They are able to ascertain what people want and need in the future and they obviously have the ability to work with people.

Planners and city managers often must provide the leadership necessary for the development of the specific goals and objectives which create the vision upon which so much depends in local government. The author of the chapter on "Promoting the Community's Future" in *The Effective Local Government Manager* asked various experienced local government managers what they found to be the most effective method of promoting their community's future. Their responses varied widely, but "several managers emphasized the importance of managerial leadership in creating community goals and priorities."[34] Robert H. vanDeusen, village manager of Glenview, Illinois, specifically noted that the city staff may have to provide training and use third-party facilitators so that local public officials can work effectively and achieve consensus on community goals.[35] He added that "achievement of consensus on goals releases a great deal of energy in the staff" and "in the process the community's future is created."[36]

Michael Carroll, who served as the planning director and then deputy mayor of Indianapolis, contends that planners must have a goal of providing input into the goals-setting process of the local political administration. He explained that in Indianapolis this meant "assisting the Mayor in preparing the state-of-the-city address; assisting the Mayor in preparing the budget message; attempting to develop consensus and then translate that consensus into decision making; and participating in the goal- and objective-setting process in the community in the way that those decisions are made."[37]

Warren Bennis, in the keynote address at the 1986 International City Management Association Conference, stated that "leadership is an art developed around a four-letter word called hope."[38] He added that "hope means choices . . . and possibilities, no matter how grim the situation is looking.[39] Similarly, Anthony Catanese suggests that planning practice works best within the politics of optimism. His concept of the essential role of hope and optimism in the practice of planning is explained as follows:

> This means that an optimistic view of the future is prerequisite, and a fitting personality is needed to run the practice. The politics of optimism is part of the American fabric and heritage. The great cities of America were built by optimistic men and women who saw the future

as better than today. They were willing to make sacrifices now for a better tomorrow. They believed that anything was possible. The planning process can be efficacious only when it is practiced by people who also think that way.[40]

Regardless of the circumstances, it is essential for the staff to exhibit a positive, upbeat attitude. For example, when Dallas was experiencing a period of economic stagnation, the city manager urged the city staff to help the community believe in itself. He stated:

> The prophets of gloom and doom need to step aside and those with more heroic dreams need to step up to bat. We've got to focus on our strengths, announce them, report them and believe them.[41]

Planners have an important role in affirming the "can do" optimism that inspires community leaders and their followers to formulate a vision of a better tomorrow. Vision can be arrived at in many ways. James Fales, Jr., city manager of Redwood City, California, explained that he attempts to develop vision for his city by scheduling an annual meeting of the city council and all city boards, commissions, and committees with the city staff "to discuss various aspects of the city's future."[42] In addition, his top management staff meets for a full day once each quarter outside the city "to brainstorm major future policy issues. . . ."[43]During the 1986 Dallas budget hearings, Philip Sieb, a local urban columnist, pointed out that city manager Charles Anderson was increasingly taking on a leadership role in the community because the council was either unwilling or unable to provide adequate direction. Sieb noted that each member of the council was capable of discussing numbers in the budget, but that "strikingly absent was any statement of that councilman's philosophy: what his intellectual approach to budget issues is and what he thinks the future of Dallas should be."[44] Sieb argued that,

> Important decisions can't evolve simply from numbers-juggling. They must be based on a vision of what Dallas should be. Failure of elected officials to articulate such a vision is one of the reasons many in Dallas today question the council's competence.[45]

Planners need to be aware that a vision that cannot be understood is the same as no vision at all. Warren Bennis contends that "a vision is dead unless it is expressed and communicated to other people in a way that is meaningful."[46] Most successful planners can communicate and express themselves in a way that is understandable and useful to their clients. They don't use jargon and they use terms with which their clients are familiar and comfortable. Consider how Robert Wegner, former planning director of Tulsa and faculty member in the Regional and City Planning Department at the Univeristy of Texas at Arlington, describes the size of an acre: "An acre is approximately the size of a football field." Most people have trouble visualizing an acre, but they can easily picture a football field. Similarly, in writing this book, we tried to use metaphors, analogies, vignettes, and even humorous stories to illustrate and help get our meaning across and hopefully to help you understand and remember our findings.

External vision is important, but effective leadership also depends on the creation and communication of an internal vision for the department or agency—a "corporate culture." Every organization has values. Successful leadership involves the effective linkage of these values to the goals and objectives of the organization. Roy Pederson, city manager of Scottsdale, Arizona, is convinced that leaders must "insist on some values—absolutely and unswervingly—and then get out of the way."[47] Peters and Waterman called it the *loose-tight principle* and described it as "the co-existence of firm central direction and maximum individual autonomy."[48] They found that "organizations that live by the loose-tight principle are on the one hand rigidly controlled, and at the same time allow (indeed, even insist on) autonomy, entrepreneurship, and innovation from the rank and file."[49]

Loose-tight management relies on a relatively simple, well-defined, and well-understood vision, value system, or organizational culture. Perhaps the clearest application of the principle was provided by city manager Bill Kirchhoff in his unswerving commitment to serving the public in Arlington, Texas. (See Chapter 3.) Such attention and obsession with the customer is one of the tightest properties of all and is one of the most stringent means of self-discipline. In Arlington, it was also accompanied by an equally strong commitment to individual autonomy, authority, and responsibility.

The value system or culture that was espoused by Norman Krumholz, former planning director for Cleveland, sustained the city's planning department through the wide-ranging political philosophies of three different administrations over a ten-year period. Krumholz proudly articulated his values in a *Journal of the American Planning Association* article:

> Regardless of who was mayor, the staff of the Cleveland planning commission consistently operated in a way that was activist and interventionist in style and redistributive in objective. Our overriding goal was to provide a wider range of choices for those Cleveland residents who have few, if any choices.[50]

In an article on surviving as a planning director, Sylvia Lewis found that "behind the strategy and tactics and all the staff effort lies an overall goal, the heart of the planning director's job" and that it wasn't a tangible product such as a plan or ordinance but rather "a personal belief or philosophy about what is best for a particular city."[51] Jerome Kaufman contends that each planning agency "needs a well-conceived set of policies to serve as normative guideposts toward which its intervention activities are directed. . . ."[52] In *Personality, Politics and Planning*, Anthony Catanese interviewed seven nationally recognized planners and found that each could easily describe an overriding goal for planning their respective cities. (See Table 5-1.) He was particularly impressed by Norman Krumholz's guiding statement and noted that it was extraordinarily useful because "it clearly defined a framework and set of constraints that give a basis for specification of daily city planning activities."[53] In an interview several years later, Norman Krumholz pointed out that a clearly defined value or culture "gives you great clarity and great power. You can think clearly about each issue: Who gets? Who pays?"[54]

When Dennis Wilson, former director of planning for Dallas, first became director of that department, he found "morale was at an all-time low, and the department was split into parochial fiefdoms." His initial response was to take a series of immediate actions designed to "establish good communications with staff and to make them feel good about themselves." Within three months of his appointment, he drafted a statement of departmental goals and objectives that focused on two goals for the planning department: (1) to provide the highest possible level of *service* to the city manager's office and other departments, to city council and other boards, commissions and committees, and to interest groups and members of the public, and (2) to provide organizational and professional *leadership* within city hall and the community at large in creating a more economically healthy city and a more attractive and functional living environment.

The four-page statement reflected Wilson's attitudes and addressed his vision of where the department should go and how he expected the staff to perform. His staff supported the proposals and was enthusiastic about developing a direction for the department.

A strong successful culture allows employees to unify behind a common purpose, deliver superior performance, and pass along skills to others. Culture building means selecting, motivating, rewarding, retaining, and unifying good employees. Strong departmental or agency cultures, like strong family cultures, come from within and are built by leaders. Hickman and Silva found that culture building involves three steps: instilling commitment, rewarding competence, and maintaining consistency.

Table 5–1

Goal Comparison

Planner - City	Goals
Eplan - Atlanta	"to make the city tolerable to live in … the basic common denominator there is to design a city where you can raise a child … and to help guide the decisions … toward a common goal…"
Krumholz - Clevland	"promoting a wider range of choice for those Cleveland residents who have few if any choices."
Carrol - Indianapolis	"input into the goals-setting process … [and] budget-making process …"
Vitt - Kansas City	"The overriding goal of the department is to help the city as a whole and each subarea … work toward performing closer to the potential that exists …"
Drew - Milwaukee	"We decided that fiscal balance would be our overall goal and the cornerstone of our comprehensive planning program efforts."
Bonner - Portland	"Less is enough is really where it is at."
Spaid - St.Paul	"The overiding goal … has two perspectives: neighborhood stability and economic viability."

Source: Catenese, <u>Personality, Politics, and Planning</u>, Sage Publications, 1978, p. 189.

Roy Pederson, city manager of Scottsdale, Arizona, warns that you must "make sure that ancillary systems support value management."[55] For instance, the newly employed planning director for Fort Worth found that the existing compensation system was at cross-purposes with the values that he was trying to instill in the department. He wanted to promote loose-tight properties with special emphasis on team building and the delegation of authority, responsibility, and autonomy to the lowest professional levels in the department. Yet the city's compensation system was based on annual across-the-board cost of living adjustments and a series of programmed annual increases that made it close to impossible to link performance with compensation. Fortunately, the city was shifting to a merit-based compensation program with salary adjustments being determined by individual performance.

Still another significant obstacle had to be faced. In Fort Worth, the formal personnel classification system for the planning department recognized three levels of professional positions below the assistant directors: senior planner, associate planner, and planner. The primary distinction between these positions was an artificial increase in supervisory duties and responsibilities. To gain a promotion involving a reclassification, it was necessary for the planner to be assigned additional supervisory responsibilities. Instead, planners should be recognized by their talents, not their titles.

The consulting firm of Parsons-Brinckerhoff has a professional associate program which recognizes and rewards excellence in performance regardless of title or supervisory responsibility. If someone wants to be the best draftsman in the world he or she is encouraged to achieve that goal; success isn't tied to becoming a project manager or department head. According to Allan Hodges, "It works!"

Peters and Austin reported that "perhaps the best and clearest signal of what's important, what is being paid attention to, especially in times of change, is who gets promoted, when, and for what."[56] In contrast to the Parsons-Brinckerhoff example, financial incentives and status symbols were being used to instill the goal of becoming a supervisor in all employees of the Fort Worth planning department. Yet with more supervisors, it was also more difficult for lower level planners to be allowed the authority, responsibility, and autonomy that the director valued. After each promotion, there invariably would also be an increased emphasis on unnecessary and undesirable supervision and a decrease in production from the individuals who had previously been exhibiting superior performance.

The director became increasingly disappointed and frustrated with the system. When a senior planner position became open, the director discovered that most of the internal applicants were seeking the position because they wanted to become supervisors. No mention was made of a desire to gain more authority and responsibility or freedom and autonomy in their work. There was little recognition of the values which the director had been articulating for the department. The last straw involved a senior planner working on a small team project who remarked that his particular assignment was not senior-level work.

With backing of the assistant city manager and the assistance of the personnel department, the planning department was reorganized specifically to support the values and vision of the director. All three classifications of planners were consolidated into a new associate planner position. The job description for this new position was rewritten to be truly reflective of the meaning of the word "associate." Under the new system, associate planners form a pool of professionals who are assigned to designated sections but also are expected to work on teams with other planners on special projects, programs, or activities. Team leaders are selected on a rotating but competitive basis that recognizes technical expertise, initiative, enthusiasm, and a commitment and ability to deliver an effective product. Salary adjustments are based exclusively on individual performance evaluations, and beyond the financial incentives is the real objective of offering a sense of mission and purpose to as many planners as possible. Every planner has the opportunity to become a pioneer, a champion, a leader and to develop a sense of being part of the best. Each can be an effective planner whose work is meaningful, respected, and valued.

Another important aspect of the Fort Worth planning department reorganization was the elimination of the word "supervise" from all of the job descriptions. Leadership and management responsibilities were required for several administrative positions, but it was emphasized that the individuals holding these positions were also responsible for performing the more complex technical studies. Equally important, they were responsible for keeping informed about emerging technologies and innovative programs, projects, and activities and for seeing them transferred and applied to the department's work program. Another adjustment was to expand the number of sections from three to five—thereby creating more opportunities for leadership and autonomy while also reducing the size of each section.

In Fort Worth, the planning director has tried to get away from what Rosabeth Moss Kanter identified in *The Change Masters* as "segmentalism" and to provide for an integrative and participative work environment. It is a fluid, nonhierarchial management structure where an individual's influence and authority are subject to negotiation and where power is willingly shared.

Other changes that the director emphasized included:

1. Encouragement of pride and increased recognition of personal and team achievements.

2. Acquisition of additional microcomputer hardware and software.

3. Reallocation of budget funds to provide for the production of more and higher quality publications.

4. Improvement of internal lateral communications.

5. Increased and earlier information about the new projects and services that were being developed.

A new employee in the Fort Worth planning department conducted a survey designed to explore various job satisfaction issues and the perceived effect that the recent reorganization had on the department's personnel. The survey revealed a high degree of job satisfaction throughout the department. More specifically, 80 percent of the planners with ten or more years of experience gave the highest ratings to morale and job satisfaction. The same cohort of planners also indicated that they had a high degree of influence on the department's procedures and policies.

The same survey also asked about the impact of the team concept approach to planning. The response from the more experienced planners was that it was "generally perceived as helping individual, division, and interdivisional productivity equally." There was a wider range of responses from the less experienced planners with the team concept being "perceived as helping individual productivity to the highest degree, with division and interdivisional productivity support being quite splintered."

The experience of the Fort Worth planning department has been consistent with the findings of Peters and Waterman that smaller entities are usually the most efficient and effective; that "the turned-on, motivated, highly productive worker, in communication (and competition) with his peers, outproduces the worker in the big facilities time and again."[57] Peters and Waterman found this to be true for plants, for project teams, for divisions, and for whole companies; we found it to be true for sections, divisions, and departments in the many local government organizations with which we are familiar.

In *Corporate Pathfinders*, Harold Leavitt noted that people's work values are influenced far more by the small groups they work with every day than by directions from distant figures at the top.[58] Peer pressure is the toughest control of all: People might be able to fool the manager but it is exceedingly difficult to fool peers. Leavitt suggested that if people can gradually be made to feel uncomfortable about their old values, and if any movement toward new values is rewarded, they will eventually come around. Peer pressure, in particular, is the best ally in this.[59]

In the Fort Worth planning department, flexibility and freedom are achieved because the management and operating "rules" have a challenging, positive cast as can be seen in the job description provided in Figure 5-1. Innovation and entrepreneurial expectations, a focus on problem solving and responsiveness to clients, an emphasis on expansion and improvement, a commitment to quality, and strong reliance on team work are all reflected. It is the sharing of these essential values that provides the tight institutional framework which, in turn, permits and even demands the autonomy, responsibility, innovativeness, and a willingness to take risks that is expected of each planner. The paradox is real: Discipline provides the framework for freedom which enables planners and planning agencies to become more effective.

Leaders rely on others to get things done. They have high expectations and they get results. They create and sustain a positive, demanding climate for their organizations. They care but they don't carry. The following is a summary of a memo from a caring but demanding city manager who expects his employees to be the best and who accepts no less:

> While the productivity and performance of many departments and/or divisions is strong, there are pockets of deterioration heretofore ignored for one reason or another. This has been exhibited by mismanaged projects, administrative incompetencies, substandard management practices, and timidity of leadership. Given your resources and

authority, responsibility for performance, good or bad, lies with the Department Head.

It was only a few months ago that this City could compete with any in terms of quality service delivery. We are now growing complacent, non-demanding, accommodative, and argumentative. We have retreat-

Figure 5-1

Typical Planning Job Description

Classification: Chief Planner

Class Summary: This position reports to the Planning Director and is primarily responsible for directing, reviewing, coordinating, and managing the work of professional, technical, and clerical employees in a major division of the Planning Department.

Examples of Duties:

1.   Develops an aggressive, innovative, and entrepreneurial annual work program and budget request for the division based on a service to the customer and client philosophy.

2.   Performs the more complex technical studies.

3.   Leads, directs, and coordinates teams involved in the production and delivery of quality products and services for the division or department.

4.   Represents the department at meetings with other agencies, city departments, and private organizations.

5.   Speaks before civic, community, governmental, and professional groups to explain and promote the products and services of the division.

6.   Participates in senior-level staff conferences.

7.   Makes recommendations on employment and is responsible for performance evaluations of employees in the division.

8.   Prepares manuscripts and articles for journals, newsletters, and other miscellaneous planning publications and presents programs and lectures at conferences.

9.   Keeps informed about emerging technologies and innovative programs, projects, and activities, and transfers and applies this information to the division's work program.

10.   Establishes challenging and measurable goals and objectives for each member of the staff and is responsible for motivating and monitoring performances.

11.   Evaluates the effectiveness of the division in responding to customer problems and concerns and is responsible for making the division and department more effective each year.

Source: Planning Department, City of Fort Worth, 1987.

ed from the necessary challenge of revitalizing and invigorating our individual shares of responsibility. We have taken on the bureaucratic tendencies we abhor.

The solution is relatively simple. First and foremost is the requirement that you demand excellent work products from your respective management teams. Your involvement, particularly where productivity is below an acceptable level, will require leadership that balances positive reinforcement with toughness when necessary. Persistence is vital and I want to underscore the necessity for immediacy of action. Your personal attention and direct intervention is an absolute necessity. It is critical that you avoid the substitution of rules, procedures, and other bureacratic tendencies for what each of us ultimately gets paid for—judgement and decision making.

In order to move the organization out of its current lethargy, personnel changes, reorganization and a redefining of duties will probably be required by the Manager's Office. From Department Heads it will require a more intensified, aggressive, and results-oriented managerial posture than has been the norm during the past months.

According to William Claire, a respected management and planning consultant, a leader/manager must constantly monitor and assess the climate of the organization. Leaders realize the importance of communication and are constantly asking for feedback.[61] Claire cites George S. Patton as a brilliant practitioner of management by walking around and offers the following observation:

His movements among his military units gave him an instant assessment of the condition, morale, and discipline of his troops. This constant vigilance also allowed him to transmit his vision of the military goals he was asked to achieve.[62]

Climate builders are extremely important to all organizations, according to Gene Bedley, noted author and educator, who also stated that they have the following characteristics:

They seek a balance between productivity and satisfaction.

They never build their own ego at the expense of others.

They influence a change toward positive climate and morale problems, rather than making excuses for them.

They have faith in people, which is evidenced by their consistent and compassionate response to others' needs.

They analyze needs by intensely listening to others. They convey that people's ideas will be carefully considered and implemented when possible.

They show special care by their interest in others' personal problems as well as job-related challenges.

They have an enthusiasm that causes others to want to work with and for them.

They enhance the climate by enabling people to reach beyond their grasp.

They have an inviting spirit.

They have a positive mental attitude that fosters both encouragement and praise toward others.

They contribute toward the cohesiveness of the organization by compromise, so as to obtain group goals.

They are the eternal learners that they want others to be.

They celebrate successes along with identifying problems.

They remember what their employer and others have done for them.

They are as intrinsically motivated to spread the good news of others' accomplishments as they are of their own.

They view problems as questions that need to be answered.

They care.[63]

Effective climate builders are committed to communication and tend to have an open-door management style. One troubled planner told us, "Oh, yeah, we have an open door policy here. If you don't like something you can open the door and leave." A valuable tool for effective communication in many organizations is the internal newsletter. We were particularly impressed with the bimonthly "Scanning Planning" newsletter published by the Dallas planning department. The typical issue included such features as a personal message from the planning director, an introduction to new employees, an in-depth interview of an employee or group of employees including some of their personal activities and interests, recognition of jobs well done, and updates and notices of various activities and equipment. This newsletter is highly personalized and it demonstrates a caring attitude toward the people in the department.

It is not simple or easy for leaders to make the changes that are needed to make people and institutions more effective. In *Strategies for Planned Change,* Zaltman and Duncan warned that "change agents concerned with altering organizations must have familiarity with change processes among individuals . . . and change agents concerned with altering the behavior of individuals must know something about change processes in organizations."[64] Their complex book provides valuable information on organizational dynamics and the dynamics of interpersonal relations. Unfortunately, as reported in a book review by Jerome Kaufman, "this is not an easy book for planners to read." But he also adds that "because it contains many insightful and useful principles, developed from a careful harvesting of the increasingly fertile fields of innovation diffusion and organizational change research, it does have value for those who want to become more effective change agents."[65]

PERSONAL STYLE AND EFFECTIVENESS

Our success lies not in ourselves—but in our relationships. HENRY C. ROGERS

Human relations is an essential aspect of effective leadership. All patterns of behavior or personal style can be effective depending on the situation and circumstance. Generally, if someone relates well to us, we describe that person's style with favorable adjectives; if not, we will tend to use unfavorable terms.

A leader who is effective in one situation may not be effective in another. You might think this conflicts with our earlier findings that most planners control the significant factors which influence or determine their effectiveness. What it simply means is that planners have to use different styles, strategies, and tactics depending on the circumstances of each situation in which they find themselves.

The key to effectiveness, according to David Merrill and Roger Reid in *Personal Styles and Effective Performance*, appears to be versatility.[66] They describe versatility as the ability "to create and maintain valuable interpersonal relationships" and to deal with others "in such a way that they come away from encounters with us feeling better about themselves, thanks to what we said and did."[67] It is the amount of effort that we put into a relationship that greatly determines our personal effectiveness. Versatility is an aspect of style. Effective planners adjust their styles to fit the environment in which they operate. Successful professionals change their styles, not their clients.

Our findings concerning style are consistent with those reported by Anthony Catanese in *Personality, Politics, and Planning*. Catanese found that personality is an important factor in the success of planners and that to be effective, "a planner needs a good style."[68] He concluded that personality and style are not acquired in school, they "are behavioral and belief patterns developed over a period of time through experience and interaction with an environment and groups within it."[69]

Case Study: We believe that Norman Standerfer exemplifies what good style in planning is all about. Several years ago, he was appointed director of the office of planning for Broward County, Florida. He was given an ordinance that had been developed to implement charter home rule subdivision authority throughout the county and told to be prepared for extremely vocal opposition at the public hearing from twenty-nine mayors, the development community, and assorted lobbyists and politicians.

Nearing the end of nearly three hours of adamant opposition to the proposed ordinance, the county administrator, sensing that the county commission's frustration level was appropriately stressed, indicated that the county's new planning director was in attendance and might have a few comments and observations to make prior to their vote. On cue, Standerfer approached the dais to make his first public appearnace before the commission and set in motion the first elements of a high-risk strategy of decisive intervention. He voiced emphatic support for the commission to implement their charter regulatory authority countywide, despite vocal opposition. He also observed that some basic problems relating to his department's ability to administer the ordinance were anticipated and that there was apparent misunderstanding by many opponents caused by the organization and format of the proposed ordinance. He concluded with a startling request that, if given ninety days, he would personally redraft the ordinance, work with representatives of the opposing forces and interests, and return with a revised ordinance that would have broad support. A ninety-day continuance was unanimously approved.

In the two weeks preceding the public hearing, Standerfer had outlined his recommendations to the county administrator. The strategy which evolved embraced multiple windows of opportunity. The first element was to claim ownership and responsibility of the planning office for the revised product and adoption process. A second element involved a reconstitution of the single-purpose platting ordinance into the format of a state legislatively enabled land development code. A third strategic issue involved immediately achieving the needed restructuring and streamlining of the county's permit and regulatory processes. None of these strategic opportunities could be achieved by the proposed ordinance.

Four days following commission continuance, Standerfer held his first of a series of all-day, two-day per week work sessions with an ad hoc group of representatives, developers, local consultants and engineers, attorney lobbyists, and environmental groups. After being introduced personally for the first time to the attending adversarial group, he distributed a one-page outline and format for his version of a new ordinance. During his opening comments, he suggested that they both had problems with the proposed ordinance and that he intended to address those problems line by line. Standerfer indicated his intention to personally redraft the ordinance within ninety days and with their help, the county commission would adopt a better ordinance. He made it absolutely clear that he would make no concessions regarding charter powers and authority or substantive regulatory or plan consistency requirements but that he intended to simultaneously develop sweeping reforms in the bureaucracy by streamlining and developing expeditious processing procedures. He also pledged to support and advocate adoption of any and all other revised language necessary to achieve the support of each adversarial group.

Standerfer appeared before the commission advocating adoption of the new ordinance on shedule. He defended—provision by provision—language designed to mitigate the concerns of those previously against portions of the ordinance. Adversary after adversary rose to support the fruits of the compromise. The ordinance, adopted in 1981 almost verbatim as transmitted, received much acclaim for its innovative provisions concerning impact fees and regulatory streamlining and was awarded the award of merit from the Florida chapter of the American Planning Association.

Participants and observers of this remarkable transformation credit Standerfer's decisive intervention, bias for action, and penchant for innovative change as the turning point in Broward County's planning and regulatory development. His skill in forging consensus solutions to seemingly no-win issues was credited for bringing "ouchless development" to Broward County. His entrepreneurial management style, disdain for bureaucracy, and his strategic "chunking" of issues to achieve significant increments of positive, innovative change led to later pioneering innovations in Broward County regarding computer automation and the "TRIPS" model for road impact fees.[70]

CARING AND TRUST

Manipulation is getting people to act for you in ways that may not neces-
sarily be for their own good. Motivation is helping people recognize mutual
interests and getting them to join the "cause" because there is a benefit for
them as well as you. ZIG ZIGLAR

In *The Transformational Leader*, Noel Tichy and Mary Devanna contend that America's scarcest natural resource is leadership and that
the entire industrialized world is in the midst of major upheaval
and transformation that requires a new type of leadership—"transformational" leadership.[71] Such leadership is based on a process
"that is systematic, consisting of puposeful and organized search
for changes, systematic analysis, and the capacity to move resources from areas of lesser to greater productivity."[72]

Transformational leaders are able to stimulate and inspire performance through a climate of openness and trust, according to
Bernard Bass in *Leadership and Performance Beyond Expectations*.[73]
Tichy and Devanna state that such leaders are characterized by the
"values of caring and trust that no one will be penalized for cooperation and that sacrifice as well as rewards will be equitable."[74]

Trust is a two-way street and without mutual trust, leadership is
not possible. From management's perspective, Peter Drucker notes
that "a relationship of trust . . . requires confidence on the part of
the superior that the subordinate manager will play to the boss's
strengths and safeguard the boss against his or her limitations and
weaknesses."[75]

"Trust," to Bennis and Nanus, "is the emotional glue that binds
followers and leaders together" and "it must be earned."[76] Roy Pederson, city manager of Scottsdale, Arizona, shares the view that to
be a leader, your employees "have to like you, trust you, respect
you."[77] Trust is essential and he argues that "you can't just say it;
you've got to act it out, you've got to do it, you've got to prove it."[78]

In the popular movie *Top Gun*, Tom Cruise played an outstanding pilot who was not trusted by his peers or his superiors. They
knew he was capable and technically competent but he was also
unpredictable, self-centered, and didn't follow the rules. In other
words, he couldn't be trusted. It was only after he himself learned
the importance of the organization's team work culture and demonstrated that he could be depended upon in a life-threatening situation that he was able to earn the trust and respect of his peers.

An individual's predictability with respect to organizational values is a key aspect of trust and one reason why it is important for leaders and organizations to have clear values that are constantly being communicated and reinforced with employees. Harold Leavitt warned that leaders *must* remember their values and enforce them.[79] Responses to both appropriate behavior or infractions must be predictable and constantly demonstrated.

Bobby Valentine, coach of the Texas Rangers, took his team from worst to almost first during the 1985 and 1986 baseball seasons. He developed a guiding vision, or culture, and successfully communicated it to the team. Within a framework of an aggressive and risk-oriented approach to the game, the players were given unprecedented authority to exercise their independent judgment and were not penalized for mistakes. But perhaps most important was the trusting, open, and truly caring relationship that he established with each of his players. The essence of trust is the feeling that you really care about people. Gary Ward, a team veteran, made the following observations about Bobby Valentine:

> All the other managers I've had stressed the game. You have to play, play, play, and that's all that mattered. Bobby's not that way. Bobby's 100 percent for baseball, but he's 110 percent for you and your family. I've talked to him a lot of times and found that he really cares about you. You can talk to him about whatever is troubling you. Bobby's the first manager to understand me, to really care about me as a person.[80]

A caring manager is a more effective leader. Jim Duncan, former director of land development services for Austin, Texas, and one of the most successful and respected planners in the country, provides an excellent example of a leader who cares. In recent years, almost sixty new employees had been added to his department because of the introduction of a sophisticated, labor-intensive zoning ordinance and a tremendous increase in the volume of permitting activity due to Austin's rapid population and employment growth.

When the growth rate subsided and development activity declined, the department budget was not able to support the high staffing levels. The new budget adopted by the council required a reduction of thirty-two employees from his department and approximately eighty from other departments. Immediately after adoption of the budget, Duncan told his assistants that they would have an increased administrative work load during the next two months because he would be spending almost 100 percent of his time assisting these displaced employees in finding new positions.

In addition to using his extensive contacts around the country to arrange for interviews, the department provided air fares and covered other related expenses such as long distance telephone charges and printing of résumés. When one planner called from Tampa and excitedly announced that he had accepted an attractive position, Duncan told him to go to the best restaurant in town, have a proper celebration, and bring him the bill.

Many city employees from the various departments had appeared at the city budget hearings to protest the proposed personnel reductions, but only one person from the planning staff spoke against the decision and he did so only after praising the director for the care and concern which he had shown to all the employees. He reported that Duncan had even spent a Saturday morning helping him develop a more effective résumé. The director's commitment to his employees was recognized and appreciated not only by the people being laid off; Duncan's caring attitude helped him earn the trust and respect of the entire staff.

Thus, the transformational leader, in the view of Bernard Bass, earns the trust and respect of staff and "inspires them to a vision of what they might accomplish with extra effort."[81] Bass surveyed ninety leaders and they identified the traits or characteristics of leaders that had influenced them, including:

Led them into working "ridiculous" hours to do more than they ever expected to do.

Inspired them to innovation.

Treated a subordinate as an equal, despite having greater knowledge and experience.

Was willing to share that greater knowledge and experience.

Encouraged the subordinate with advice, help, support, recognition, and openness.

Was a good listener.

Gave autonomy to subordinates and furthered their self-development.

Could be formal at work when necessary.

Was firm and would reprimand when necessary.

Could be counted on to stand up for his people.[82]

The Golden Rule—do unto others as you would have them do unto you—is another way of stating the fact that consideration for others is essential to the foundation of openness and trust upon which good employee relations depend. Such relationships can be built on both a collective or individual bases, but the importance of personal relationships cannot be minimized. Roderick P. Deighen, head of the Patrick-Douglas Outplacement Firm in Cleveland, Ohio, reports that "an important feature of executive success and survival is the conscious development of personal power basing with the company" and that the key ingredient "is personal support of others, be they peers, superiors, or subordinates."[83] Sometimes it is hard to differentiate between leadership and fellowship.

Effective planning leaders are adept at creating and sustaining good interpersonal and social relationships. Jerome Kaufman says that planners "should have the capacity to span the boundaries, or reduce the distances, between themselves and other actors in the decision process."[84] He has found that if plans are going to be accepted and acted upon then "planners of all persuasions must become involved in social relations with others."[85]

Public sector employees want from their managers the same things that people in the private sector want. Bill Jamieson, Jr., former chairman of the governor's cabinet in Arizona says they want "to make a good living for their family, to have pride in their work, to believe in what they do, and to have some job satisfaction and some fun."[86] He adds that "public employees want to have good leaders" and they "want you to respect them professionally."[87]

Competence is an essential prerequisite for trust. Senate Majority Leader Robert Byrd of West Virginia noted that "without competence . . . government will have a tough time earning the nation's trust, and government without trust is government without power."[88] While there are many proven ways to earn the trust and respect of others, Sally Reed believes that first and foremost "that person has to earn his or her own self-respect, as a manger, as a leader, and as a person in the position he or she holds."[89] Each individual must decide if he or she is really ready and capable of leading an organization. If the answer is yes and it reflects an understanding of the integration of leadership and management practices discussed here, then that person is in a position to be the leader of an effective planning agency.

A leader of a planning organization also must earn the trust and confidence of the public officials who are being served. What specific actions can planners take to build trust and respect? Robert Einsweiler developed trust by delivering a product or service that worked. People respect results, but sometimes results are not enough. The successful leader "not only has to try to get the right things done, he or she must show how it is done and convince the governing body and the public that the job *is* being done well."[90]

The following story illustrates this point. After the planning staff had completed updating the twenty-five-year-old Beaumont Zoning Ordinance, the retiring mayor told the planning director that he wanted to hear and read about their success. Subsequently, articles and references appeared in *Urban Land, TML Texas Town & Cities, Planning, Zoning and Planning Law Report,* an American Planning Association *PAS Report,* and an International City Management Association book, *Shaping the Local Economy.* The director also spoke about the success of their local effort at various regional, state, and national conferences on land use regulations. The zoning ordinance became an issue in the following election and a member of the planning commission who had been a champion of the new ordinance was overwhelmingly elected as mayor. The planning director and the department had delivered a quality product and had aggressively and successfully campaigned for and earned the community's respect and affirmation. Their success was verified by the election results.

Success renews the sense of respect and self-worth. Returning to the earlier example of Bobby Valentine and the Texas Rangers, the team's general manager commented that "not only are we making strides with wins and losses, but we have renewed the respect the fans have for this organization."[91] Pete O'Brien, who plays first base for the Rangers, added that "the players are proud of what the organization is doing. What is going on helps everybody out as a human being. It gives them a sense of self-worth."[92]

THE DEVELOPMENT OF SELF

If you think you've completed your education (and it doesn't matter when), you are on a fast track to personal obsolescence. DENNIS WAITLEY and ROBERT TUCKER

In their research and analysis of ninety leaders, Bennis and Nanus found that these individuals had an extraordinary commitment to learning and that "leaders are perpetual learners."[93] More specifically, they concluded that "learning is the essential fuel for the leader, the source of high-octane energy that keeps up the momentum by continually sparking new understanding, new ideas, and new challenges."[94] Jack Rains, former chairperson of the Houston-based 3D/International design and management consulting firm and currently Texas secretary of state, possesses these characteristics. He has worked as a night disc jockey, merchant seaman, steelworker, and lawyer. He is proud of his accomplishment and says "I don't fit into neat molds. My test is, am I learning something every day and is it fun? I'm always into challenges."[95]

Dennis Waitley and Robert Tucker, in *Winning the Innovation Game*, found that successful innovators were lifelong learners and that "their love of learning springs from a natural curiosity."[96] They added that innovators want to know not just *how* but *why* and they described their hunger for knowledge as follows.

> Their pattern of learning tends to approximate what is known in eating circles as "binging"; they become fascinated with a topic and delve into it headlong, reading all the books they can find on the subject, amassing dozens of articles, and seeking out the top experts.[97]

In an attempt to learn more about success—how people attain it, how they handle it, and what it means to them—George Gallup, Jr. and Alec Gallup surveyed more than 1,500 achievers listed in Marquis's *Who's Who in America*.[98] One of the common characteristics was a specialized knowledge of their field. "Do your homework," advised one particularly successful leader, noting that "nothing helps success more than knowing what you're doing."[99]

Almost all of us learn new things each day so you might be asking yourself, "What's so special and important about learning as it relates to leaders and leadership?" Bennis and Nanus found that "leaders have discovered not just how to learn," but more importantly, "how to learn in an organizational context."[100] In essence, leaders concentrate and focus their energies on the areas which matter most to their organizations. Equally important, leaders are able to inspire others to expand their knowledge and skills. Learners must be recognized and rewarded by their organizations.

In *Making City Planning Work*, Allan Jacobs pointed out that developing a competent staff was an important first step in building the influence and power of a planning agency.[101] Sylvia Lewis's article on surviving as a planning director stated that the top planners she interviewed all agreed that technical competence comes first.[102] The director who fears having a competent staff and who is threatened by individuals showing initiative and entrpreneural behavior will not have an effective agency.

Many young graduates from planning schools are content to rest on their new degrees. They don't realize that a degree is just

the beginning and that the degree, *with* experience *and* a commitment to continuing education, makes it possible to develop the
management skills and knowledge necessary to be an effective
planner. Several planners we talked to blamed their lack of success
on an inadequate education; they assumed that something was
wrong with the school they attended and its programs. Over the
years there has been a steady stream of criticism about the technical scope and quality of education provided by graduate planning
programs. We believe that most planning curriculums can be
strengthened as suggested in the beginning of this chapter, but we
are more interested in reminding educators of the importance of
instilling in students a respect, if not a love, for continuing education. Mortimer Adler, chairman of the board of directors of *Ency-
clopaedia Britannica*, has suggested that "the very best thing for our
schools to do is prepare the young for continued learning in later
life by giving them the skills of learning and the love of it."[103]

Several years ago, Ross Perot told a group at the Harvard Business School that he would give the University an A-plus for the
quality of the students it attracts and an F for what it does to them.
But he assured the students that in due course most of them would
shrug off their educational experience and go out and be successful. The gist of Perot's speech was "that if they (the students) don't
come out of school and get dirty, they won't learn the skills they
need . . . to become successful."[104]

Allan Hodges contends that if planners are going to advance in
the profession they must understand that "the master's degree in
planning is no longer sufficient as an end product" and they must
"build on that foundation by enrolling in continuing education
courses to acquire skills needed for higher-level positions."[105] Peter
Drucker has suggested that "individuals will increasingly have to
take responsibility for their own continuous learning and relearn-
ing, for their own self-development, and for their own careers."[106]
Yet only a few planners are responding to the practical continuing
education programs that have been developed by the American
Planning Association, the American Institute of Certified Planners, and various universities. There, unfortunately, is great truth
in the ancient saying that awareness of ignorance is the beginning
of wisdom, and it was Jean Toomer who noted that "most novices
picture themselves as masters—and are content with the picture.
This is why there are so few masters."

It is essential to never cease learning, and the best possible graduate of the best possible school needs to continue learning as much as the least educated. When we shared this opinion with one planner he said, "That's good advice but it's like me going home and telling my dog to get smart. What do you recommend for people who really are interested and want to know how to learn?" In our view, the most important thing a planner can do to further his or her learning and to increase effectiveness is to read and discuss. Read everything available. But, as Mortimer Adler noted, "never just read, for reading without discussion with others who have read the same book is not nearly as profitable."[107] Discussion is the key. It is no accident that this book was written by two people. Our views and ideas were developed, refined and perfected by vigorous give-and-take exchanges. Learning and working together, we achieved what we could not have done as individuals.

Philip Crosby, corporate vice-president of ITT and author of several management books, offered the following advice on how to learn:

> Read at least one magazine every day and three or four books a month (on any subject from history to sex). Dig up several good conversations each week . . . It's not possible to know what you need to learn. Therefore, you have to constantly seek out new experiences and exposure. Some of the new magazines, or movies, or cultures may turn you off. But they are real. They need to be understood a little, if only so you can know how to deal with them or the effect they create.[108]

Another important ingredient of the learning process is a willingness to take risks and even fail based on an understanding that you can learn and prosper from the experience. This is a recurring theme in our work that has been touched upon in other chapters. Joe Paterno, who has compiled one of the best records in college football as Pennsylvania State's head coach, stated that having a bad start in his first year on the job was probably the best thing that ever happened to him. He concluded that "had we been moderately successful, I never would have questioned the way I was coaching. Now I constantly question everything I do."[109]

Paterno also believes that even when you lose you must continue to believe in yourself and to play with extreme confidence or you will lose again. Losing can become a habit and too many planners are good losers. For successful leaders like Paterno, failure is a springboard to success.

In the preface, we noted that most successful planners show initiative, take risks, make mistakes, and most important of all, learn from their failures and become more effective. We must admit that we were surprised at the ease and eagerness with which successful planners shared their not-so-successful stories with us.

In contrast to our experience with these achievers, we found that less successful planners had few, if any, failures to tell us about. These underachievers did have victories that they were proud of, but in a surprising number of cases, we concluded that their claims were either false or significantly distorted. This reinforced our view that a strategy of timidity produces both fewer significant victories and fewer losses—in other words, no pain, no gain.

We also found that many successful planners were self-critical almost to the extreme. They constantly questioned themselves and they have a unique ability to objectively review their strengths and weaknesses. They harshly rebuke themselves when they fail and they are obsessed with doing it right and doing it better than anyone else.

Effective planners welcome challenges, take risks, and exhibit a high level of confidence in themselves and the planning profession. Corinne Gilb, professor of urban studies at Wayne State University and former planning director for Detroit, offered this description of the approach she followed in advancing her career in planning:

> It was trial by fire, but I live best under pressure and respond best to exotic and extreme challenge. That's when I feel my oats.[110]

Many lower level planners have the confidence, ability, and willingness to take the initiative if and when they are given the chance. The development of a competent staff depends on the creation of a decentralized working environment that encourages the delegation of authority, autonomy, and responsibility. Some planning directors assume too many responsibilities. They become too involved in directing and managing individuals and projects and do not delegate. A steady stream of employees is constantly checking in with them and seeking approval for past work or permission to proceed.

When Dennis Wilson was the director of planning for Dallas, he tried to increase each staff member's sense of personality, responsibility, and ownership for the work performed. He was an outspo-

ken advocate of decentralization and he gave us the following explanation in support of his position. "No one individual can
handle every item that is the responsibility of a large city planning
office. That is why it is so important to train and support staff to
make decisions and take actions without fear of reprisal. Staff then
develops into very competent professionals and the work accomplished by the department expands exponentially."

We found that one of the most common characteristics of an effective planning agency was a commitment to decentralization in
decision making and a belief in the competence of the staff. Several
planning directors shared with us their almost religious conver-
sion from a philosophy of dictatorship to one of delegation. The
following is from *Inc.* magazine and is representative of what we
heard.

> So I started on a new regimen. When people came to me with a ques-
> tion, I didn't offer an answer as I had before, but rather asked a ques-
> tion of my own: "What do you recommend?" It wasn't very long before
> the parade into my office thinned out. People began to think through
> their questions and the possible solutions before coming to me, and in
> the process they came up with their own answers. My staff began to
> think more like managers and to become more self-reliant. And since
> they were closer to the problem than I was, their solutions tended to be
> better than anything I might have suggested.[111]

While decentralization was a popular philosophy with all the
planners we talked to, some were more sincere and more committed to this strategy than others. One of the strongest advocates was
Joseph Vitt, Jr., who described the "star system" he had developed
years ago in Kansas City, Missouri:

> . . . a planner comes in and is assigned a project that is his to manage.
> Our job is a coaching job to help that person do his best to be successful.
> We are not competing with these planners because we have been
> through that route before. We know how to do those things. What we
> are trying to do now is make the staff successful, and so we are basically
> in a coaching capacity. We do not get on the field to play very often. We
> let the planning staff do that.[112]

In their book *Managing for Excellence*, David Bradford and Allan
Cohen concluded that to achieve excellence, a manager has to believe in the importance of tapping subordinates' talents, excite
them about their mission, build effective teams, and be willing to
share joint responsibilities for success.[113] They noted that "at the

same time that the manager works to develop management responsibility in subordinates, he or she must help develop the subordinate's abilities to share management of the unit's performance."[114] Metaphorically, they describe the image of this type of leader as "a very demanding but supportive and inspirational coach, who works hard to bring the team along, insisits on high standards and rigorous efforts, but passes on all the knowledge that will help the athletes grow."[115] In our search, we found that Joseph Vitt, Jr., was an outstanding example of this model. In addition to actually describing himself as a coach and demonstrating his commitment to the sharing of authority and responsibility with his staff, he was also committed to hiring and developing highly skilled professionals for his department.

We were also impressed with the way Dennis Wilson ran the Dallas planning department. An excellent communicator, he did a superior job in delegating responsibility to his staff and was committed to their professional development. We were particularly impressed with his policy that *every* professional staff member should have a project that he or she is responsible for and that everyone also had backup or support responsibility for someone else's project. We found that Wilson's management style had a positive influence on his staff, which began staying after work and coming in on weekends to complete assignments. The staff also began doing state-of-the-art technical work, as evidenced by the awards received from the American Planning Association.

Most planning organizations have a number of individuals who are contributing less than their capacity. In personal surveys we have taken over the years, a surprising majority of planners have indicated that they do not work as hard as they could and that they could do more. We have never tried to quantify the lost opportunities and the potential benefits that could have been acted upon, but they appear to be enormous. The real tragedy is that there are so many people ready, willing, and able to contribute so much more to their organizations and to themselves. It is the challange for leaders like Dennis Wilson to effectively engage and tap these human energies and resources. And while such leaders are a luxury in good times, they are, in fact, a necessity for survival and success in hard times.

Not everyone is going to be successful in meeting challenges and opportunities, but the effective planner is a learner and will benefit from almost any experience. As Nietzsche said, "What doesn't kill you makes you stronger." When a planner is passed over for a promotion or a position with another agency, that individual should attempt to learn from the experience. Some people are unwilling to accept any blame or responsibility for their failures. When football great Paul Hornung was caught stubbing out a cigarette by Frank Leahy, his coach at Notre Dame, a quick dialogue developed. Leahy: "Do you see what I see near your shoe, Paul?" Hornung: "Yeah, coach, I see. But you take it. You saw it first."

Many planners become angry or bitter about rejection and they don't stop to think that perhaps the decision makers could be right. Maybe they didn't have as much experience, or education, or perhaps they just didn't compete as well during the selection process. If you can't be effective in selling yourself, then how effective will you be in promoting your agency? Successful planners learn from failure. They ask for guidance from the people involved in the selection process and learn to correct their weaknesses and build on their strengths. They work harder than their competition and learn to overcome obstacles, be they personal or professional.

What successful leaders such as Corinne Gilb and Jack Rains really value in a job is a sense of challenge, excitement, adventure, and importance. In our interviews they talked about "solving problems," "exercising power," and "making a difference." They enjoyed what they were doing. They sought positions of authority and responsibility for the opportunity to become more effective— to make a difference. In almost every instance, the financial aspects of the jobs were a secondary and often insignificant factors in their decisions to accept positions. In this respect, many successful planners exhibit the altruistic characteristics of an earlier generation.

In *Come As You Are: The Peace Corp Story*, Coates Redman tells the story of how Sargent Shriver recruited Beverly Hills tax lawyer Frank Mankiewicz for a middle-management position in the Peace Corps.

In 1961, Mankiewicz hid out in the Rockies while trying to decide on which federal job to take. But he couldn't escape Shriver's phone calls.

Mankiewicz found Shriver in El Paso presiding over the first graduation of Peace Corps volunteers, soon to be heading to Tanganyika (now Tanzania). There in a motel room Mankiewicz succumbed to Shriver's enthusiasm, as most people Shriver wanted did.

Mankiewicz turned to leave, and Shriver asked, "Hey, don't you want to know what the job pays?" Mankiewicz said, "Well, yeah, I guess so. I mean, sure. How much does it pay?"

"I haven't the foggiest idea," said Shriver with a great cackle.[116]

Norman Krumholz believes that "the payoffs in our profession, if we are serious about our work, cannot be limited to increases in salaries, or contracts gotten, or tenure achieved, or articles or books published."[117] He contends that "the payoffs have to be in the actual improvement of the management of cities and in the lives of city residents—particularly the lives of those city residents who are most in need."[118]

While there is no question that the Kennedy administration created a unique environment for individuals in government service, we found that most successful leaders of planning agencies also possess the ability and personal resources to inspire and motivate their employees. Ineffective managers do not become effective simply by an infusion of fiscal resources. And, just as a side note, compensation should almost always be based on performance and contribution—not on longevity.

Motivated planners have a sense of mission and purpose. Without some form of guiding inspiration, attitudes suffer and decay sets in. We interviewed one frustrated and distraught director of planning in a large city who complained that his senior-level staff frequently spent time arguing over such insignificant bureaucratic issues as the management of the departmental bulletin board, the organization of office supplies, the interpretation of compensatory time guidelines, or most important of all, whose turn it was to make the coffee. He could not understand why his staff preferred bureaucratic squabbling to actually doing domething to resolve difficult planning issues.

William McGowan, founder and chairman of MCI, a long-distance telephone service, is a strong advocate of decentralization and an adversary of bureaucracy. His views are clearly communicated by the remarks he makes when he greets a group of new management employees:

I know that some of you, with your business school backgrounds, are out there already beginning to draw up organization charts and starting to write manuals for operating procedures. As soon as I find out who you are, I'm going to fire every last one of you.[119]

Planners who are constantly involved with internal bureaucratic issues are not going to be committed to excellence in the pursuit of effectiveness. They certainly won't be reading this book, because planning to them is a job, not a profession. They measure their effectiveness by the size of their paychecks or the number of reports on their shelves.

Often, planners become interested in bureaucratic affairs because they have time on their hands. Despite having ability, they lack motivation to focus their energies on activities that would make them more valuable to their organization. Such people are blindly content with the status quo and oblivious to the need to do more. An anecdote that illustrates our point was provided by Mike McGee, a basketball player for the Los Angeles Lakers. As McGee walked off the court after a Lakers practice, coach Pat Riley, unhappy with the way McGee had been playing, said in a loud voice, "You know, I keep calling, 'Mike McGee, Mike McGee,' but there's never anybody home." McGee turned and said, "I'm usually home, Coach, what time you been calling?" Subsequently, McGee was traded to another team.

Guidelines to Effective Office Management – Sample Regs

by Will Flush, Supervisor

In the past, employees were permitted to make trips to the restroom under informal guidelines. Effective January 1, 1987, a Restroom Trip Policy (RTP) will be established to provide a consistent method of accounting for each employee's restroom time and to ensure equal treatment of all employees. Under this policy, a "Restroom Trip Bank" will be established for each employee. On the first day of each month, employees will be given a Restroom trip credit of 20. Restroom trip credits can be accumulated from month to month.

Currently, the entrances to all restrooms are being equipped with personal identification stations and computer-linked voice print recognition. During the next three weeks, each employee must provide two copies of voice prints (one normal, one under stress) to

Personnel. The voice print recognition stations will be operational, but not restrictive, for the month of November; employees should acquaint themselves with the stations during that period.

If an employee's restroom trip bank balance reaches zero, the doors to all restrooms will not unlock for that employee's voice until the first of the next month.

In addition, all restroom stalls are being equipped with timed paper roll retractors. If the stall is occupied for more than three minutes, an alarm will sound. Thirty seconds after the alarm sounds, the roll will retract, the toilet will flush, and the stall door will open.

If you have any questions about the new policy, please ask your supervisor.

Reprinted with permission from The Western Planner.

Planners in successful agencies are motivated to expend their energies on devising ways to increase their effectiveness. They don't wait for their name or number to be called, they make their own opportunities. They have confidence, pride, and respect for the importance of their work, and they are striving to live up to the director's and decision maker's expectations. Such planners are valued contributors to the success of the organization and they are constantly seeking ways to become even more valuable to the people with and for whom they work.

Bennis and Nanus developed a unified theory of management based on the concept of positive self-regard and what they call the Wallenda factor.[120] Positive self-regard means that you believe in yourself and are justifiably confident of your competence. The Wallenda factor refers to the experiences of Karl Wallenda, a tightrope walker who fell from success when he became more concerned about losing than winning.

Bennis and Nanus propose that successful leadership requires "a fusion between positive self-regard and optimism about a desired outcome."[121] Their theory goes a long way toward explaining the lack of effectiveness which is characteristic of too many planners and planning agencies. They explain the negative implications of their theory:

> People can give up trying because they seriously doubt they can do what's required. That is negative self-regard. Or they may be assured of their competencies but give up trying because they expect their efforts to produce no results whatsoever.[122]

Some planners have a negative self-regard for their ability to comprehend and solve the complex problems that they are employed to handle. Others are supremely confident of their technical capabilities but have limited expectations of eventual success. They believe that their ultimate effectiveness is dependent on external factors that are beyond their control; for them, success seems a matter of luck and circumstance.

One of the major objectives of our work has been to demonstrate that there are strategies and tactics that competent planners can use to become more effective and that, in fact, we should be expecting and demanding more from planning professionals. Planners who are unwilling to accept a positive perception of the role of planning in successfully influencing the outcome of events are doomed to perpetual ineffectiveness.

Most of us believe that we are winners. But according to the findings of Peters and Austin in *A Passion for Excellence*, "most of our organizations go out of their way to disconfirm that daily."[123] Fran Tarkenton offered the following related observations in his book, *How to Motivate People*:

> We've found that most people will do a good job about four times as frequently as they will do lousy work. . . . It makes sense, then, that managers who want improved results should recognize that workers do a good job about 80 percent of the time, and thus we should motivate and demotivate people in about the same proportion, praising them about four times as often as dumping on them.

> But we find exactly the opposite happens. Eighty percent of the typical manager's comments to his workers focus on that 20 percent of the time they are performing under par. That means a lot of the time that they work well will go by without comment. What's the effect on the individual? He's gong to conclude that if he doesn't screw up, nobody is going to notice he's there. And he may even be encouraged to perform badly, because that at least will get him noticed.[124]

One surefire way to recognize and reinforce positive behavior and instill a sense of self-worth and pride in individuals is to help them set and achieve goals. Edwin Locke, an internationally known industrial organizational psychologist, and Gary Latham, who researches and teaches at the University of Washington, concluded in their book, *Goal Setting: A Motivational Technique That Works*, that goal setting can clarify management expectations, relieve boredom, increase satisfaction with task and performance, and strengthen self-confidence.[125] Their book provides an excellent guide to assist managers in working with their staff to develop goals and to create a climate of success.

In establishing goals for each individual, initially concentrate on what can be achieved. According to Peters and Austin, it is the small initial win that "allows the average person to find that there is a star within him."[126] Each person benefits from the opportunity to put several victories under his or her belt, which helps generate momentum and create a winning tradition. "Change," as noted by Rosabeth Moss Kanter in *The Change Masters*, "requires a leap of faith, and faith is so much more plausible on a foundation of successful prior experiences."[127] Simply put, success breeds success.

The trick to building confidence is to set carefully balanced, realistic goals that are challenging, achievable, and, most important,

The Theory of the Small Win

How often have you wished you could start over from the beginning – your family, your education, or your job ? If you had new subordinates, a new state-of-the-art control system, and a fresh group of rational and helpful peers and superiors, you could accomplish any thing.

Starting over, or doing a major restructuring, appeals to all of us. But businesses don't work that way. Changes are usually created by doing a series of "consistent, moderate size, clear-cut out comes – patterns of small wins," according to Thomas J. Peters in Organizational Dynamics.

The author has found this pattern of change repeatedly in the literature of business and politics. In all these cases, small wins led to a change in the ongoing pattern of interaction and decision-making in the enterprise.

How do managers bring about these "small wins?" Peters reports eight strategies that are so mundane or ordinary that they have seldom been studied in business literature. Yet they prove ultimately far more effective than some ponderous approaches as structural overhauls.

Rule 1: Spend time.
Interpretation: Spending time exerts, in itself, a "claim" on the decision making system.

Rule 2: Persist.
Interpretation: Having more patience than other people often results in adoption of a chosen course of action.

Rule 3: Exchange status for substance.
Interpretation: Gather support for programs by rewarding allies with visible tokens of recognition.

**Rule 4: Facilitate opposition
              participation.**
Interpretation: Often those outside the formal decision centers overestimate the feasibility of change. Encouraged to participate, they often will become more realistic.

Rule 5: Overload the system.
Interpretation: Bureaucracies chew up most projects although some pass through. Merely launching more projects is likely to result in more successes.

Rule 6: Provide garbage cans.
Interpretation: Organizations endlessly argue issues. To induce desired outcomes, put "throw away" issues at the top of agendas to absorb debate and save substantive issues for later.

Rule 7: Manage unobtrusively.
Interpretation: Certain actions can influence the organization pervasively but almost imperceptibly. Moreover, the resulting changes will persist with little further attention.

Rule 8: Interpret history.
Interpretation: By articulating a particular version of events, the leader can alter people's perception of what has been happening. The person who writes the minutes influences the outcome.

Suggestion: To bring about change, aim for a series of small wins. Use these methods to achieve a series of modest but clear cut successes.

Reprinted with permission from The Pryor Report, Vol. 3, No. 5, January 1987.

---

owned by the employees. People don't resist goals that they help develop and that represent their own aspirations. There is a big difference between being given a goal or objective and being asked to help set the desired outcome.

In Arlington, Texas, the planning director told her regulatory staff that there was a growing backlog of unprocessed zoning cases and that the planning commission and development community were complaining to the city council. Rather than ordering the staff to increase their processing productivity, she asked them if it was possible to help her out by processing more cases each month. Several planners responded to the request and they were able to achieve a 50 percent increase in output—a figure that was much higher than the objective that the director would have established. Inspired by these planners' achievements, other planners were also able to increase their production. An organization's vision may be set at the top, but it is the people who actually decide what, how, and by when work will be done.

Leaders have positive expectations, a sense of confidence and self-worth, and an ability to transfer these feelings to their followers. William Claire contends that leaders and managers must create and maintain an encouraging, supporting, and stimulating environment for their staffs.[128] Brian Tracy, a professional motivator and trainer, has found that the key to superior performance in an organization "is the creation of an environment where people feel free to give the best to the organization, where they feel motivated and committed about the organization and themselves."[129]

Fran Tarkenton has stated that "if you want the best from your people in business, you've got to do exactly what all the great coaches have done. You've got to turn your people on." Tarkenton contends that "people don't change their behavior unless it makes a difference to them to do so" and that the managers need to remember three rules: (1) behavior that is reinforced by positive consequences tends to continue or improve, (2) behavior that is demotivated by negative consequences tends to decrease, and (3) good, productive behavior that goes unnoticed tends to decrease over time.[130]

Managers must have a positive effect on their supporting staff if they are to be respected and accepted as leaders. Bill Russell, a basketball player who won the most valuable player award during three consecutive years in the NBA suggested that to be good you have to make your teammates respond to you in a positive fashion. He believes that teammates react not only out of respect but also how they see you as a person.

Chuck Yeager, a great test pilot and the first man to fly faster than the speed of sound, was recognized in his career with the U.S. Air Force as an outstanding leader. He related his success as a leader to the fact that he was able to earn the respect and confidence of the people in his command. He found that "once they saw I was really good, they would follow my leadership—not just obey orders—because I had proved that I knew what I was talking about."[131] Leonard Sayles, author of *Leadership: What Effective Managers Really Do . . . and How They Do It*, noted that effective managers gain acceptance by demonstrating superior abilities—technical skills and organizational sophistication.[132] This is remarkably consistent with the findings of Anthony Catanese who concluded in *Personality, Politics, and Planning* that "the success of the planning director would seem to hinge upon the achievement of a proper balance of technical presentation and political astuteness."[133]

Ron Short, former executive director of the Hillsborough City-County Planning Commission in Tampa, Florida, is but one of many successful planners who is recognized as a leader in the profession. His technical competence and enthusiasm is known and valued by his staff and his peers, and his commitment to education and learning is truly extraordinary. People who work with Short are exposed to a steady stream of opportunities for continuing education. He believes that self-development is a critical aspect for both personal and organizational success. Like other successful leaders, Short helps his staff believe that he is dependent on them. He is committed to raising each individual's level of aspiration and to strengthening his or her self-confidence. Short holds planners in high esteem and he knows from experience that their actions can change the community in which they practice.

Robert Morris, the former publisher of the *Dallas/Fort Worth Business Journal*, found in his experience with successful CEOs that they "establish high standards for themselves and for their employees and then do everything humanly possible to meet those standards."[134] Chuck Yeager stated that "in training my bunch to be the best squadron in the wing, I had high performance standards and because the men respected me, they stretched to reach them."[135]

More planning directors need to understand the value and importance of earning their staff's confidence and respect. Few planners have the education and training to be managers, much less leaders, but the best managers and leaders are usually the best workers. It is a rare phenomenon when a technically incompetent planner can become a successful agency leader. Harland Cleveland, in *The Knowledge Executive*, suggested that a leader "is very likely to be unsuccessful unless he or she has, earlier in life, been a first-rate specialist."[136] Ross Perot describes this principle simply as "knowing your business." In truth, successful leaders usually have worked harder and know the fundamentals of their businesses better than their staff.

When defensive city or county managers appoint trusted individuals—who have administrative skills but do not have planning knowledge or technical competence—to direct a planning department, they hurt themselves, their organizations, and their communities. Most of these unqualified planning directors tend to be lame ducks because they are perceived to be mostly interested in serving their time before moving to a higher management position. They often pride themselves on not being planners and even go out of their way to let others know it. They exhibit little care or respect for the people they manage; leadership is nonexistent. These individuals may be skilled troubleshooters and good administrators but the vast majority are not managers of change—in fact, they tend to perpetuate the status quo and tolerate no deviation from the norm. Such individuals are both a curse to the profession and betrayers of basic human rights. Employees, including planners, have the right to be respected and to be allowed to make productive and meaningful contributions to their organizations and communities. Inadequate administrators who fail to use planners to help manage change are themselves in line to become victims of change.

How does a planner know if he or she has "the right stuff" to be a manager and a leader within the planning profession? When Chuck Yeager was asked if he had the right stuff, he gave the following brief but profound answer:

> All I know is I worked my tail off to learn how to fly, and worked hard at it all the way. And in the end, the one big reason why I was better than average as a pilot was because I flew more than anybody else. If there is such a thing as "the right stuff" in piloting, then it was experience.[137]

A leader has to work harder than anyone else in the organization according to Herbert Kelleher, president and chairman of the board for Southwest Airlines. He questions how you can get people to feel what they're doing is important unless you demonstrate that it is important to you.[138]

Many planners and educators complained to us about the decline in the intellectual levels and academic quality of the students who were being attracted to graduate planning schools. But in our experience with the profession, we found that there was little correlation between intelligence and effectiveness. In fact, we found several instances where brilliant individuals were strikingly ineffective. For example, one particularly ineffective planning director belonged to Mensa—he told us that his goal was to have a job where he worked no more than twenty hours a week and could devote the rest of his time to thinking.

This director spent most of his day behind closed doors or out of the office. He was inaccessible, unwilling to delegate, and fearful of his staff. He was lazy, but his strength was the public's perception that he was intelligent and had a pleasing personality. He talked a good game, but he was like a baby mockingbird: A whole lot of mouth and very little bird. His companionship was highly valued by the planning commission and its chairperson took great pride in pointing out that their director was so popular that he could recommend denial of a rezoning request and make the applicant like it. Our research did not find many instances where he had ever recommended denial of anything. He was weak, ineffective, and the integrity of the planning department had been used to purchase his popularity and financial security. The various planning products that were produced by the department were only a sop to public opinion and easily ignored by the decision makers.

The planner had an impressive vocabulary and interviewed well and despite his limited experience, he was selected to be the planning director in another city that had a reputation for innovative and effective planning. For the first time in his professional life, he was in an environment that expected and demanded excellence and maximum effectiveness. He was unable to provide either. His new staff, commission, and city manager soon became disillusioned with his management style and obvious lack of substance. He was forced to resign in less than two years.

An awareness of the need for and a commitment to self-development by the director and staff is central to the evolution of an effective organization. Intelligence, knowledge, and imagination become effective only through hard work. As the leader of the agency works to be more effective, there is another impact: Aspirations are raised and individuals are motivated to higher performance and higher dedication. Peter Drucker concluded in *The Effective Executive* that "organizations are not more effective because they have better people. They have better people because they motivate to self-development through their standards, through their habits, through their climate. And these, in turn, result from systematic, focused, purposeful self-training of the individuals in becoming effective. . . ."[139]

Executive Focus Self-Examination

	Always	Often	Seldom	Never
1. Do you approach activities with your full, undivided attention ?	4	3	2	1
2. Do you restrict your focus to activities at which you can excel ?	4	3	2	1
3. Can you shift focus quickly and completely from one activity to another ?	4	3	2	1
4. Do you list and rank your interests in order of importance ?	4	3	2	1
5. Do you list and rank your people's interests in order of importance?	4	3	2	1
6. Do you get your employees extremely interested in a project before you attempt to implement change ?	4	3	2	1
7. Are you able to remain interested in a project, keeping your focus intense over along period of time ?	4	3	2	1
8. Do you make sure there is a "felt need" among your people before you embark on change ?	4	3	2	1
9. Do you identify a respected individual or group advocating the change before you proceed ?	4	3	2	1
10. Do you lay out all the specific details of what will affect and be affected by the change before you implement it?	4	3	2	1

A score of 30 or less indicates a need for improvement.

In *Peak Performers: The New Heroes,* Charles Garfield states that "individual peak performers—not the organization man or woman—will shape America's future."[140] Garfield reports that peak performers are committed to results in the service of a compelling mission and they use their jobs toward their own personal development. He believes that "only when individuals are encouraged

How Good a Manager Are You?

Select the one answer for each question that best expresses your feelings.

1. You discover that your associate keeps a diary on a half-hour basis. What is your reaction ?
   (a) It's a good idea if it's done consistently.
   (b) Probably he or she is on and off. I start one myself, but then I neglect it.
   (c) I think it's a waste of time. Things have a way of changing too much anyway.
   (d) It's ridiculous. There is no privacy left.

2. Do you keep a calendar ?
   (a) I use it only to look at today's date.
   (b) Yes, also for next year and the year after.
   (c) My calendar is kept up to date for a month, but no more.
   (d) I don't even have one !

3. When you are about to visit another company's offices and do not have exact instructions on how to get there, what do you usually do?
   (a) I ask for exact instructions and mark them on a road map.
   (b) I just drive more or less in the direction of where I remember their offices are – and I often get lost.
   (c) I stop on the way a few times and ask for directions.
   (d) I have a good sense of direction and seldom get lost, even in foreign places.

4. You plan to have things done for a particular day or week.
   (a) I usually get things done as planned.
   (b) It hardly ever works out as planned. Something always goes wrong.
   (c) I plan in such a way that there is leeway for some changes.
   (d) I hardly ever make any plans.

5. You have the following tasks to accomplish. Arrange them in the order by which you get them all done in the least time and with out mishaps.
   (a) Pick up a parcel. It is heavy, and the place closes at 11 a.m.
   (b) Buy ice cream cake to take home.
   (c) Stop at the bank to get money.
   (d) Stop at a gas station to fill up.
   (e) Have glasses repaired. The optometrist promised to have them ready in an hour if they are dropped off in time.
   (f) Pick up a customer at the railroad station. The train arrives at noon.
   (g) Pick up repaired glasses.

Scoring and Interpretation

1.	2.	3.	4.	5.
(a) = 3	(a) = 2	(a) = 2	(a) = 3	(a) = 1*
(b) = 2	(b) = 1	(b) = 1	(b) = 2	(e) = 2
(c) = 4	(c) = 4	(c) = 4	(c) = 4	(c) = 3
(d) = 1	(d) = 3	(d) = 3	(d) = 1	(f) = 4
				(d) = 5
				(g) = 6
				(b) = 7

*This version scores 5 points. Pretesting showed, however, other alternatives. If the order permits ice cream to melt or taking too long or missing a closing date, each mistake counts for one point to be deducted from the total score of 5.

The highest score is between 17 and 21. In some cases we granted a lower score for a too perfect and almost compulsive solution, although it sounded like a more perfect answer. For example, in item 1(a), half-hour diaries are overly efficient; item 2(d) received a 3 despite the apparent inefficiency; and item 3(c) was granted a score of 4 because it permitted some inefficiency. A score below 17 shows too little planning.

to pursue their self-development on the job can both individuals and organizations succeed."[141] He suggests that peak performers share the following attributes:

> They all have a strong sense of mission, well-defined goals, a capacity for self-analysis, the ability to bring out the best in others, the mental agility to steer through complex situations and the foresight to adapt to major changes without losing momentum.[142]

Are we asking too much from the managers and leaders in the planning profession? Are we setting our standards high enough? Are we wrong to be concerned when a planning director says that she lacks confidence in her ability to handle certain topics and that she's more comfortable being a manager than a technician? Are we wrong to criticize the placement of a professional administrator who has no successful experience as a planner to head a planning agency? The body of evidence we have accumulated provides a loud and resounding *no*.

We began this chapter by noting that leadership can be learned. Our sincere hope is that the information we have researched and presented will help challenge, motivate, and perhaps even inspire planners to become leaders and more effective managers. Each of us can learn to become more effective, and most of us can make a difference in the community where we live and work.

John Wooden, the only man ever enshrined in the basketball hall of fame as both a player and coach, always emphasized constant improvement and steady performance. He believed that the mark of a true champion was to always perform near your own level of competency and to do that by never being satisfied with the past and by always planning for the future. He found that while it may be possible to reach the top of one's profession on sheer ability, it is impossible to stay there without hard work and character. In evaluating character, Wooden looked for young men who would play the game hard, but clean, and who would always be trying to improve themselves in order to help the team. He learned that with character and ability, the championships would take care of themselves.[143]

6

Caveat Emptor

There is no reason to believe that business managers, put in control of service institutions, would do better than the "bureaucrats." PETER F. DRUCKER

This book is not based on the premise that government should be run like a business or that, as Woodrow Wilson suggested in his pioneering essay, that "the field of administration is a field of business." We do not suggest that private sector management practices and techniques are a cure-all for the many operational problems faced by planning agencies. The public sector operates under political limitations and constraints that preclude any straight transfer of private sector management principles and practices. Richard Snelling, former Vermont governor, noted that "the list of dissimilarities between business and government is much, much longer than the list of similarities, but we ought to apply what we can from management to running government."[1]

Despite the obvious differences between the public and private sectors, we have found that the efficiency and effectiveness of planners and planning agencies can and have been improved by using basic private sector management principles and practices. In summary, our surveys and research of planning literature show that successful planning agencies share many of the most common traits and characteristics of successful businesses.

But planners need to be cautious as they begin to adapt private sector principles and practices to the public sector. Government, or the process of public government, can be viewed like a business but not as a business. Even though public and private managers, and this includes planners, perform similar functions, have similar clients, and even have similar management problems, there are many important contrasts in how they manage and what they are managing. One major contrast concerns the basic purpose of each entity.

The purpose of government and those who serve in government is to provide authority over rights of those being governed. There is a parallel here to private business, but it is often not well understood. In a business, stockholders give to a corporation some of their assets. In return, the corporation promises to manage those assets in a manner which will be profitable to the stockholder. The corporation then does with the stockholders' assets as it sees fits but it has an obligation, a trust, to manage those assets in a profitable way. The basis of the trust between the corporation and the stockholders is monetary.

Under a government, individuals relinquish authority over some of their rights and, in return, the government promises to ensure that all of their rights will be protected. This is the basis for police power, taxation, regulation, and the provision of services. The government then has a trust to protect those rights. It protects the right to health by providing water and sanitary sewer services; it protects the right for pursuit of happiness by providing parks. The important point is that the basis for the trust between government and those being governed is not monetary, but individual rights.

Of course, government cannot protect these rights without some monetary exchange, and this is why government is like a business. To provide this protection, and fulfill the trust, it does with those rights as it believes is best. One thing it does is exert its authority over the right of personal possession so that in order to own or use property, individuals must pay a tax. But a government still is not a business and it is the nature of its trust that makes it different.

Planners, probably more than any other public officials, are strongly involved in the governing aspects of public administration. Planners must contend with and manage several factors that are related to the purpose of government, representation, authority, and justice. These are characteristics which are not part of the basic purpose of most businesses, but are major forces in public government and the administration of that government. "A theory of public administration means in our time a theory of politics also."[2] Recently, particularly during the Reagan administration, there has been much attention as to how government can be operated like a business and ways that "good management" can be used to improve efficiency. But much of this attention has strayed from the intent of government.

This attitude is reflected in a report prepared by the Grace Commission.[3] In March 1982, Reagan appointed J. Peter Grace, CEO of W. R. Grace & Co., a leading international chemical, natural resource, and consumer services company, to chair the President's private sector survey on cost control. The report prepared by this commission strongly criticized federal public administration as being inefficient, costly, and unproductive. Many of the issues and conditions raised by this report have been greatly acclaimed, while others have been criticized for being inaccurate and unrealistic. The report roots out many examples of waste and inefficiency in federal government spending and thus merits attention by public administrators, but the underlying tone of the report does not recognize that the basic purpose of government is to govern. The report "implies that cutting federal spending can be accomplished easily, if only Congress would stop spending money on politically motivated activities."[4] This concept that politics, and thus representation, authority, and justice, should not enter in the decision-making process, is a trap planners must avoid.

As planners begin to apply many of the techniques discussed here, they should avoid losing sight of the public trust that they have been granted. Planners must constantly review their actions in relation to the purpose of government authority, representation, and justice, and the constraints that are placed upon them.

An example of the inappropriate application of a businesslike approach to local government was provided by the Port of New York Authority. This agency was established in the 1920s to manage automotive and truck traffic throughout the two-state area where the port was located. The authority was well managed and businesslike but Peter Drucker pointed out that in this case such an approach to public service had serious negative consequences to the general public.

> It (the Port of New York Authority) did not concern itself with transportation policy in the New York metropolitan area even though its bridges, tunnels, and airports generate much of the traffic on New York's streets. It did not ask, "Who are our constituents?" Instead it resisted any such questions as political and unbusinesslike. In the end it has come to be seen as the villain of the New York traffic and transportation problem.[5]

When a public planning agency begins to chunk its activities or begins to emphasize a bias for action, it is easy to lose sight of its public purpose. An agency striving to build a reputation as a "problem solver" attacks those problems that are most obvious and for which results are clear and immediate. A pitfall to avoid is neglecting the long-range issues. Planners, as problem solvers, must be prepared to advise their public chief executive officer about the long-range implications of existing trends and short-range strategies. Planners must identify possible future problems and solve them before they become visible and more difficult to manage. For the planner, this often is not as rewarding as putting out those "raging forest fires." The importance of fixing something that is not broken is obscure at best, and often its importance is unrecognized and the deed goes unrewarded. Still, public agencies should not compromise their long-range planning efforts in the name of action; instead, they must maintain a balance between them.

The planning department in Arlington, Texas, has a conscious bias for action and makes a concerted effort to be prepared to quickly advise the city manager, planning commission, and city council on possible action plans to address current planning problems. However, much of this preparedness is based on the department's ongoing comprehensive planning program. When an action plan is presented, the comprehensive and long-range implication of the plans is either discussed or it is emphasized that it must be examined and the results presented at a later date. Such an approach provides a bias for action while keeping prominent the importance of long-range view.

Planners also need to avoid the squeaky wheel pitfall when chunking or working toward developing plans for action. Often those issues that are considered hot are generated by political concerns and problems that may not be of much political significance can easily be forgotten. However, public planning has an obligation to fairly address a community's issues. As planners "chunk" their workload, they need to be conscious of all the community's problems, not just those that are politically significant. Action plans should be developed to address problems that are representative of the community as a whole. This is often difficult because legislators on all levels reap their greatest rewards from solving those problems that are of most benefit to their political careers. Granted, this is natural because a legislator serves his constituency, but the planner must serve the community as a whole, including those who choose not to participate in the political process.

Serving the community as a whole is also a pitfall of getting close to the customer. The public planner has a variety of customers, some easily identifiable, others less obvious. Here again is a major difference between the private and public sectors. Planners, unlike business people, cannot choose the market that they want and feel they can most efficiently serve. The planners' marketplace is the public and it includes current and future voters, nonvoters, young, old, whites, blacks, Hispanics, Orientals, homeowners, renters, and visitors. Some of these so-called customers are easy to get close to while others are more difficult, if not impossible, to thoroughly understand. Yet the planner must plan for and be concerned about all of these clients. As planners begin to learn more about their customers and develop market niches and specialized products, more obscure segments of the public should not be alienated or abandoned.

One area where the public can be denied information and be effectively locked out of the decision-making process is cost. Although recouping costs for value-added products can result in significant incomes for planning agencies, there should be special consideration for groups that cannot afford such costs. Low-income, minority, homeowners, nonprofit groups, and other similar groups should be permitted inexpensive access to planning documents and data. "Knowledge is power," wrote Francis Bacon in 1597, and such power should not be allocated on the basis of the ability to pay. When planners assess the "cost that the market will bear," they should examine who will be locked out of this market.

Planners also have customers who are not considered part of the public, but rather are part of the government system itself. Planners often produce products and services that are used by other public agencies or departments. In turn, planners use products and services provided by these public agencies. Competition often generates new and innovative solutions, but within public bureaucracy it can also generate ill will that generally is more detrimental than any positive results generated. Planners need to be aware of this and make extra efforts to avoid such difficulties. One way to do so is to make these other agencies feel like they are clients. Getting close to them as the planner would any other customer and finding out how they use planning information and how such information could be made more valuable to them can only help. Identify how planners can help solve their problems.

In both Corpus Christi and Beaumont, Texas, the planning departments established a client-like relationship with the park and recreation departments and then produced park and open space plans that reflected the departments' needs. The Beaumont plan received a national award from the U.S. Department of Interior and was successfully used to obtain competitive grants and public support for bond issues. In contrast, the Seattle, Washington, planning department was ineffective in establishing supporting client relationships and was unable to fulfill its planning responsibilities. As noted by Linda Dalton, former chair of the Seattle City Planning Commission, their planning department:

> . . . was not able to coordinate planning with line departments because line department staff members resented the high-handed way that relatively inexperienced OPP (Office of Policy Planning) members intruded in departmental operations.[6]

Under the comprehensive planning program in Arlington, Texas, other city departments are treated just like the commission, city council, and special interest groups. They are asked to participate in all issue and goal identification and ranking surveys. They receive the same documents as the commission and council, and are asked to comment on their contents. Finally, much of the effort undertaken as part of the comprehensive planning process is focused on providing these departments with better data or tools to conduct their daily business. They, like the public, are truly clients of the comprehensive planning process.

We began this chapter with a quote from Peter Drucker to the effect that the system is the problem in government, not the people delivering the services. Yet we frequently heard educators and many experienced planners complain that planning had declined because the best and brightest people are no longer attracted to planning. There was a consensus that government often moves too slowly for real entrepreneurs and that they become discouraged and move on to more rewarding careers. However, in *Innovation and Entrepreneurship*, Peter Drucker notes that the real problem is not the quality of people in local government service but rather the nature of most public service institutions. He has found that "the most entrepreneurial, innovative people behave like the worse time-serving bureaucrat or power-hungry politician six months after they have taken over the management of a public-service institution, particularly if it is a government agency."[7]

In his classic work, *Management: Tasks, Responsibilities, Practices,* Drucker argued that service institutions did not need to be more like business but rather needed to be more like hospitals, universities, governments, and so forth, depending on their own specific functions, purposes and missions.[8] He concluded that service institutions do not need better people, they need better managers "who focus themselves and their institutions puposefully on performance and results."[9] More important, Drucker believes above all else that "they need effectiveness, that is, emphasis on the right results."[10] We must not make the mistake of confusing our support for effective performance with a belief that government should be run like a business. The simple premise that we have repeatedly stressed is that the efficiency and effectiveness of planning can and has been improved by using basic private sector management principles and practices. Use what works for you and reject the rest.

7

Developing a
Winning Game Plan

*Nobody really listens. We all have something to say, and we keep search-
ing for someone to listen to it.* PHILIP B. CROSBY

The people we talked to and the articles, papers, and books we read
in conducting our research for this book offered hundreds of valuable lessons for planners. In our own search for excellence, we
tried to absorb the content and intent of much of what was being
said, add our own ideas, thoughts, and experiences and then reformulate it to help motivated planners become more effective.

This book is about how planners can take control of what happens to them and their planning organizations. We have covered a
lot of ground in just a few pages and have offered many ideas and
perhaps even a fresh perspective that should enable planners to increase their effectiveness on the job. Some of our suggestions will
require significant changes in attitude and behavior, while others
might require only a simple adjustment.

Our purpose here is to reinforce our findings. This chapter is
not a summary and it is not a substitute for the rest of the book.
Some planners will want to be able to pick this book up and in just
a few minutes gain the information that will make them the next
planning directors of their agencies. We wish it were so, but excellence and effectiveness are not superficial characteristics; they
must be earned and purchased with perseverance, dedication, and
commitment.

In the movie *The Hucksters,* Clark Gable spent his last $20 on a tie
to impress Sidney Greenstreet. Gable got the job and the audience
got a message about the importance of style. We don't have such
simple, quick fixes. Instead, we have tried to focus on critical, substantive areas and we believe that what has been produced can
really help planners become more effective. Simply employing the
proper mix of strategies and tactics we have discussed can improve

a planner's win/loss record, but we believe that a deeper understanding and commitment to the basic philosophy of excellence is an essential requirement for ultimate effectiveness—both for planners and for the planning profession.

We are confident that as an increasing number of planners work toward becoming more effective the performance levels of individual planning organizations and the planning profession will raise. Our mission has been to motivate and perhaps inspire planners to take control of their destinies, to understand the vision of opportunity that exists in the profession, and to make a difference. Effectiveness can be learned; it also *has* to be learned.

A WINNING GAME PLAN FOR YOUR ORGANIZATION

You don't have to be a sports fan to know that every organization, including your own, is a team. ROBERT KEIDEL

In *Game Plans: Sports Strategies for Business,* Robert Keidel, a senior fellow at the Wharton Applied Research Center at the University of Pennsylvania, points out that "different team sports have different requirements for teamwork and coaching and these differences have remarkable parallels to business."[1]

We believe this analogy can also be extended to local government. Keidel contends that sports models can help make sense of any kind of organization, big or small, and that success, no matter what the game, depends on a team effectively carrying out staffing, planning, and operating tasks. He states that: "*Staffing* is deciding which players will be on the team and in the game; *planning* is specifying in advance how the game should be played; *operating* deals with influencing the proces or flow of the game."[2]

Over the years we have had the opportunity to formulate and reformulate game plans for a number of planning agencies and no two plans were alike. The initial step in developing a game plan should be to analyze the internal and external environments and determine what can be changed and what must be adapted to and overcome. Next, review the numerous strategies and tactics that are discussed in this book and select the ones that are appropriate for your circumstances and the objective of your program. Your plan must reflect a balance between the need for change and the capacity of the organization to change.

Differing strategies may be used simultaneously, in sequence, or both. However, as noted by Gerald Zaltman and Robert Duncan in *Strategies for Planned Change,* care must be exercised that one strategy does not cancel out the effects of another strategy used earlier, being used simultaneously, or to be used later.[3] The difficulty of developing the proper mix and use of strategies shouldn't be underestimated. And above all else planners must be sensitive, flexible, and responsive to both internal and external changes in the environment. After all, insensitivity is what causes most of us to get in trouble in the first place.

There is a simple but critically important point that must be grasped by planners who are trying to become more effective: What worked last year or even last week may not work—in fact probably won't work—tomorrow or next year. Conditions constantly change and planners must monitor and adapt the mix of strategies and tactics to maintain satisfactory performance levels and to take advantage of emerging opportunities.

Success often breeds complacency and provides the seeds for destruction. We found that some successful planners are often like some successful athletic coaches in that once they develop an effective operating strategy based on what has worked for them over the years, they tend to stick with it. In football parlance, it is referred to as "dancing with the one that brung you." Of course, when the strategy fails to work, it is described as "going to the well once too often." Some planners fail to understand that the success of different strategies and tactics depends on a combination of internal and external factors that are constantly changing. This means that the effectiveness of most planning organizations should be in a constant state of flux. Yet we were shocked by the number of planners and respected educators who were unaware of the significance of this. We also talked to a number of planners who were confused and frustrated by the lack of consistency on the part of the decision makers for whom they work. Over and over, we heard planners bitterly complain about the schizophrenic character of their managers and elected officials. They complained that they were in trouble this year for doing something the very same way they had done it before. But after thinking, they could easily identify several significant changes in the community that probably were influencing the way managers or public officials were making decisions.

In *Planners and Local Politics,* Anthony Catanese found that "it is incorrect to assume that the same set of inputs will result in similar output consistently over a period of time, and the effective and astute participant in or observer of the political system must be aware of the critical nature of timing."[4] Still, many planners, researchers, and educators have failed to come to grips with the temporal nature of the formulation and implementation of the various strategies and tactics that are used to determine the effectiveness of an organization. It is not uncommon for someone to report the success of a particular project and then later someone else will reexamine the situation and find failure. In our research, we found that, more often than not, both evaluations were correct! How could this be? The answer is simple: In many cases, success had evolved over time into failure. But here is where we disagree with some colleagues. Many researchers are too quick to conclude that a project was always a failure because it wasn't a success when they evaluated it. They ignore, downplay, or even worse, report early successes as outright failures. In truth, there are many early successes that for various reasons result ultimately in failure being snatched from the jaws of victory. A primary culprit is often a failure to seek out, listen, and respond to feedback from the clients being served. Self-satisfaction and overconfidence can be fatal to almost any planning project or program.

In formulating a wining game plan, there must be a recognition of and a commitment to the changes that are needed to steadily move the planning organization toward excellence and increased effectiveness. These changes should be based on such factors as a bias for action, a desire to serve, an interest in innovation and entrepreneurship, a willingness to take risks, political sensitivity and awareness, and leadership opportunities and responsibilities. Perhaps most important of all there must be a commitment to the most valuable resource—the people on your team.

A WINNING GAME PLAN FOR YOURSELF

People will change their behavior—do a better job—only when it makes a difference to them to do so. FRAN TARKENTON and TAD TULEJA

We now come to the final question. What specific steps can you take to become more effective and to get ahead in the profession? The following are what we believe to be the 25 components of a winning strategy for personal success:

1. *Aim for action now.* Focus your efforts on a limited number of products and activities and produce tangible, action-oriented results in a timely fashion. Be willing to get your hands dirty and help execute your projects. Carry a list of current projects and

check it during any free moments. If your day is slipping away with nothing being done on any of them, then look at what you can do at that moment or try to squeeze in some time to work on a project before the day is over.

2. *Be sensitive and responsive to political considerations.* Develop the skills and knowledge of the various political relationships which Dennis Rondinelli identified in his classic article, "Urban Planning as Policy Analysis." Such development is needed to successfully intervene in and become a part of the political decision-making process. If you cannot understand and respect the personalities and characteristics of public officials, you cannot be an effective service provider.

3. *Take reasonable risks.* You must be prepared to "mix it up" and assume the risks associated with standing up for your point of view if you are going to be effective. If you are passive and only try to avoid making mistakes, you won't have a meaningful role in the decision-making process. Be willing to take risks, to make mistakes, and to learn from failure.

4. *Listen to, hear, and learn.* Spend time in the community, seek out potential clients, get close to them, listen to them and learn what problems they are experiencing. Planners are specifically trained in problem-solving skills and the products and services you provide should make it possible for their unique problems to be solved. Let people "push you around" and learn to like it.

5. *Exploit your skills.* Find out what you are good at and look for areas where you can be particularly useful and effective in meeting the needs of various client groups. But be balanced in your approach to serving special niches in the marketplace.

6. *Work with, not for, people.* People are not a burden or nuisance to the planning process. Their participation actually is essential to the development of effective products and services. Be aware of the growing public interest in volunteerism, self-help, and co-production and use it to increase public involvement in, understanding of, and support for your activities.

7. *Sell planning.* Promote planning in general and the specific plans, projects, and services that you are responsible for at every chance you get. This helps build public understanding and support for planning and contributes to the development of speaking skills that are so essential to professional advancement.

8. *Delivery quality.* Sell your services on the basis of quality, not price. Superior quality *is* valued by almost all planning clients. Look at developing quality products and services that will generate revenues for your organization. Make sure that quality and value go into a product before your name goes on it.

9. *Do more with less.* Look at what you are doing and how you are doing it. Abandon obsolete and ineffective products and services and pursue coproduction opportunities. Coproduction can improve both the quantity and quality of public services at any budgeting level.

10. *Be innovative.* Systematically and purposely monitor and pursue the seven sources of opportunity identified by Peter Drucker in *Innovation and Entrepreneurship.* Thinking up ideas is not enough, they must be used. The proof of their value is only in their implementation. There is no shortage of creativity but there is a shortage of innovations that can make things happen. Demonstrate that you have the know-how, energy, daring, and staying power to successfully implement ideas.

11. *Become better and more valuable.* Start by asking yourself what you can do to help your organization, the people you work for and with, and the people that work for you. Ann Landers once wrote in her advice column that the secret to a successful marriage was mutual need. So it is with the relationship between you and your organization. Look for deficiencies in your organization and provide for unmet needs. Learns to complement the strengths of your organization and the person for whom you work. Be a team player.

12. *Make yourself more valuable.* Recognize responsibility for making yourself more valuable. This increased value can only happen when you stretch yourself, develop new skills, teach yourself, and channel your talents and energies into *mutually* beneficial areas and opportunities.

13. *Critically inventory yourself.* Thoroughly and objectively look at your strengths and weakneses and work on enhancing your capabilities and self-esteem. It was Robert Burns, the Scottish poet, who longed for the gift "to see ourselves as other see us." The ability to be self-critical is an essential trait of effective planners.

14. *Peform at a higher level.* Try to do the work associated with the next highest position in your organization. Demonstrate that you can handle the imaginary opening one rung higher on the organization's ladder. Do more than is requested—not just because

you are trying to get ahead, but because you want to satisfy yourself.

15. *Be caring and trusting.* Good personal relationships are important. One key to success is your ability to understand your boss's personality traits. Learn his or her idiosyncrasies, likes, dislikes, habits, family situation, character strengths, and weaknesses. Gaining the ear of your boss is an important first step in getting your ideas across and accepted. Care about people and develop empathy with them. Learn to identify and empathize with others. Try putting the needs of others ahead of your own.

16. *Adopt your boss's value system, but don't be hypocritical.* Maintain your integrity and self-respect. Remember Shakespeare's advice: "To thine own self be true." If you don't admire, trust, and respect your boss find a new position—fast! Seek out the best, brightest, most aggressive, and successful director you can find. Your goal should be to work for an achiever who makes things happen and who you can trust, respect, and emulate.

17. *Formulate a professional development program for yourself.* Establish a goal of what and where you want to be in five years and determine what knowledge and skills are needed in that capacity. Work toward getting the specific experience and education that is required for advancement. Read, read, read, discuss, and learn from others. If you don't read all the time, then we doubt that you can become an effective planner.

18. *Publicize how good you are.* Write articles and papers and deliver lectures at conferences. Share credit with others. Remmember to take special care to see that your promotional efforts don't alienate people. Being aggressive and generous in sharing credit with your teammates and using coauthors for your articles are excellent ways to promote harmony and goodwill within your organization and demonstrate your commitment to teamwork.

19. *Improve your thinking processes.* Norman Vincent Peale concluded in *The Power of Positive Thinking* that it is how we direct, control, and channel our thinking that ultimately shapes our self-image and our lives. You must learn to become a more creative thinker and a more effective problem solver. Success in planning will increasingly depend on the ability to develop innovative and creative solutions to problems for which there are often no precedents.

20. *Become a student of change.* In *Winning the Innovations Game,* Dennis Waitley and Robert Tucker noted that as the world becomes more interconnected, events outside a person's narrow field have an impact upon his or her field, career, family, and pocketbook. Without an understanding of the world, you'll only be able to react and to avoid. Waitley and Tucker recommend taking the offensive. Be alert to early warning signs of change. Aggressively look for changes in your work, your profession, and your community and use them to your advantage.

21. *Pay attention to details.* Demonstrate that you can overcome bureaucratic obstacles, follow through, and complete projects. Learn to schedule and prioritize and to get the right things done. Above all else, make sure that things do get done and that they are done well.

22. *Exhibit initiative, motivation, and drive.* Fran Tarkenton said that "if you don't have that fire in your belly when the game starts, you're going to get your tail beat by a ninety-pound weakling who does." This is true in more than sports. Accomplishments speak louder than words and you can demonstrate your initiative by successfully overcoming obstacles and impediments to the development and implementation of your plans, projects and services. Employers don't want to hear excuses, they want people who accept and adapt to constraints and make good things happen.

23. *Become a leader.* Managers do things right, but leaders do the right things. You must adapt to the environment and work within the context of things as they are, not as you wish them to be. Recognize the importance of vision and relate your daily activities to a longer term perspective. Develop and communicate values that are consistent with the needs of your organization and your community. Understand the mission of your organization and relate your activities to its goals and objectives. Lead, but also be on the team.

24. *Develop emotional maturity.* If you don't have it, you need to get it fast. Unfortunately, it has to be worked for and earned over time. Characteristics such as personal integrity, honesty and ethical behavior, and high standards of personal conduct are indicators of the kind of maturity that is essential to lasting success in any profession.

25. *Guard against overconfidence.* Everything is relative. In *Smokey and the Bandit,* Burt Reynolds noted that "How smart you are depends on where you are." The more we traveled, read, and collected information for this book, the more we found out how little we knew. If you quit learning, you will quickly become obsolete.

GETTING OUT OF THE PLATEAUING TRAP

Redefinition of goals and resentment on the part of lower level planners may reflect a combination of relatively high expectations encouraged by planning education, present low status in an agency, and limited prospects for advancement within that agency. HOWELL S. BAUM

In a reversal of the Peter Principle, which holds that people rise to a level where they are incompetent, many planners have not been able to rise to the level where they would be competent. The boom years of growth in employment opportunities for planners has passed. Long gone are the unusual historical conditions that led to rapid promotions and advancements for so many younger planners. Yet the profession is still paying the price for having promoted many younger, inexperienced, unqualified, and immature planners into positions of responsibility and authority.

Today, we have an impressive number of extraordinarily well-educated and well-qualified younger planners competing for a limited number of advancement opportunities. This has resulted in increasingly fierce competition both within the baby boom generation and between it and the older generation. History is no longer on the side of the ambitious. It's an often bitter struggle for personal survival and the odds are awful. In truth, there are far more qualified candidates than there are upper level positions in the planning profession, and the gap will continue to grow. Many well-qualified planners now in their thirties are having to face the reality that they may have already reached the ceiling in their professional careers.

Judith Bardwick in her insightful book, *The Plateauing Trap*, provided a list of words and phrases that come to mind when you think of plateaued people.[5] She notes that the list, provided below, is piercingly judgmental and the negative image that is portrayed is inescapable.

in the closet	deadwood
peaked	slug
coasting	moss-back
out of runway	over the hill
a shelf sitter	pumping gas
obsolescent	out to lunch
on an in-plant vacation	when you get close enough,
a *Wall Street Journal* retiree	you hear an echo
a spare wheel	a goofoff
old what's-his-name	playing defense

an empty suit

walking wounded

on the shelf

out of the running

incompetent

a coat rack

lack-a-wanna

POP (pissed on and passed over)

burned out

a spare wheel

retired in place

rocks

cadavers

Are you plateaued? Have you exhausted your supply of competitiveness and ambition and given up believing in yourself and your ability to control your life? Can you be described by one or more of the words and phrases that Bardwick has collected?

Giving up illusions is not the same thing as giving up hope. Coming to terms with plateauing means developing realistic ca-

reer goals and taking the necessary steps to achieve them. Bard-wick notes that "although most people first see only what they cannot do, who they will never be, and what they will not achieve, that is only the first step toward really seeing what *else* we can achieve, we can experience, we can be."[6] She adds that:

> Paradoxically, when we accept the limits of reality, we are psychologi-cally free to experiment and grow. Doing that, we discover capacities we weren't aware of before. The truth is the only thing that sets us free.[7]

If you are plateaued, you need to change your professional aspi-rations and to pursue the 25 specific steps that we believe will in-crease your effectiveness and make you more successful. Bardwick contends that "when you have the courage to act, to make the changes you need, you will create a future for yourself."[8]

A FINAL WORD

Millions of ordinary, psychologically normal people will face an abrupt collision with the future . . . many of them will find it increasingly painful to keep up with the incessant demand for change that characterizes our time. ALVIN TOFFLER

Many of our planning colleagues have labored so long and so hard but have so very little to show for their efforts. In the face of often astronomical odds and a long list of adversities, they have contin-ued to toil in the fields of our profession and to take pride in their sometimes meager accomplishments. In many ways, these plan-ners are like Grover and Edna Turrill, the resilient characters of Robert Flynn's short story, "The Great Plains," who endured a life-long series of incredible hardships and tragedies as farmers in ru-ral west Texas. After one of their final heartbreaks, a dejected Gro-ver looks over a desolate prairie under a starlit sky and offers this lament:

> "Damn country. Washes away every time it rains. Blows away every time there's a wind. Hail or grasshoppers every year. I've sweated over it. I've broken my back. It has taken everything I have and given me nothing."

> "Yeah," Edna said, looking out over the miles and years they have trav-eled together. "But ain't it purty?"[9]

Strategy can be defined as skillful mangement in getting the better of an adversary or attaining an end. We have found that the most dangerous adversaries to the goal of effective planning are the status quo, complacency, and outright resistance to change. Planners must be willing to change. In fact, they must aggressively embrace change if they are going to make a difference in this world. How planners respond to the opportunities and risks presented by change will determine their ultimate success or failure.

Our principal theme in this book has been that most planners and planning organizations can employ a variety of strategies and tactics that will significantly influence or even determine their effectiveness. Planners can manage the variables that they can influence or control—such as how hard they work and the projects they work on—while they adapt to and overcome the variables beyond their control. Too much of what we have seen as planners hasn't been pretty. But there is still time for planners to take control of their destinies and to make a difference. We have done it, others have done it; you can do it, too.

Notes

Preface

1. Anderson, *The Effective Local Government Manager* (International City Management Association, 1983), p. 10.

2. Altshuler, *The City Planning Process: A Political Analysis* (Cornell University Press, 1965), p. 354.

3. Roeseler, *Successful American Urban Plans* (Lexington Books, 1982), p. xviii.

4. *Webster's New Collegiate Dictionary* (G & C Merriam Company, 1979).

5. Ibid.

6. Planning Position Paper (League of Women Voters of Atlanta-Fulton County, Inc., 1984).

7. Marcuse, "On the Feeble Retreat of Planning," *Journal of Planning Education and Research* (Association of Collegiate Schools of Planning, September 1983), p. 52.

8. Id. at 53.

9. Reissman, "The Visionary: Planner for Urban Utopia," *Urban Planning Theory* (Dowden, Hutchinson & Ross, Inc., 1975), p. 24.

10. Lindbloom, "The Science of Muddling Through," *Urban Planning Theory* (Dowden, Hutchinson & Ross, Inc., 1975), p. 523.

11. Peters and Waterman, Jr., *In Search of Excellence* (Harper & Row, 1982), p. 142.

12. Catanese, *The Politics of Planning and Development* (Sage Publications, 1984), pp. 27–8.

13. Kanter, *The Change Masters* (Simon & Schuster, Inc., 1983), p.306.

14. Mason et al., "Ross Perot's Crusade," *Business Week* (McGraw-Hill, Inc., October 6, 1986), p. 60.

Chapter One

1. Steiner, *Strategic Planning* (The Free Press, 1979), p. 5.

2. See Walker, *The Planning Function in Urban Government* (The University of Chicago Press, 1941).

3. Tomazini, "The Logic and Rationale of Strategic Planning" (paper presented at the 1985 annual meeting of the Association of Collegiate Schools of Planning).

4. Cratsley, "How to Improve Service and Cut Costs," *Nation's Cities Weekly* (National League of Cities, May 12, 1986), p. 4.

5. McDowell, "Strategies for Adapting Regional Councils to New Federalism" (paper presented at the 27th Annual Conference of the Association of Collegiate Schools of Planning, 1985).

6. Ibid.

7. Ibid.

8. Schon, *The Reflective Practitioner: How Professionals Think in Action* (Basic Books, Inc., 1983).

9. Altshuler, *The City Planning Process* (Cornell University Press, 1965), p. 354.

10. Slater, *Management of Local Planning* (International City Management Association, 1984), p. 54.

11. Id. at 55.

12. Peters and Waterman, Jr., *In Search of Excellence* (Harper & Row 1982).

13. Ibid. pp. 13–16.

14. Nissenbaum, "Tracking the Pursuit of Excellence," *PM Public Management* (International City Management Association, May 1986), p. 13.

15. Id. at 14.

16. Ibid.

17. Kuehl, "American Planning Association: Member and Non-Member Market Surveys" (American Planning Association, 1984).

18. Rapp and Patitucci, *Managing Local Government for Improved Performance: A Practical Approach* (Westview Press, 1977), p. 21.

19. Vitt, Jr., "Kansas City: Problems and Successes of Downtown Development," *Personality, Politics, and Planning* (Sage Publications, 1978), p. 106.

20. Hodges, "Career Advancement in Spite of a Planning Education," *Journal of the American Planning Association* (American Planning Association, Winter 1985), p. 4.

Chapter Two

1. Peters and Waterman, Jr. *In Search of Excellence* (Harper & Row 1982), p. 134.

2. Bonner, "Portland: The Problems and Promise of Growth," *Personality, Politics and Planning* (Sage Publications, 1978), p. 153.

3. See N.1 *supra*.

4. Williams, Jr., *American Land Planning Law*, Volume 1 (Callaghan & Company 1974), p. 42.

5. Altshuler, *The City Planning Process* (Cornell University Press, 1965), p. 377.

6. Ibid.

7. Id. at 379.

8. See N.1 *supra* at 126.

9. Ibid.

10. Bradford and Cohen, *Managing for Excellence* (John Wiley & Sons, 1984), p. 170.

11. Herchert, "Organizational Excellence Based on Ideals," *Public Management* (International City Management Association, August 1984), p. 22.

12. Black, "The Team Approach," *Public Management* (International City Management Association, May 1984), p. 21.

13. See N.1 *supra* at 127.

14. Hayes and Watts, *Corporate Revolution.*

15. Spaid, "Professionalism and Timing of Planning," *Personality, Politics and Planning* (Sage Publications, 1978), p. 168.

16. Naisbitt and Aburdene, *Re-Inventing the Corporation* (Warner Books, 1985).

17. Andrews, "Municipal Productivity Improvements Are a Way of Life in Phoenix," *National Civic Review* (National Municipal League, May-June 1986), p. 150.

18. Reprinted with permission from Bradford and Cohen, *Managing for Excellence*, copyright 1984 by John Wiley & Sons.

19. Meck, "Look Before You Leap," *Planning* (American Planning Association, March 1986), p. 22.

20. Kanter, *The Change Masters* (Simon & Schuster, Inc., 1983), pp. 17–142.

21. Darrington, "My Philosophy of Management," *Public Management* (International City Management Association, August 1986), p.11.

22. Walker, *The Planning Function in Urban Government* (The University of Chicago Press, 1941).

23. Catanese, *The Politics of Planning and Development* (Sage Publications, 1984), p. 18.

24. Meshenberg, *The Language of Zoning: A Glossary of Words and Phrases* (American Society of Planning Officials, 1976), p. 25.

25. Harmon, "Citizen Keys on Involvement," *The Western Planner*, November-December, 1986, p. 5.

26. Ibid.

27. Ibid.

28. Allor, *The Planning Commissioners Guide* (Planners Press, 1984), p. 11.

29. Milbrodt, "Costly Comprehensive Strategic Planning," *Public Management* (International City Management Association, April 1983), p. 20.

30. Catanese, *Planners and Local Poli-*

tics (Sage Publications, 1974), p. 45.

31. See N.5 *supra* at 1.

32. Conot, "Tracking John Friedman," *Planning* (American Planning Association, February 1984), p. 25.

33. Fulton, "Six Standouts," *Planning* (American Planning Asociation, April 1986), p. 8.

34. Koontz and O'Donnell, *Principles of Management: An Analysis of Managerial Functions* (McGraw-Hill, 1972), p. 113.

35. Ackoff, *A Concept of Corporate Planning* (Wiley-Interscience, 1970), p. 1.

36. Knack, "Moving Into the Fast Lane," *Planning* (American Planning Association, July 1984), p. 28.

37. Dark, "Lessons in Louisiana," *Public Management* (International City Management Association, April 1984), p. 19.

38. Smith and Cooper, *Elements of Physics* (McGraw-Hill Book Company, 1979), p. 296.

39. Bueche, *Principles of Physics* (McGraw-Hill Book Company, 1982), p. 589.

40. Eplan, "Atlanta: Planning, Budgeting and Neighborhoods," *Personality, Politics, and Planning* (Sage Publications, 1978), p. 45.

41. Id. at 55.

42. *Mid-South Conservation and Revitalization Plan* City of Fort Worth (Department of Planning and Growth Management, November 1986), p. 2.

43. Drucker, *Management: Tasks, Responsibilities, Practices* (Harper & Row, Publishers, 1973), p. 128.

44. Id. at 129.

45. Fulton, "Los Angeles: Prime Time," *Planning* (American Planning Association, February 1986), p. 10.

46. Kaplan, "Citizens Want a Hand In Zoning," *Los Angeles Times*, April 6, 1986.

47. Wesnick, "City's K mart Decision Right," *The Billings Gazette*, June 4, 1986.

48. Ibid.

49. See N.46 *supra*.

50. See N.5 *supra*.

51. Bair, "Planning for Action,"

Planning Cities (American Society of Planning Officials 1970), p. 144.

52. Lindbloom, "The Science of Muddling Through," *Urban Planning Theory* (Dowden, Hutchinson & Ross, Inc., 1975), pp. 521–522.

53. Walter and Choate, *Thinking Strategically: A Primer for Public Leaders* (The Council of State Planning Agencies, 1984), p. 13.

54. See N.40 *supra*.

55. Webber, "A Difference Paradigm for Planning," *Planning Theory in the 1980s* (Center for Urban Policy Research, 1978), p. 157.

56. See N.15 *supra* at 171.

57. Ibid.

58. Peattie, "Politics, Planning and Categories Bridging the Gap," *Planning Theory in the 1980s* (Center for Urban Policy Research, 1978), p. 84.

59. Catanese and Farmer, *Personality, Politics and Planning* (Sage Publications, 1978).

60. Dalton, "Politics and Planning Agency Performance," *Journal of the American Planning Association* (American Planning Association, Spring 1985), p. 189.

61. Id. at 195.

62. Lineberry and Sharkansky, *Urban Politics and Public Policy* (Harper & Row Publishing, 1978), p. 96.

63. Rondinelli, "Urban Planning As Policy Analysis: Management of Urban Change," *Journal of the American Institute of Planners* (American Institute of Planners, January 1973), p. 13.

64. Id. at 19.

65. Baum, *Planners and Public Expectations* (Schenkman Publishing Company, Inc., 1983), p. xiii.

66. Friedmann, "A Conceptual Model for the Analysis of Planning Behavior," *Administrative Science Quarterly* (September, 1967), p. 227.

67. Kaufman, "The Planner as Interventionist in Public Policy Issues," *Planning Theory in the 1980's: A Search for Future Directions* (Rutgers University 1978), pp. 191–2.

68. Patton and Sawicki, *Basic Methods*

of Policy Analysis and Planning (Prentice-Hall, 1986), pp. 129–30.

69. Knack and Peters, "Where Have All the Radicals Gone?" *Planning* (American Planning Association, October 1985), p. 15.

70. Rademan, "Viewpoint," *Planning* (American Planning Association, October 1985), p. 42.

71. Ibid.

72. Gelfand, "Rexford G. Tugwell and the Frustration of Planning in New York City," *Journal of the American Planning Association* (Sprng 1985), p. 153.

73. Id. at 160.

74. Id. at 154.

75. Peterson, "The Nation's First Comprehensive City Plan," *Journal of the American Planning Association* (Spring 1985), p. 134.

76. Id. at 148.

77. See N.22 *supra*.

78. Knack, "Woman's Work," *Planning* (American Planning Association, October 1986), p. 29.

79. Ibid.

80. Carroll, "Indianapolis: Fragmentation and Consolidation," *Personality, Politics, and Planning* (Sage Publications, 1978), p. 88.

81. Shirvani, "Insider's View on Planning Practice,"*Journal of the American Planning Association* (American Planning Association, Autumn 1985), p. 493.

82. Martel, *Mastering Change: The Key to Business Success* (Simon and Schuster, 1986), p. 302.

83. Merritt, "A Man and His City: B. Gale Wilson, Fairfield's City Manager," *Public Management* (International City Management Asociation, August, 1986), p. 18.

84. See N.52 *supra* at 522.

85. Vitt, Jr., "Kansas City: Problems and Successes of Downtown Development," *Personality, Politics and Planning* (Sage Publications, 1978), p. 109.

86. Ibid.

87. See N.81 *supra* at 492.

88. Stollman, "The Values of the City Planner," *The Practice of Local Government Planning* (International City Management Association, 1979), p. 16.

89. See N.5 *supra* at 400.

90. Id. at 401.

91. Id. at 400.

92. Id.

93. Steiner, *Strategic Planning: What Every Manager Must Know* (The Free Press, 1979), p. 14.

94. So, "Strategic Planning: Reinventing the Wheel?" *Planning* (American Planning Association, February 1984), pp. 16–21.

95. Kaufman and Jacobs, "A Public Planning Perspective on Strategic Plannng," (paper presented at the 1986 Annual Conference of the American Planning Association), p. 7.

96. Bolen, "Emerging Views of Planning," *Journal of the American Institute of Planners* (Volume 33, Number 4, 1967); Myerson and Banfield, *Politics, Planning and the Public Interest* (The Free Press, 1955); and Catanese, *Planners and Local Politics* (Sage Publications, 1974).

97. Bonner, "Portland: The Problems and Promises of Growth," *Personality, Politics and Planning* (Sage Publications, 1978), p. 150.

98. Nash, *Direct Marketing—Strategy/Planning/Execution* (McGraw-Hill Book Company, 1986), p. 16.

99. Catanese, *Planners and Local Politics* (Sage Publications, 1974), p. 170.

100. Mier, Moe, and Sherr, "Strategic Planning and the Pursuit of Reform, Economic Development and Equity," *Journal of the American Planning Association* (American Planning Association, Summer 1986), pp. 299–309.

101. Id. at 306.

102. See N.95 *supra*.

103. Hickman & Silva, *Creating Excellence* (New American Library, 1984), p. 232.

104. See N.98 *supra*.

105. Silver and Burton, "The Politics of State-Level Industrial Policy," *Journal of the American Planning Association* (American Planning Association, Summer 1986), p.277.

106. Tomazini, "The Logic and Rationale of Strategic Planning," (paper presented at the 1985 Annual Confer-

ence of the Association of Collegiate Schools of Planning), p. 14.

107. See N.100 *supra* at 307.

108. Ibid.

109. See N.15 *supra* at 168 and 169.

110. See N.51 *supra* at 145.

111. See N.85 *supra* at 107.

112. Levin, "Planning Agencies: Surviving in Hard Times," *Planning* (American Planning Association, January 1985), p. 22C.

113. See N.85 *supra* at 112.

114. See N.1 *supra* at 142.

115. Weaver and Babcock, *City Zoning: The Once and Future Frontier* (Planners Press, 1979), p. 168.

116. Forrester, "Wyoming (Ohio) Concurs," *Public Management* (International City Management Association, May 1984), p. 17.

117. Greene, "Learning You're Not a Hero," *The Dallas Morning News* (A. H. Belo Corporation, October 1986), p. 17A.

118. Se N.31 *supra* at 149.

119. See N.115 *supra* at 172.

120. Slater, *Management of Local Planning* (International City Management Association, 1984), p. 148.

121. Id. at 149.

122. Hedrick, "Serving the Planning Profession," *Planning* (American Planning Association, May 1986), p. 26D.

123. Austin, *Texas Business* (Commerce Publishing Corporation, March 1986).

124. Ibid.

125. Petersen, "Turning a Crisis into a Triumph," *USA Today*, June 5, 1986.

126. Finkler, "Avoiding Scorch City," *Planning* (American Planning Association, May 1985), p. 20.

127. Ibid.

128. Nichols, "Turning Forty in the Eighties," (W. W. Norton and Co., 1985).

129. Ibid.

130. See N.125 *supra*.

131. Ibid.

132. Se N.126 *supra*.

133. See N.115 *supra*.

134. Krumholz, "Make No Big Plans . . . Planning in Cleveland in the 1970's," *Planning Theory in the 1980s* (Center for Urban Policy Research, 1978), p. 38.

135. Ibid.

136. Id. at 39.

137. Jacobs, *Making City Planning Work* (American Society of Planning Officials, 1978), p. 313.

138. Ibid.

139. See Hoch and Cibulskis, "Planning Threatened: A Preliminary Report of Planners and Political Conflict," (paper presented at the 1986 Annual Conference of the American Planning Association in Los Angeles, California), p.22.

140. Gould, "Thrown Out of the Game After Hitting a Home Run," *The Wall Street Journal* (Dow Jones & Company, Inc., October 20, 1986), p. 21.

141. Ibid.

142. See N.139 *supra* at 23.

143. Milbrodt, "Curmudgeon Comes Forth," *Public Management* (International City Management Association, May 1984), p. 21.

144. See N.30 *supra* at 69.

145. Sprecher, "Sharing the Excellence," *Public Management* (International City Management Association, May 1984), p. 16.

146. See N.61 *supra* at 198.

147. See Fulton, "Henry Cisneros: Mayor as Entrepreneur," *Planning* (American Planning Association, February 1985).

148. Lindsay, "The New Planning," *Planning 1970* (American Society of Planning Officials, 1970), p. 17.

149. Ibid.

150. Bolen, "Managers and Leaders: Are They Different?" *Public Management* (International City Management Association, May 1985).

151. See N.30 *supra* at 72.

152. Memo from City Attorney to Mayor and City Council, "Legal Review of Adult Entertainment Use Regulations," dated February 8, 1985, City of Arlington, Texas.

153. Roeseler, *Successful American Urban Plans* (Lexington Books, 1982), p. xvi.

154. Slater, *Management of Local Planning* (International City Management Association, 1984), p. 8.

155. Ibid.

156. Stillman, "Local Public Management in Transition: A Report on the Current State of the Profession," *The Municipal Year Book—1982 (International City Management Association, 1982), p. 171.

157. Jacobson, "Anderson Scolds City Planners," *Dallas Morning News* (June 27, 1986), p. H-2.

158. Cleveland, *The Future Executive* (Harper & Row, 1972), p.22.

159. Schmidt, *Attorney's Dictionary of Medicine and Word Finder* (Matthew Bender and Company, 1984), p. T-54.

160. Meier, "An Anatomy of Risk," *Journal of the American Institute of Planners* (American Institute of Planners, October 1978), p. 487.

161. Ibid.

162. Cleveland, *The Knowledge Executive* (Truman Talley Books, 1985), p. 168.

163. Lewis, "How to Survive as a Big City Planning Director," *Planning* (American Planning Association, December 1983), pp. 12–15.

164. Drucker, *Innovation and Entrepreneurship* (Harper & Row, Publishers, 1983), p. 180.

165. See N.163.

166. Ibid.

167. Zaltman and Duncan, *Strategies for Planned Change* (John Wiley & Sons, 1977), p. 200.

168. "Turning Ideas into Action in the Municipal Environment," *TML Texas Town and City* (Texas Municipal League, June 1986).

169. Anderson, "The First Six Months," *Public Management* (International City Management Asociation, September 1981).

170. Bentley, *The Process of Government* (Harvard University Press, 1967), p. 208.

171. Franks, "Terms of Endearment," *Texas Business* (Commerce Publishing Corporation, March 1987),

pp. 32–3.

172. See N.30 *supra* at 26.

173. McClendon, "Making More Effective Public Presentations," *Planning* (American Planning Association, November 1986), pp. 24A–B.

174. Forester, "Planning in the Face of Power," *Journal of the American Planning Association* (American Planning Association, Winter 1982), p. 67.

175. Steinberg, "Are You An Ethical Public Employee," *Public Management Magazine* (International City Management Association, May 1982), pp. 20–21.

176. Pierce, "Revolving Doors Snare Cities, Counties," *Public Administration Times* (American Society for Public Administration, July 1, 1986), p. 2.

177. Ibid.

178. Ibid.

179. ibid.

180. Jaben, "Preventing Corruption," *American City and County* January 1986, pp. 24–30.

181. Ibid.

182. Marcuse, "Professional Ethics and Beyond: Values in Planning," *Journal of the American Insitute of Planners* (American Institute of Planners, July 1976), p. 264.

183. Id. at 267.

184. Kaufman, "Ethics and Planning: Some Insights from the Outside," *Journal of the American Planning Association* (American Planning Association, April 1981), p. 199.

185. Barrett, "What Do Planners Think on Ethical Issues," *Student Planner* (American Planning Association, Winter 1986), p.4.

186. Ibid.

Chapter Three

1. Levitt, "Marketing and the Corporate Purpose," *The Marketing Imagination* (The Free Press 1983), p. 5.

2. Zaltman and Duncan, *Strategies for Planned Change* (John Wiley and Sons, 1977), p. 55.

3. Spaid, "St. Paul: Professionalism and Timing of Planning," *Personality, Politics, and Planning* (Sage Publications,

1978), p. 165.

4. Moore, "Why Allow Planners to Do What They Do? A Justification for Economic Theory," *Journal of the American Institute of Planners* (American Institute of Planners, October 1978), pp. 387–97.

5. Ibid.

6. Bennis and Nanus, *Leaders—The Strategies for Taking Charge* (Harper & Row, Publishers, 1985), p. 162.

7. McGowan and Stevens, "Local Government Management: Reactive or Adaptive," *Public Administration Review* (American Society for Public Administration, May/June 1983), p. 20.

8. Boyer, "President of CBS News Says Cutbacks Inevitable," *The Dallas Morning News* (A. H. Belo Corporation, August 27, 1986).

9. Ibid.

10. See N.6 *supra*.

11. Ries and Trout, *Positioning: The Battle for Your Mind* (McGraw Hill, 1981), p. ix.

12. Id. at 5.

13. Trachtenberg, "Autodoms Persistent Bad Image," *Forbes* (Forbes, Inc., August 1986), p. 124.

14. Alsop, "Famous Brands Go Gourmet, But Consumers May Not Bite," *The Wall Street Journal* (Dow Jones & Company, Inc., December 18, 1986), p. 23.

15. See N.1 *supra* at xii.

16. Knack, "Moving Into the Fast Lane," *Planning* (American Planning Association, July 1984), p. 29.

17. Drucker, "How to Manage the Boss," *The Wall Street Journal* (Dow Jones & Co., August 1, 1986).

18. Staiger, "Viewpoint," *Planning* (American Planning Association, May 1985), p. 42.

19. Peters, "Houston Gets Religion," *Planning* (American Planning Association, May 1985), p. 42.

20. Boyce, Day and McDonald, *Metropolitan Plan Making* (Regional Science Research Institute, 1970).

21. Id. at 98.

22. Waterston, "Resolving the Three-Horned Planning Dilemma,"

Planning 1971 (American Society of Planning Officials, 1971), p. 164.

23. Anderson, *The Effective Local Government Manager* (International City Management Association, 1983), p. 157.

24. Id. at 158.

25. Id. at 152.

26. Beatty, "Did You Know They Hired a Woman?" *Public Management* (International City Management Association, September 1981), p. 16.

27. Meyer, "First Manager in Town," *Public Management* (International City Management Association, September 1981), p. 10.

28. King, "The New Manager in Town," *Public Management* (International City Management Association, September 1981), p. 5.

29. Conot, "Tracking John Friedman," *Planning 26* (American Planning Association, February 1984), p. 26.

30. Hickman and Silva, *Creating Excellence* (New American Library, 1984), p. 37.

31. Baum, "Politics, Power and the Profession," *Planning* (American Planning Association, December 1983), p. 19.

32. Id. at 19–20.

33. Ibid.

34. Ibid.

35. Rondinelli, "Urban Planning as Policy Analysis: Management of Urban Change," *Urban Planning Theory* (Dowden, Hutchinson & Ross, Inc., 1975), p. 529.

36. Nesbitt and Weinstein, "How to Size Up Your Customers," *American Demographics* (Dow Jones & Company, Inc., July 1986), p. 34.

37. See N.2 *supra*.

38. Peters and Waterman, Jr., *In Search of Excellence* (Harper & Row 1982), p. 183.

39. Bolton and Bolton, *Social Style/Management Style* (American Management Association, 1984), p. 106.

40. See N.38 *supra* at 184.

41. Howard, "The Local Planning Agency: Internal Administration," *Principles and Practice of Urban Planning*

(International City Management Association, 1968), p. 546.

42. Drucker, *Management: Tasks, Responsibilities, Practices* (Harper & Row, Publishers, 1973), p. 146.

43. Id. at 145.

44. Vitt, Jr., "Kansas City: Problems and Successes of Downtown Development," *Personality, Politics, and Planning* (Sage Publications, 1978), p. 111.

45. Ibid.

46. Webber, "A Different Paradigm for Planning," *Planning Theory in the 1980's* (Center for Urban Policy Research, 1978), p. 160.

47. See N.2 *supra* at 197.

48. Heskett, *Managing in the Service Economy* (Harvard Business School Press, 1986), p. 10.

49. Ibid.

50. Rohe and Gates, *Planning with Neighborhoods* (The University of North Carolina Press, 1985), p. 120.

51. Id. at 192.

52. Id. at 193.

53. *A Developer's Handbook*, Department of Environmental Services, Multnomah County, Oregon (1977).

54. *Neighborhood Notebook*, Dallas Department of Urban Planning, Dallas, Texas, 1974.

55. See N.38 *supra* at 189.

56. Id. at 184.

57. Sawicki, "Microcomputer Applications in Planning," *Journal of the American Planning Association* (American Planning Association, Spring 1985), pp. 209 and 214.

58. Waitley and Tucker, *Winning the Innovations Game* (Fleming H. Revell Company, 1986), p. 48.

59. Gil and Lucchesi, "Citizen Participation in Planning," *The Practice of Local Government Planning* (International City Management Association, 1979), p. 554.

60. See N.29 *supra* at 156.

61. Loughery, *Energy Planning Network* (Energy Planning Division of the American Planning Association, Spring, 1985), p. 6.

62. McClendon and Lewis, "Goals for Corpus Christi: Citizen Participation in Planning," *National Civic Review* (National Municipal League, Inc., February 1985).

63. Gelfand, "Rexford G. Tugwell and the Frustration of Planning in New York City," *Journal of the American Planning Association* (American Planning Association, Spring 1985), p. 156.

64. Moses, "Are Cities Dead?," *Metropolis: Values in Conflict* (Wadsworth Publishing Company, Inc., 1965), p. 55.

65. See N.38 *supra* at 156.

66. Id. at 165.

67. Drew, "Milwaukee: Planning for Fiscal Balance," *Personality, Politics, and Planning* (Sage Publications, 1978), p. 135.

68. Friedman, "Dupont Trims Costs, Bureaucracy to Bolster Competitive Position," *The Wall Street Journal* (Dow Jones & Company, Inc., September 25, 1985).

69. "Supersalesman Chuck Sussman," *Inc.* (Inc. Publishing Corporation, February 1986), p. 44.

70. Levine, "Citizenship and Service Delivery: The Promise of Coproduction," *Public Administration Review* (American Society of Public Administration, March 1984), p. 181.

71. Ibid.

72. Ferris, "Coprovision: Citizen Time and Money Donations in Public Service Provision," *Public Administration Review* (American Society for Public Administration, July/August 1984), p. 331.

73. See *The Sector Planning Program-City of Fort Worth*, Planning Department, 1971.

74. Catanese, *Personality, Politics, and Planning* (Sage Publications, 1978), p. 200.

75. Argyrs, *Intervention Theory and Method* (Addison-Wesley, 1970), p. 16.

76. Baum, *Planners and Public Expectations* (Schenkman Publishing Company, Inc., 1983), p. 241.

77. "Corporate City Arlington—Its Mission, Value System and Organization," Office of the City Manager, Ar-

lington, Texas.

78. "Policy Memo: Employee Relations with Citizens," Office of the City Manager, July 18, 1985.

70. Hansell, "Ideals for Excellence in Community Management," *Public Management* (International City Management Association, August 1984), p. 14.

80. Wright, "Crowds Flock to Management Plenary, How-To Workshops," *Nation's Cities Weekly* (National League of Cities, December , 1986), p. 4.

81. See Woodhouse, "Virginia Municipal League Achievement Awards," *Nation's Cities Weekly* (National League of Cities, September 22, 1986), p. 8.

82. See N.38 *supra* at 170.

83. *1983 Dayton Program Strategies* Office of Management and Budget, City of Dayton, Ohio, 1983, p. 3.

84. *Annual Budget 1979–80* (Finance Department, City of Galveston, Texas 1979), p. 4.

85. Ibid.

86. See N.78 *supra* at 13.

87. Cratsley, "The Workshops: How to Improve Service and Cut Costs," *Nation's Cities Weekly* (National League of Cities, May 12, 1986), p. 4.

88. Crosby, *Quality is Free* (McGraw-Hill Book Company, 1979), p. 3.

89. Ibid.

90. Peters and Austin, *A Passion for Excellence* (Random House, 1985), p. 99.

91. See N.44 *supra* at 111.

92. See N.3 *supra* at 159 and 160.

93. Colman, "Fresno County's Strategic Direction," *Public Management* (International City Management Association, April 1983), p. 19.

94. Peiser, "Does It Pay to Plan Suburban Growth," *Journal of the American Planning Association* (American Planning Association, Autumn 1984), p. 425.

95. Zucker, *The Management Idea Book* (West Coast Publishers, 1983), p. 103.

96. See "Neighborhood Planning Position Update: Follow Up Briefing" (League of Women Voters of Atlanta-Fulton County, Inc., 1984), p. 7.

97. Fukuhara, "Improving Effectiveness: Responsive Public Services," *Managing with Less* (International City Management Association, 1979), p. 101.

98. Id. at 105.

99. See N.38 *supra* at 193–194.

100. See N.78 *supra* at 14.

101. Steadman, "Planner of the Month," *The Western Planner* (Western Planner, September/October 1986), p. 5.

102. "Director 'Makes People Tick'," *Public Management* (International City Management Association, March 1986), p. 15.

103. "Cleveland Residents Share in Shaping Future," *Nation's Cities Weekly* (National League of Cities, November 19, 1984).

104. Lineberry and Sharkansky, *Urban Politics and Public Policy* (Harper & Row Publishers, 3rd Edition, 1978), p. 97.

105. Lippman, *The Phantom Public* (Harcourt, Brace and Co., 1925), pp. 320–25.

106. See N.104 *supra* at 17.

107. See N.38 *supra* at 186.

108. So, *The Practice of Local Government Planning* (International City Management Association, 1979), pp. 552–575.

109. Rodgers, Jr., *Citizen Committees* (Ballinger Publishing Company, 1977), pp. 19–20.

110. Black, "The Comprehensive Plan," *Principles and Practices of Urban Planning* (International City Managers Association, 1968), p. 350.

111. Toll, *Zoned American* (Grossman Publishers, 1969).

112. *Land Use Law and Zoning Digest* (American Planning Association, May 1980), p. 4.

113. Naisbitt, *Megatrends* (Warner Books, 1982), p. 129.

114. Gil, *Neighborhood Zoning: Practices and Prospects*, Planning Advisory Service Report No. 311 (American Society of Planning Officials 1975).

115. League of Women Voters, *SuperCity/Hometown, USA: Prospectus for a*

Two-Tier Government (Prager 1974), pp. 31-32.

116. Vernon's Ann. Rev. Civil Stats. of the State of Texas, Ch. 4, Art. 1011k (1945).

117. See Nesbitt, *Megatrends* for a more complete discussion on the national trend toward decentralization and a self-help philosophy.

118. *Zoning News* (American Planning Association, March 1985), p. 4.

119. Levine, *Managing Fiscal Stress: The Crisis in the Public Sector* (Chatham House Publishers, 1980), p. 305.

120. Id. at 306.

121. See N.79 *supra.*

122. Quoted in Levine, "Police Management in the 1980's: From Decrementalism to Strategic Thinking," *Public Administration Review* (American Society for Public Administration, November 1985), pp. 697-8.

123. Colby, "What is Alternative Service Delivery and What Do We Know About It?" *Management Science and Policy Analysis* (Vol. 3, No. 4 (Spring 1986), p. 6.

124. Heins, "Government Is On the Defensive," *Forbes* (Forbes, Inc., December 15, 1986), p. 128.

125. Naisbitt, *The Year Ahead 1986* (Warner Books, 1986), p. 107.

126. Ferris and Graddy, "Contracting Out: For What? With Whom?," *Public Administration Review* (American Society for Public Administration, July/August 1986), p. 342.

127. See N.124 *supra.*

128. Andrews, "Municipal Productivity Improvements Are a Way of Life in Phoenix," *National Civic Review* (National Municipal League, Inc., May/June 1986), p. 149.

129. See N.125 *supra* at 106.

130. Heskett, *Managing in the Service Economy* (Harvard Business School Press, 1986), p. 19.

Chapter Four

1. Osborne, "The Most Entrepreneurial City in America," *Inc.* (Inc. Publishing Corp., September, 1985), pp. 55-6.

2. Sawicki, "Planning Curricula: Adapting to Change," *The Student Planner* (American Planning Association, Spring 1985), p. 8.

3. *Webster's New World Dictionary*, Second College Edition (The World Publishing Company, 1970).

4. Kanter, *The Change Masters* (Simon & Schuster, Inc., 1983), p. 153.

5. Waitley and Tucker, *Winning the Innovations Game* (Felming H. Revell Company, 1986), p 51.

6. Quoted in Peters and Waterman, Jr., *In Search of Excellence* (Harper & Row 1982), p. 200.

7. Ibid.

8. Drucker, *Innovation and Entrepreneurship* (Harper & Row, Publishers, 1973), p. 255.

9. See N.6 *supra* at 201.

10. Saporta, "The City's Development Maze," *The Atlanta Constitution*, March 1, 1985.

11. "Is Development Chaos Necessary," *The Atlanta Constitution*, March 5, 1985.

12. See N.6 *supra* at 216.

13. Ibid.

14. Id. at 218.

15. Id. at 223.

16. Id. at 200.

17. Id. at 203-204.

18. " 'Outlaw' Principals Called Key to Good Schools," Fort Worth Star Telegram, September 27, 1985.

19. Ibid.

20. Ibid.

21. See N.6 *supra* at 207.

22. Id. at 106.

23. See N.6 *supra* at 208.

24. Id. at 211.

25. Peterson, "The Nation's First Comprehensive City Plan," *Journal of the American Planning Association* (Spring 1985).

26. Id. at 134.

27. Gelfand, "Rexford G. Tugwell and the Frustration of Planning in New York City," *Journal of the American Planning Association* (Spring 1985), pp. 153 and 159.

28. Ibid.

29. Kets de Vries, "The Dark Side of Entrepreneurship," *Harvard Business Review* (Harvard Business School, November-December 1985), p. 160.

30. Id. at 166.

31. See N.29 *supra* 160–167.

32. Dalton, "Politics and Planning Agency Performance," *Journal of the American Planning Association* (American Planning Association, Spring 1985), p. 194.

33. Lewis, "How to Survive as a Big City Planning Director," *Planning* (American Planning Association, December 1983), p. 14.

34. Vitt, Jr., Kansas City: Problems and Successes of Downtown Development," *Personality, Politics, and Planning* (Sage Publications, 1978), p. 111.

35. See N.33, *supra*.

36. As quoted in Lewis, N.33 *supra*.

37. Drucker, "The Entrepreneurial Mystique," *Inc.* (Inc. Publishing Corporation, October 1985), p. 56.

38. Culler, "Most Federal Workers Need Only Be Competent," *The Wall Street Journal* (Dow Jones & Company, May 21, 1986), p. 24.

39. Drucker, *Management: Tasks, Responsibilities, Practices* (Harper & Row, Publishers, 1973), p. 139.

40. Brownstein, "So You Want to Go Into Politics?" *Inc.* (Inc. Publishing Corporation, November, 1985), p. 98.

41. Banfield and Wilson, *City Politics* (Vantage Books, 1966), p. 265.

42. Id. at 269.

43. Raymond, "The Role of the Physical Urban Planner," *Planning Theory in the 1980's* (Center for Urban Policy Research, 1978), p. 4.

44. Ibid.

45. Drucker, "Setting Up Entrepreneurial Units," *Inc.* (Inc. Publishing Corporation, November, 1985), p. 22.

46. See N.39 *supra* at 146.

47. See N.6 *supra* at 222.

48. Id. at 223.

49. See N.1 *supra* at 56.

50. Ibid.

51. Ibid.

52. See N.8 *supra* at 198.

53. See N.6 *supra* at 223.

54. Ibid.

55. Hansell, "The Fabulous Flops Award or In Search of the Perfect Failure," *Public Mangement* (International City Management Association, December 1984), p. 3.

56. Ibid.

57. Croce, "Corporate Culture Run Amok," *Public Management* (International City Management Association, December 1984), p. 5.

58. Hansell, "Ideals for Excellence in Community Management," *Public Management* (International City Management Association, August 1984), p. 14.

59. Gittler, "Decisions Are Only as Good as Those Who Can Change Them" *The Wall Street Journal* (Dow Jones & Co. Inc., October 7, 1985).

60. Alsop, "Coke's New Soft Drink Poses Problem" *The Wall Street Journal* (Dow Jones & Company, Inc., April 24, 1985), p. 2.

61. Porter, "Growth Management: Requiem or Reprise?," *Urban Land* (Urban Land Institute, March 1986), p. 34.

62. See N.58 *supra*.

63. Miller and Gray, "Why Businesses Often Sink In Decisional Quicksand," *The Wall Street Journal* (Dow Jones & Company, Inc., December 15, 1986), p. 29.

64. Zaltman and Duncan, *Strategies for Planned Change* (John Wiley & Sons, 1977), p. 197.

65. Id. at 199.

66. See N.8 *supra* at 35.

67. *Baseline Data Report - Microcomputers* (International City Management Association, Volume 15, No. 7, 1983).

68. See N.8 *supra* at 254.

69. Peters and Austin, "A Passion for Excellence," *Fortune* (Time, Inc., May 13, 1985), p. 24.

70. Ibid.

71. Ibid.

Chapter Five

1. Rabinowitz, "Viewpoint," *Planning* (American Planning Association, January, 1984), p. 46.

2. Catanese, *The Politics of Planning*

and Development (Sage 1984), p. 97.

3. See. N.1 *supra.*

4. Lewis, "How to Survive as a Big City Planning Director," *Planning* (American Planning Association, December 1983), p. 16.

5. Hodges, "Career Advancement in Spite of a Planning Education," *Journal of the American Planning Association* (American Planning Association, Winter 1985), p. 4.

6. Ibid.

7. Kaufman, "The Planner as Interventionist in Public Policy Issues," *Planning Theory in the 1980's* (Center for Urban Policy Research, 1978), p. 186.

8. Vitt, Jr., "Kansas City: Problems and Successes of Downtown Development," *Personality, Politics, and Planning* (Sage Publications, 1978), p. 104.

9. Borras, "What Makes a Leader," *Public Management* (International City Management Association, August 1986), p. 2.

10. Bennis and Nanus, *Leaders: The Strategies for Taking Charge* (Harper and Row, 1985), p. 22.

11. Kelleher, "Managers and Leaders: Are They Different?" *Public Management* (International City Management Association, May 1985), p. 6.

12. See N.10 *supra* at 55–56.

13. See N.11 *supra* at 7.

14. Reed, "Managers and Leaders: Are They Different?" *Public Management* (International City Management Association, May 1985), p. 8.

15. Ibid.

16. "Marketing Wiz James McManus," *Inc.* (Inc. Publishing Corporation, September 1986), p. 46.

17. Ibid.

18. See N.14 *supra.*

19. Ibid.

20. Bob Bolen, "Managers and Leaders: Are They Different?" *Public Management* (International City Management Association, May 1985), p. 9.

21. Hickman and Silva, *Creating Excellence* (New American Library, 1984), p. 23.

22. See N.10 *supra* at 26–27.

23. Scalf, "Leadership, Management and the Local Government," *Public Management* (International City Management Association, August 1986), p. 6.

24. See N.20 *supra.*

25. Fiordalisi, "Cisneros: Power Through Persuasion," *City and State* (Crain Communications Inc., September 1986), p. 18.

26. Ibid.

27. See N.21 *supra* at 160 and 161.

28. Peters and Austin, *A Passion for Excellence—The Leadership Difference* (Random House, 1985), p. 284.

29. Id. at 285.

30. Leavitt, *Corporate Pathfinders* (Dow Jones-Irwin, 1985), p. 2.

31. See N.2 *supra* at 101.

32. Barnett and Miller, "Edmund Bacon: A Retrospective," *Planning* (American Planning Association, December 1983), p. 7.

33. Rudnitsky, "A One-Man Revolution," *Forbes* (August 25, 1986), p. 40.

34. Anderson, "Promoting the Community's Future," *The Effective Local Government Manager* (International City Management Association, 1983), p. 163.

35. Id. at 157.

36. Ibid.

37. Carroll, "Indianapolis: Fragmentation and Consolidation," *Personality, Politics, and Planning* (Sage Publications, 1978), p. 89.

38. Bennis, "Leaders: The Strategies for Taking Charge," *Public Management* (International City Management Association, January 1987), p. 12.

39. Ibid.

40. Catanese, *The Politics of Planning and Development* (Sage Publications, 1984), p. 31.

41. Anderson, "City Manager Charles Anderson," *Dallas Morning News* (A. H. Belo Corporation, September 28, 1986), p. 15A.

42. See N.34 *supra* at 160.

43. Ibid.

44. Sieb, "Dallas Councilmembers Refusing to Face Issues Squarely," *Dallas Morning News* (A. H. Belo Corporation, September 3, 1986), p. 23A.

45. Ibid.

46. See N.38 *supra.*

47. Pederson, "Solving the Management Equation," *Public Management* (International City Management Association, August 1986), p. 8.

48. Peters and Waterman, Jr., *In Search of Excellence* (Harper and Row, Publishers, 1982), p. 318.

49. Ibid.

50. Krumholz, "A Retrospective View of Equity Planning: Cleveland 1969–1979," *Journal of the American Planning Association* (American Planning Association, Spring 1982), p. 164.

51. Lewis, "How to Survive as a Big City Planning Director," *Planning* (American Planning Association, December 1983), p. 15.

52. See N.7 *supra* at 186.

53. See N.40 *supra* at 188.

54. See N.51 *supra.*

55. Se N.47 *supra.*

56. See N.28 *supra* at 9.

57. See N.48 *supra* at 321.

58. See N.30 *supra* at 89.

59. Ibid.

60. Kirchhoff, city of Arlington, Texas, Jan. 7, 1987.

61. Claire, "How's Your MBWA? Improving the Climate of Your Organization," *Planning* (American Planning Association, September 1985), p. 20c.

62. Ibid.

63. Id. at 20c and 21c.

64. Zaltman and Duncan, *Strategies for Planned Change* (John Wiley & Sons, 1977), p. vii.

65. Kaufman, "Strategies for Planned Change," *Journal of the American Institute of Planners* (American Institute of Planners, October 1978), p. 492.

66. Merrill and Reid, *Personal Styles and Effective Performance,* p. 89.

67. Ibid.

68. Catanese, *Personality, Politics, and Planning* (Sage Publications, 1978), p. 205.

69. Id. at 206.

70. See "The Politics of Automating a Planning Office," *Planning* (June 1983).

71. Tichy and Devanna, *The Transformational Leader* (John Wiley & Sons, 1986), p. viii.

72. Ibid.

73. Bass, *Leadership and Performance Beyond Expectations* (The Free Press, 1985).

74. See N.71 *supra* at x.

75. Drucker, "How to Manage the Boss," *The Wall Street Journal* (Dow Jones & Company, Inc., August 1, 1986), p. 20.

76. See N.10 *supra* at 153.

77. See N.47 *supra* at 9.

78. Ibid.

79. See N.30 *supra* at 194.

80. Ringolsby, "Win or Lose, 86 a Success for Rangers," *Dallas Morning News* (A. H. Belo Corporatin, September 5, 1986), p. H-2.

81. See N.73 *supra.*

82. Ibid.

83. Joyce Lain Kennedy, "Personal Alliances are Vital on the Job," *Dallas Morning News* (A. H. Belo Corporation, September 29, 1986), p. 7E.

84. See N.7 *supra* at 187.

85. Ibid. For more discussion on this pont, see Richard Bolan, "The Social Relations of the Planner," *Journal of the American Institute of Planners* (November 1971).

86. Jamieson, "Government: A Profoundly Human Affair," *Public Management* (International City Management Association, May 1985), p. 20.

87. Ibid.

88. Birnbaum, "Democrats Give Policy Outline for the Nation," *The Wall Street Journal* (Dow Jones & Company, Inc., January 28, 1987), p. 54.

89. Reed, "Managers and Leaders: Are They Different?" *Public Management* (International City Management Association, May 1985), p. 8.

90. Anderson, "On Being an Effective Local Government Manager," *The Effective Local Government Manager* (International City Management Association, 1983), p. 10.

91. See N. 80 *supra.*

92. Ibid.

93. See N.10 *supra* at 188.

94. Ibid.

95. Nichols, "Clement's Pick for

State Post Known as Doer," *The Dallas Morning News* (A. H. Belo Corporation, December 21, 1986), p. 52A.

96. Waitley and Tucker, *Winning the Innovations Game* (Felming H. Revell Company, 1986), p. 47.

97. Ibid.

98. See Gallup and Gallup, *The Great American Success Story* (Dow Jones-Irwin, 1986).

99. Ibid.

100. See N.10 *supra* at 189.

101. See Jacobs, *Making City Planning Work* (Planners Press, 1983).

102. Lewis, "How to Survive as a Big City Planning Director," *Planning* (American Planning Association, December 1983), p. 13.

103. Adler, "True Education Begins Long After Schooling Ends," *Fort Worth Star Telegram* (December 3, 1986), p. A-23.

104. Rowan, *The Intuitive Manager* (Little, Brown and Company, 1986), p. 19.

105. See N.5 *supra* at 4.

106. Drucker, *Innovation and Entrepreneurship* (Harper & Row, Publishers, 1985), p. 264.

107. See N.102 *supra*.

108. Crosby, *Quality is Free* (McGraw-Hill Book Company, 1979), p. 154.

109. Paterno, "On Staying Power," Panhandle Eastern Corporation.

110. Knack, "Woman's Work," *Planning* (American Planning Association, October 1986), p. 26.

111. Suters, "Managing People," *Inc.* (Inc. Publishing Corporation, November 1986), p. 116.

112. Se N.8 *supra* at 112.

113. Bradford and Cohen, *Managing for Excellence* (John Wiley & Sons, 1984), p. 60.

114. Ibid.

115. Ibid.

116. Wren, Jr., "If It Failed, There Still Was Glory," *The Fort Worth Star-Telegram* (November 13, 1986), p. E-9.

117. Krumholz, "Cleveland: Problems of Declining Cities," *Personality, Politics, and Planning* (Sage Publications, 1978), p. 10.

118. Id. at 70 and 71.

119. Naisbitt and Aburdine, *Re-Inventing the Corporation* (Warner Books, 1985).

120. See N.10 *supra* at 77.

121. Id. at 79.

122. Ibid.

123. See N.28 *supra* at 310.

124. Tarketon, *How to Motivate People* (Harper and Row, 1986).

125. Locke and Latham, *Goal Setting: A Motivational Technique that Works!* (Prentice-Hall, Inc., 1984).

126. See N.28 *supra* at 296.

127. Kanter, *The Change Masters* (Simon & Schuster, Inc., 1983), p. 151.

128. See N.61 *supra* at 200.

129. Sifford, "Professional Motivator Offers Advice for Bosses, Workers," *Fort Worth Star Telegram*, November 28, 1985.

130. See N.124 *supra*.

131. Yeager, *Yeager* (Bantam Books, 1985), p. 298.

132. See Sayles, *Leadership: What Effective Managers Really Do . . . and How They do It* (McGraw-Hill, 1979).

133. See N.67 *supra* at 183.

134. Morris, "Publisher's Notes," *Dallas/Fort Worth Business Journal* (Scripps-Howard Business Publications, June 22, 1986), p. 6.

135. See N.130 *supra* at 300.

136. Cleveland, *The Knowledge Executive* 11 (Truman/Talley Books, 1985).

137. See N.130 *supra* at 407.

138. See N.11 *supra* at 6 and 7.

139. Drucker, *The Effective Executive* (Harper Colophon Books, 1966), p.170.

140. Gottschalk, Jr., "The Dancing Toll Taker and Other Successes," *The Wall Street Journal* (Dow Jones & Company, Inc., March 17, 1986), p. 15.

141. Ibid.

142. Ibid.

143. See Wooden, "On Staying Power," Panhandle Eastern Corporation.

Chapter Six

1. Marcuse, "On the Feeble Retreat of Planning," *Journal of Planning Education and Research* (Association of Collegiate Schools of Planning, September, 1983), p. 52.

2. Gaus, "Trends in Theory of Administration," *Public Administration Review* (1950) 164, p. 10.

3. President's Private Sector Survey on Cost Control, Office of the President, 1983.

4. Hartle, "Sisyphus Revisited: Running the Government Like a Business," *Public Administration Review* (March/April, 1985), p. 342.

5. Drucker, *Management: Tasks, Responsibilities, Practices* (Harper & Row, Publishers, 1973), p. 138.

6. Dalton, "Politics and Planning Agency Performance," *Journal of the American Planning Association* (American Planning Association, Spring 1985), p. 194.

7. Drucker, *Innovation and Entrepreneurship* (Harper & Row, Publishers, 1985), p. 178.

8. See N.2 *supra* at 166.

9. Ibid.

10. Ibid.

Chapter Seven

1. See Keidel, *Game Plans: Sports Strategies for Business* (E.P. Dutton, 1985) Soundview Executive Book Summaries.

2. Id. at 2.

3. Zaltman and Duncan, *Strategies for Planned Change* (John Wiley & Sons, 1977), p. 167.

4. Catanese, *Planners and Local Politics* (Sage Publications, 1974), p. 40.

5. Bardwick, *The Plateauing Trap* (American Management Association, 1986), p. 4.

6. Id. at 10.

7. Ibid.

8. Id. at 180.

9. Flynn, *Seasonal Rain and Other Stories* (Corona, 1986).

Index

271

Addendum

After *Mastering Change* was first published, the authors conducted a series of workshops on planning agency management. What follows are some of the questions that were asked during those workshops—and the answers the authors supplied.

I may not win very often, but I am a good planner and do my job well. Why do you put so much emphasis on winning?

We emphasize winning because this trait is universally valued and admired—and because it will make you a better, more effective planner. Our profession needs heroes; heroes are winners.

Some winners are lucky, but most create their own luck. Franz Klammer was the last skier in the men's downhill race in the 1980 Winter Olympics. The course was covered with icy ruts created by previous skiers, and fog made it impossible to see more than two flags ahead. To win Klammer had to beat his previous best time by .3 seconds. Yet Klammer *did* win. When asked how he did it, Klammer answered, "When I left the gate, I decided that I would win or die."

You become a winner by phasing out failures while phasing in success. You establish measurable goals and critically evaluate your performance. A basic rule is, "What gets measured, gets done." Know your batting average and challenge yourself to become better.

What is your specific definition of winning (that is, effective planning)?

Effective city planning is planning that makes a difference. It yields a high return on the amount of resources that were invested in the process. One of the key characteristics of effective planning is meaningful citizen participation. Partnerships, networking, consensus building, negotiation, and compromise are hallmarks of effective citizen participation. To be effective, in other words, the planning process must empower clients to solve their problems. They must be united in purpose and believe in themselves and their ability to improve their situation. They should have a vision of a better tomorrow, believe that it will happen, and have developed measurable, step-by-step objectives to get there. In short, they must have ownership of a plan that is based on social, economic, and political reality.

In truth, most planners know just how effective they and their programs are. Winning planners can point to results; losers make excuses. Most planners know their winning percentages on zoning cases and on their recommendations for the various plans, studies, reports, and projects they are working on. They know if their plans are adopted. They know if their proposals are being implemented. They may not like the results, but they are usually aware of them.

You suggest downsizing plans, reports, and studies into smaller, more attractive documents. Don't we need to give the public all the information we have? If we condense the final product won't people question the time and cost it took to produce it?

We advocate what we call dehydrated planning—products reduced to their essence. The real challenge is how to take a broad stream of raw data and analyze and refine it into knowledge that can be acted on. Planners' mission is not to show people how hard we have worked in collecting data or how technically sophisticated we are in analyzing it; our job is to give them the essential information they need to make decisions and solve problems. Filtered information is what people really want.

With the vast amount of information available today, it's clear that there is real value to the person, service, or product that can sort through data and get clients what they need to know. Further, because different clients need different types of information—and in different styles or formats— it is important to customize documents.

Most users need *less* than planners feel comfortable in delivering. This is especially true of consultants. One consultant we know says his competitors would gain an advantage if he tried to reduce the size or complexity of his products. Our response was that the needs of the clients should prevail. The secret is to pack more perceived value into a smaller space. Consultants should offer more useful products, not bigger, more complex ones. Plans that are too big to be carried around will be left behind; portable ones will be used.

You say that planners should get closer to their customers. But most planners already know how to sell their products and services. Are you making a distinction between marketing and selling?

Absolutely! Selling focuses on the needs of the seller; marketing tries to satisfy the needs of the customer. Market-oriented planners create items their customers will want, even *demand*. In other words, customers will suggest the form of the product or service, how it is to be created, and how and when it is to be delivered.

This approach to planning requires planners to focus first on improving the effectiveness of products and services and then on the efficiency of the planning process. This approach may sound simple, but it is a challenge to convert technical information into usable products or services that are satisfying to the customer.

The choice between becoming a master of technology or a master of markets is easy if you are committed to effective public service. Just keep in mind that products must be tailored to the capabilities of your clients. Products that are too complex or sophisticated for the intended users have limited value. Customers want products they can use, not monuments to planners' technical expertise.

Putting the customer first requires more than good intentions and mission statements. It takes vigorous leadership to push this philosophy into every nook and cranny of an organization. Employees must be carefully selected and trained to believe in the importance of customer service—and they must check with customers constantly to make sure they are on the right track.

You urge planners to create high-quality products and services but at the same time you want us to work faster and with less data. How do you explain the contradiction?

Two points need to be made. First, our goal is to increase planners' effectiveness. Quality products and services will increase effectiveness, but quality does not depend on the amount of money or time spent. Quality should be a direct function of our clients' needs; it should not be dictated by staff. If you can deliver a workable solution in two months, then why would you take four months to produce a technically superior solution that arrives too late to be used?

Second, we have found that planners too often equate quality with extensive data collection and analysis. Consider the views of Terry Moore, who teaches in the Department of Planning, Public Policy, and Management at the University of Oregon. Writing in the Autumn 1988 issue of the *Journal of the American Planning Association*, Prof. Moore contended that planners spend too much time reconfirming and documenting the obvious. "By passing quickly over the preliminary steps and developing concrete policy alternatives, planners can avoid much of the tedium that precedes real policy analysis, encourage substantive citizen invovement, and get better policies quicker," said Prof. Moore. We agree.

You suggest that one of the important goals of strategic planning is positioning to take advantage of change. What kind of changes do you foresee in the way city planning will be practiced in large planning organizations in the future?

Some of the following changes are *already* taking place:

- Planning organizations will be smaller, will employ a few highly educated specialists, and will be much more respected than they are today.

- These organizations will have two primary functions: visioning and problem solving.

- Specialized knowledge will exist not at the top but at the bottom of the organization. Planning specialists will be self-directed and responsible for both internal and external relationships and communications.

- Planning specialists will report to the planning director and not to intermediate managers.

- Civil service will be reformed so that planners will be held accountable for performance.

- Career opportunities will be more limited. Aspiring, ambitious planners will have to move from city to city as they move from organization to organization within a specialty. Advancement into management will be the exception rather than the rule. Planning will not be a lifetime profession.

- Fewer resources will be available for comprehensive planning. More emphasis will be placed on strategic planning and implementation.

- Timely responses will be more valued than comprehensiveness. In the eyes of the practitioner, standards will be lowered.

- Fewer resources will be committed to data collection, but more data will be available and planners will be expected to convert it quickly into relevant, useful information through sorting and sifting services.

- Plans, programs, and services will be expected to produce measurable results and client satisfaction.

- Products and staff will be evaluated constantly, and organizations will make programming decisions on the basis of clients' needs.

- Citizen involvement, volunteerism, and self-help will dominate the planning process. Most of the planning will be done by unpaid staff. Nuturing clients and helping them become self-reliant will be an essential responsibility for planners.

- Conflict resolution, consensus building, deal making, and teaching will also be prevalent responsibilities for most planners.

- The planner will no longer be an autonomous problem solver. Privatization and co-production will be typical in the development and delivery of most planning products and services.

- Almost all planning will be a form of advocacy planning.

Change is inevitable. As planners we must believe in the possibility and desirability of change in almost everything, including ourselves and the planning profession. We must develop a better sense of tomorrow if we want to be effective planners today.